THE JAPANESE DISCOVERY OF EUROPE

An early Japanese use of a European invention
(from Saikaku, *Kōshoku Ichidai Otoko*, 1682)

THE JAPANESE
DISCOVERY OF EUROPE

HONDA TOSHIAKI
AND OTHER DISCOVERERS
1720–1798

---

by
DONALD KEENE

GROVE PRESS—NEW YORK

*First published in
the United States in* 1954
by Grove Press
795 *Broadway, New York City*

*Made and printed in Great Britain
by William Clowes & Sons Ltd
London and Beccles*

TO MY MOTHER

CONTENTS

CONTENTS

ILLUSTRATIONS

ix

ILLUSTRATIONS

INTRODUCTION

IT is the temptation of any translator to exaggerate the glory and importance of his subject. Perhaps such faith is necessary if the long and often exasperating work of translation is to be accomplished. In the case of a writer of some fame, there is a less urgent compulsion to explain the justice of the translator's decision to render his works into another tongue. But in the case of a writer whose name is barely mentioned in Western books and whose works are little known in Japan, there is indeed some need to show whether the translation represents a real discovery or merely so much digging in the boneyard of a forgotten past.

Perhaps the best way to come upon the works of Honda Toshiaki (1744–1821) would be after months spent studying the essays of seventeenth- and eighteenth-century Japanese philosophers of the orthodox Confucian schools. A page of any one of Honda's writings would suffice to show that with him one has entered a new age, that of modern Japan. One finds in his books a new spirit, restless, curious and receptive. There is in him the wonder at new discoveries, the delight in widening horizons. Honda took a kind of pleasure even in announcing that Japan was, after all, only a small island in a large world. To the Japanese bourgeois who had thought of Chinese civilisation as being of immemorial antiquity, he declared that Egypt's was thousands

J.D.E.—I   I

of years older and far superior. The world, he discovered, was full of wonderful things, and he insisted that Japan take advantage of them. Honda looked at Japanese institutions as he thought a Westerner might, and he saw things that had to be changed, terrible drains on the nation's moral and physical strength. Within him sprang the conviction that Japan must become one of the great nations of the world.

Honda's chief works, *A Secret Plan for Managing the Country* and *Tales of the West*, contain his solutions for the problems that were tormenting Japan at the end of the eighteenth century, as well as proposals for the Japan of the future. By way of introduction to the translation of major parts of these two works, I have presented an account of the growth and uses of Western learning in Japan between 1720 and 1798. These are the dates of the beginning of official interest in Western science in Japan and of the composition of Honda's principal essays. The three-quarters of a century included by the two dates was a most important period in Japanese history, and one which has been relatively little discussed. It was a time when intellectuals, rebelling at the isolation of their country, desperately sought knowledge from the West. The amazing energy and enthusiasm of such men made possible the later spectacular changes in Japan, which are all too often credited to the arrival of Commodore Perry.

In describing the activities of the Dutch, the source of Japanese information about the West in the eighteenth century, I realise that I may seem at times unnecessarily harsh. I am perfectly well aware that similarly unattractive portraits might be drawn of other Western merchants in the East. It is nonetheless difficult for one who reads with nostalgia of Japan before Europeanisation to restrain his indignation at the indifference and hostility of the Dutch to the colourful surroundings in which they lived. But, as they might well have answered, it was their example which inspired Honda Toshiaki and many other progressive men to their vision of a new Japan, and for this the nation was ever to be in their debt.

Here, then, is a study of that most interesting phenomenon of recent centuries, the meeting of East and West, as it occurred in eighteenth-century Japan in the mind of an original thinker.

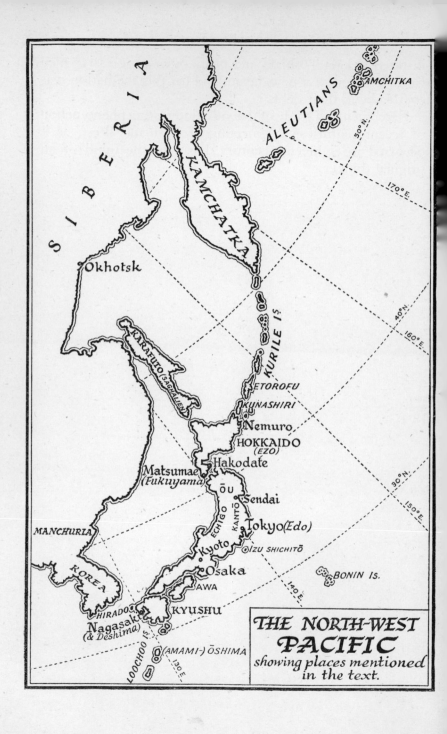

THE NORTH-WEST
PACIFIC
showing places mentioned
in the text.

Chapter One

THE DUTCH IN JAPAN

A T the end of the eighteenth century, when a few Japanese began with immense effort the serious study of the civilisation of Europe, the centre of their interest was the tiny island of Deshima in Nagasaki Harbour. There, in the rather mean buildings of a trading station, lived a dozen or so Dutchmen, the sole Europeans permitted to enter the Japanese islands.

The nation had not always been thus isolated from the West. During the little less than a century between the discovery of Japan by the Portuguese in 1542 and their expulsion in 1639, the Japanese had had considerable opportunity to examine Western ways, and some of them had even made journeys to Europe and America. But although the government was aware of the advantages of trade with the foreigners, the ever-growing menace of Christianity (introduced as early as 1549 by St. Francis Xavier) led to the enaction of a series of laws which culminated in the expulsion of all Europeans but the Dutch.

It was not the theological aspects of Christianity, or more particularly of Catholicism, which had so disturbed the Japanese government, but the fear that native converts to the religion might have divided political loyalties, and might even

5

facilitate the invasion of the islands by a European power. The example of the Philippines, conquered by the Spaniards on the heels of missionary activity, served as warning to the Japanese, and the successive revelation of supposed plots to endanger Japanese sovereignty caused the government to banish first the Spaniards and then the Portuguese. Of the other nations which had traded with Japan, England had left voluntarily, finding the business unprofitable. The Dutch, with a superior flair for trade perhaps, remained.

Although the Japanese government was absolutely determined to erase every trace of Christianity within the realm, there had been adequate proof of the innocuousness of the Dutch variety of the religion. In 1637-8, when tens of thousands of Japanese Christian converts banded together on the peninsula of Shimabara in a desperate last stand, the Dutch had obligingly lent artillery support to the government forces. They were not overly concerned at having to play a part in the destruction of the Christian religion in Japan, for they were friends neither of Catholicism nor of the Portuguese, their deadly rivals in the East and the people most likely to benefit commercially by Christian successes in Japan. The support that the Dutch lent helped to persuade the Japanese that they had come exclusively for trade, and though there was nothing in the world for which the Japanese military leaders officially had greater contempt than commerce, they preferred to deal with docile Dutch merchants than with proud and unruly Portuguese soldiers.

In 1641 the Japanese government ordered the Dutch to move their trading station, or factory, as it was known, from Hirado at the western end of Kyushu to the island of Deshima.[1] At first the Dutch welcomed the change to the more convenient harbour of Nagasaki, and they may even have felt as they took over the buildings erected originally for the Portuguese that the act was symbolic of the passing of supremacy in the Orient from Portugal to Holland. The Dutch, indeed, were rising to the height of their glory, and their successes were due as much to the efforts of their merchants as to the prestige of Dutch arms.

Vondel, the greatest of Dutch poets, in an ode written on the occasion of Marie de' Medici's visit in 1639 to the Amsterdam East India House, described the achievements of the Dutch traders:

> 'Twas not enough they'd won the field in Netherlands;
> They sailed the earth to distant and exotic lands,
> As far as shines the sun, resolved the sun would see
> Their mighty deeds. Our Holland serves as granary
> For all the Indies grow. The North has filled its ships
> With Eastern crops. The Winter Prince who warms his lips
> With pepper, guards in these domains the boast
> Of all that heav'nly fires of summer cook and roast.
> Arabia of incense-burners gives the best.
> The commerce with the Persians ever keeps abreast;
> They trade their silks and all their cotton-ware.
> Great Java shares with us her treasures fair,
> And China, porcelain. We Amsterdammers journey
> Where Ganges casts its waters down into the sea:
> Wherever profit leads us, to every sea and shore,
> For love of gain the wide world's harbours we explore.[2]

It was the 'love of gain', the motive of all Holland's far-flung ventures, that enabled the Dutch merchants in Japan to endure the repeated humiliations to which they were subjected. Already in their Hirado days they had humbled themselves to save their necks and their business: a newly erected warehouse was torn down to appease an official who had noticed the Christian date on the cornerstone. But if they had any illusions that Deshima would be better than Hirado, the Dutch were soon made aware of the manner of living which they would be expected to follow. They were prisoners, free only to walk up and down the two streets of their tiny isle, watched, guarded and spied on. Once a year, in the spring, the factory director and a few of his assistants journeyed to Edo (modern Tokyo) in order to offer presents to the shogun and thus demonstrate their fealty. Accounts of the embassies in the years 1691 and 1692 have been preserved in the *History of Japan* by Engelbert Kaempfer, a German physician serving with the factory during those years. Kaempfer related,

Having waited here upwards of an hour, and the Emperor having in the mean while seated himself in the hall of audience, Sino Cami and the two Commissioners came in and conducted our Resident into the Emperor's presence, leaving us behind. As soon as he came thither, they cry'd aloud Hollanda Captain, which was the signal for him to draw near, and make his obeisances. Accordingly he crawl'd on his hands and knees, to a place shew'd him, between the presents rang'd in due order on one side, and the place, where the Emperor sat, on the other, and then kneeling, he bow'd his forehead quite down to the ground, and so crawl'd backwards like a crab, without uttering one single word.3

The shogun (whom Kaempfer called 'the Emperor') was not contented with these formalities alone, but summoned the Dutch embassy for a second interview, during the course of which he had the foreigners interrogated on a great variety of subjects. Then, to end the entertainment properly, 'he order'd us to take off our Cappa, or Cloak, being our Garment of Ceremony, then to stand upright, that he might have a full view of us; again to walk, to stand still, to compliment each other, to dance, to jump, to play the drunkard, to speak broken Japanese, to read Dutch, to paint, to sing, to put our cloaks on and off. Mean while we obey'd the Emperor's commands in the best manner we could, I join'd to my dance a love-song in High German. In this manner, and with innumerable such other apish tricks, we must suffer ourselves to contribute to the Emperor's and the Court's diversion.'4

It was not only in Japan, of course, that the Dutch were willing to submit to such indignities in the hope of profit. In China they did not hesitate to kowtow three times and then nine times before the Emperor when their trade mission visited Peking in 1685.[5] The view of the Dutch merchants was that anything which would benefit the Company must be performed. In justification of their acts of submission they could point to the fact that mighty princes of Japan prostrated themselves before the shogun, and the monarchs of distant nations paid reverent homage to the Chinese emperor. It must be noted, however, that representatives of other European nations were not always willing to demean themselves (as they considered) in this manner. A Russian envoy to the Court of Peking, for example, once refused to kowtow to the Emperor because he 'only knelt to God'. The Chinese court was offended, and the mission accordingly suffered.[6]

The treatment of the Dutch by the Japanese grew somewhat more lenient as the years passed and as the fear of Christianity gradually subsided, but as late as 1804 Captain Krusenstern, who had brought a Russian envoy to Nagasaki, was unable to find words to express how shameful and barbarous the conduct of the Dutch appeared to him and 'how much it is to be regretted that an enlightened European nation, owing its political existence to a love of freedom, and which has acquired celebrity by great actions, should so far debase itself from a desire of gain as to attend with submission and devotion to the hateful commands of a set of slaves.' At an order from the interpreter, 'Mr. Factory-Director, make your compliment to the High Official!' the Dutchman was required to incline his body until it formed nearly a right angle, and was forced to remain in this position with his arms extended until the official at length gave him permission to stand in his natural posture. After one brief and unsuccessful attempt to induce the Russians to bow in a similar manner, the Japanese gave no more trouble on that score.7 But, as the Dutch may well have argued, the Russians went home empty-handed.

The glory of Holland, of which Vondel had sung, was already much faded in Kaempfer's time. The people which had risen to greatness by driving the Spaniards from their country had so given themselves to the commercial spirit that 'when Louis XIV was actually advancing in the conquest of their country with the most rapid success, he was regularly supplied with gunpowder and ammunition by this nation of merchants.'8 In the eighteenth century conditions in Holland grew steadily worse. The fleets which had swept up the Medway and Thames in 1666 and which had tolerated no rivals in the seven seas could no longer afford adequate protection to Dutch merchant shipping. There was constant quarrelling among the men in high position, and 'there were in every city men, who wished more for the plunder than the prosperity of their country.'9

The decline in the fortunes of the Dutch nation was paralleled by that of its East India Company. All the sins of the home government were reproduced by the Company, and to them were added the variations and enlargements made possible by the atmosphere of the colonies. The corruption and greed of the officials has been described by one eminent Dutch scholar as 'putting in the shade the worst that has been attributed to oriental peoples'.10 In Japan, where strict regulations curbed the *élan* of the Dutch merchants, there was nevertheless considerable smuggling. Indeed, as the eighteenth century advanced and there was less and less profit to be derived from the legitimate trade at Deshima, the chief excuse for maintaining the factory was the private smuggling in which the Dutch engaged.

Few skilled or learned men entered the service of the Company in the eighteenth century. The 'surgeons' were usually no more than barbers' apprentices, and the chief qualification of a director was apt to be his family relationship to other directors.11 In Batavia, the overseas headquarters of the East India Company, one governor founded a Latin school in an attempt to bring some culture to his organisation, but the school was short-lived. The dregs of the Dutch nation, for that was what most of the Company's men represented, could not have been expected to respond to such efforts. Their sole purpose was to make money, and to this end they devoted themselves with unbounded energy and complete ruthlessness. Even when measured by the eighteenth-century yardstick of economic exploitation, the activities of the Dutch company in the Indies cannot fail to horrify us. In 1740 occurred the massacre of 10,000 Chinese in Batavia, a senseless and barbarous step by the Company. Many Dutchmen in Holland were profoundly shocked when they heard this news, and one of them wrote a long poem in which he revealed the full brutality of his compatriots abroad.[12]

From such misfortunes Japan was spared by the severe treatment she afforded the Dutch. Insolent and overbearing in Batavia, where they held military power, the Dutch were servility itself on Deshima. Already in the eighteenth century they had gained notoriety in Europe for their behaviour in Japan. It was commonly believed, although it does not appear to have been true, that the Dutch were made to trample on pictures of the Virgin and Child to prove their indifference to the Christian religion. Swift in *Gulliver's Travels* did much to give this story currency, but even among Dutch writers the Deshima businessmen were sometimes criticised for their lack of religious principles. In the play *Agon, Sultan of Bantam* (1769), for instance, an Indonesian princess is made to reply to the boastful remarks of a Dutchman with the words

Th'enslavement of a Race may be by Fate compelled,
But ere the Dutch arrived the East had not beheld
Free Men who in Japan themselves do base Slaves make,
And but for Gain their God on Deshima forsake.[13]

The Dutchmen on Deshima were typical of the Company. Not many more than a half dozen of them (and these were chiefly foreigners) can be singled out as men of culture and intelligence of all those who visited Japan during the two hundred and fifty years of the factory's existence. Most of them were completely uninterested in Japan, and regarded it as a great imposition if they were required to attend a local festival, or indeed do anything which kept them away from their accounts. The pages of the factory journals kept by the successive directors form a dreary succession of business calculations, with seldom a word to suggest that the Dutch were living in what was one of the most fascinating countries in the world. The Swedish scientist C. P. Thunberg, who served as surgeon of the Dutch factory in 1775-6, declared that a European who was condemned to pass the rest of his life on Deshima would be buried alive. There was not the slightest intellectual stimulation to relieve the dull monotony of the days.

Here, just as in Batavia, we pay a visit every evening to the chief, after having walked several times up and down the two streets. These evening visits generally last from six o'clock to ten, and sometimes eleven or twelve at night, and constitute a very disagreeable way of life, fit only for such as have no other way of spending their time than droning over a pipe of tobacco.[14]

There were, it is true, numerous obstacles placed by the Japanese in the way of Dutchmen who sought to learn more about the country in which they were living, but such men as Kaempfer and Thunberg who really wished to spend their time more profitably than 'droning over a pipe of tobacco' overcame official opposition to their projects.[15] From the rest little or nothing reached Europe to enlighten an exploration-mad society. As Krusenstern complained of Holland, 'Europe owes nothing to this nation with respect to a knowledge of the Japanese empire . . . I cannot help attributing this reserve of the Dutch to a ridiculous, mean, and at all events a very useless policy, contrary to the spirit of a philosophical age, and unbecoming a republican government.'[16]

But even when the point is reached at which the nullity, if not the viciousness, of most of the representatives of the East India Company becomes perfectly apparent, one cannot but remark that the Japanese were fortunate to have the Dutch, of all the Europeans, as their mediators with the West. The fact that the Japanese were spared the outrages inflicted on the native populations of the Indies was in large part due to the skill with which they handled the Dutch, but had the factory at Deshima been English or Russian, the Japanese would probably have been forced, to the detriment of their country, to yield greater concessions than the Dutch enjoyed. Had, on the other hand, a weak nation like Spain or Portugal been the channel of information, the Japanese would have been able to learn very little about modern advances in science. Holland, in spite of her decline in grandeur, possessed in Leiden one of the important centres of medical research, and students from all parts of Europe gathered there to work under the celebrated Boerhaave and others. Some of the achievements of Dutch science were transmitted directly to the Japanese by the factory doctors, and much was also learned from books as Japanese came gradually to read Dutch.

Apart from those fields in which the Dutch still maintained some of their old eminence, there was still much they could teach the Japanese. It did not matter to the Japanese, for example, that the eighteenth-century Dutch painters were not as good as Rembrandt or Vermeer; the techniques of perspective and shading, which even the most mediocre of their painters could handle, were in themselves profound discoveries to the Japanese. Hundred-year-old Dutch books of astronomy or navigation were as exciting to such men as Honda Toshiaki as if they had just been written. Even the ignorant, money-minded merchants on Deshima knew a thousand things with which no one else in Japan was familiar.

The great problem lay in establishing communication between the Dutch and their would-be Japanese students. The earliest dealings with the Dutch had been conducted in Portuguese, the then *lingua franca* of the Orient, but as that language lost its importance, there were fewer Dutchmen who could use it easily, and the Japanese realised that they would have to talk to the Dutch in their own language. The study of Dutch began in Nagasaki during the second half of the seventeenth century, and by 1670 there were interpreters who could not only speak but read the language.[17] This is not to say that Portuguese was at once entirely abandoned; there continued to be Portuguese interpreters into the eighteenth century, as well as experts in Chinese (of several varieties), Corean, Loochoo, Siamese and the languages of other countries with which Japan permitted herself to have commercial relations.

The Nagasaki interpreters were government officials who enjoyed hereditary positions. Their abilities of course varied from man to man, but on the whole their achievements were not impressive. We possess a kind of report card for the 1693 interpreters: 'Barely knows any Dutch at all'; 'Because he is either stupid or lazy, he knows only the slightest amount of Dutch in spite of the fact that he has been studying for years'; 'He, like his father, has a reputation for being an interpreter of Portuguese, but he has not the slightest comprehension of the language.'[18]

These were not very good marks for the aspiring interpreters to receive from their Dutch teachers. To aid these frail vessels in the comprehension of their communications, the Dutch for a time sent Chinese translations along with the originals. These can scarcely have been of much help to the Japanese, however, for they are in such bad Chinese that they are virtually unintelligible unless one already knows what the Dutch text means.

In their defence, it must be said that the problems confronting the interpreters were enormous. They had no dictionaries save for rough-and-ready lists of words and phrases, no grammars and no competent teachers. As one of the interpreters put it to a prospective student of Dutch, it was easy enough to learn the Dutch word for wine, and one might in time learn to say 'I drink wine', but it was extremely difficult to acquire such phrases as 'I enjoy drinking wine', let alone any more subtle expression.[19] It was not only a matter of learning a language with a totally dissimilar grammatical structure, but also of attempting to pronounce complicated series of consonants and vowels with the simple open Japanese syllables. And Japanese were presumably no better linguists in those days than at present.

Although interest in the West among Japanese scholars (as opposed to the interpreters) did not die out entirely after the 'Christian century', it became increasingly difficult to obtain any information. The government, it is true, was furnished each year with a report on happenings (*fūsetsusho*) by the Dutch factory director on his annual visit to Edo, but only those high in the administration had access to them. From time to time the Dutch also presented the court in Edo with maps and illustrated books. These were accepted along with the more usual offerings of cotton cloth and strong liquors, and were then carefully stored away. In 1717 a factory director was asked, to his surprise, to translate the title of a zoology book presented by the embassy of 1663. The same book, still looking quite new, reappeared in 1741, and questions were again asked about its contents.[20]

The Japanese attitude towards Western books continued to be influenced by the fear and hatred of Christianity, even when that religion no longer presented any threat to the security of the country. It was fear of Christianity which dictated the policy of banning books written in Chinese by the Jesuit priests and converts in Peking, regardless of whether or not the works had to do with religious matters. In 1630 a decree was issued forbidding the importation of thirty-two religious and scientific works by Matteo Ricci and other Jesuit scholars. Copies already in Japan were confiscated and either burnt or secretly stored by the government. Included among these books were translations of Euclid's *Elements* and Cicero's *On Friendship*, as well as geographies and astronomical treatises.[21]

The period of greatest severity in the censorship of Chinese books began in 1685 when a zealous official in Nagasaki discovered a book relating to Christianity aboard a Chinese ship. He was rewarded for his diligence by being made censor of all books imported from China, and went to great lengths to prove that his position was not a sinecure. His office either destroyed or sent back to China with the offending passages blotted out any work which mentioned Christianity in whatever context. When censorable books were discovered aboard a Chinese vessel, the captain and crew were cut off from contact with other ships, the cargo could not be unloaded, and the chief officers of the ship were generally forbidden to return to Japanese waters. But however careful a Chinese captain might be to see that no objectionable literature was aboard his ship, he could not have been expected to know, for example, that the Japanese censor would take umbrage at a novel because it contained the words 'Lord of Heaven' (*tenju*), a term commonly used by Christians for God, when the words did not actually have that meaning in the book.[22] To such lengths was the anti-Christian censorship carried.

The banning of Chinese books on European religion and science had the effect of cutting off Japanese scholars almost entirely from the achievements of the West. A few copies of the forbidden books were hidden in private libraries, and some even circulated in manuscript, but such works were prized chiefly for their bibliophilic value rather than for their contents. It was not felt necessary to prohibit the importation of books in European languages because no one in Japan, apart possibly from a few interpreters, could read them. Occasionally some Chinese translation of a Western scientific work was tacitly permitted into the country on account of its manifest practical value, but the number of such books was trifling.

It was not until 1720 that any general relaxation of the restrictions occurred. In that year the shogun decreed that banned books which did not actually expound Christian doctrine might circulate in Japan. This shogun, Tokugawa Yoshimune, was greatly interested in the sciences, particularly mathematics and astronomy, and his decree is traditionally associated with his desire to obtain an improved calendar. In Japan, as elsewhere in the orbit of Chinese civilisation, the calendar held an importance second to none in the administration of the state. It was the obligation of the ruler 'to give the time to the people'; that is, to promulgate a calendar which was in keeping with the observable motions of the planets and stars, and thus to ensure that rites took place at the proper time. In addition, the calendar served as an almanac for the nation, with information as to the correct days to plant crops, lucky days for beginning enterprises, etc. Yoshimune, as a good Confucian ruler, felt it incumbent on him to give the people a flawless calendar, and his scientific training permitted him to recognise that the current one was carelessly made and full of mistakes.

A Kyoto silversmith named Nakane Genkei was recommended to Yoshimune as a calendar expert, and thereupon was invited to Edo for an examination. Nakane's responses pleased the shogun so much that he was requested to punctuate for Japanese reading a recently imported Chinese calendar study.[23] Nakane executed the order, but on presenting the punctuated book, reported that it was only an extract from a longer Western study, and that unless he could see the complete work, it would be impossible for him to give a clear explanation of the meaning of the text. A copy of the Chinese version of the original was eventually secured, on the basis of which Nakane compiled his calendar. He was still not satisfied with his work, however, and informed the shogun that it would be necessary to consult other Western books in order to gain a real understanding of the correct methods of making calendars. The prohibition placed on all books containing the word 'Lord of Heaven' or the name of Matteo Ricci prevented Japanese scholars from advancing in their studies. Nakane concluded his plea with the suggestion that if it was the shogun's desire to place calendar-making on a scientific basis in Japan, the severe restrictions on the importation of Western books in Chinese translation must be relaxed.[24]

Yoshimune's decree of 1720 represented a necessary first step in the direction of the acquisition of a knowledge of Western science, but the number of books in Chinese on the subject was very limited. It was not until 1741, however, that Yoshimune decided to encourage the study of the Dutch language, when he ordered Noro Genjō and Aoki Konyō to learn the language, the former for scientific purposes, the latter in order to make a dictionary. The two men did not begin their studies until the following year, when they were given some lessons by the interpreters accompanying the Dutch embassy to Edo. Since they were able to receive instruction only during the few days of each year that the Dutch were in the capital, it is small wonder that they did not progress very rapidly.[25] Noro managed by 1750 to compile his *Japanese Explanations of Dutch Botany*[26] from conversations with members of the Dutch embassies and from translations made for him of European botanical studies. Aoki's dictionary was not completed until 1758. Although this was not an impressive work, certainly not for a prominent scholar, it possessed considerable historical importance.

More significant than these achievements of Noro and Aoki was the cachet of respectability given to Dutch studies. It was no longer possible to dismiss 'barbarian learning' as an unworthy pursuit when two of the most distinguished men in the country with the encouragement of the shogun were devoting themselves to its study. Dutch learning was thus extended from the small circle of Nagasaki interpreters to the shogun's palace itself, and before many years had elapsed there were students of the West in every part of Japan.

NOTES

1. *Cf.* Boxer, *Jan Compagnie in Japan 1600–1817*, p. 4. This work contains valuable information on the early period of the Dutch factory, only briefly treated here.

2. Vondel, *Werken*, vol. 3, pp. 628–9.

3. Kaempfer, *History of Japan*, vol. 3, pp. 87–8.

4. Kaempfer, pp. 93–4.

5. Vixseboxse, *Een Hollandsch Gezantschap naar China*, p. 67.

6. Ch'en, *Sino-Russian Diplomatic Relations since 1689*, p. 488. This was Spafari's mission of 1676.

7. Krusenstern, *Voyage Round the World*, vol. 1, pp. 257–62. It should be noted, however, that this ungainly 'compliment' was far less humiliating than the bow on hands and knees exacted of Japanese subjects, or of the Dutch in Kaempfer's day.

8. *History of the Internal Affairs of the United Provinces*, p. 24.

9. Playfair, *Inquiry into the Permanent Causes, etc.*, p. 68.

10. C. Snouck Hurgronje, quoted in Du Perron, *De Muze van Jan Companjie*, p. 13.

11. Feenstra Kuiper, *Japan en de Buitenwereld in de Achttiende Eeuw*, p. 40.

12. W. van Haren, *Gedicht op den moord gepleegd aan de Chineesen te Batavia*. (Quoted in Du Perron, p. 164.) The poem contains such lines as this description of the murder of a Chinese family. The father begs

his Dutch assailants to spare his child's life, if not his wife's or his own:

> For an answer he feels the steel slash his vitals,
> And sees while still dying his dearest ones perish.
> They seize the poor child by his tender and chubby legs
> And swing him thrice through smoke and flames,
> And dare to crush him thus, still moaning, against the wall,
> So that brains and blood stain the executioner's face.

13. Quoted in Du Perron, p. 198. The author of the play was O. Z. van Haren.

14. Thunberg, *Travels*, vol. 3, p. 64.

15. Titsingh (factory director between 1779 and 1784) declared that it was want of initiative which kept the directors from learning about Japan, not lack of opportunity. But the Company replied to his suggestions for the selection of directors that it was 'a general rule in these parts to sacrifice to Mercury, but never to Pallas.' *Vide* Boxer, '*The Mandarin at Chinsura*', p. 4.

16. Krusenstern, vol. 1, p. 252.

17. Itazawa, *Rangaku no Igi*, etc., pp. 460–1.

18. Itazawa, p. 466.

19. *Cf.* Sugita, *Rangaku Kotohajime*, pp. 38–9.

20. Itazawa, pp. 150–2.

21. *Vide* Sakanishi, *Prohibition of Import of Certain Chinese Books.* The fullest account of the banned books is Nakamura, *Edo Bakufu no Kinsho Seisaku.*

22. Nakamura, p. 203.

23. The work was the *Li-suan Ch'üan-shu* (*Rekisan Zensho*), a collection by Mei Wen-t'ing (1633–1721) compiled from various Western works. This was a pre-Copernican study, but the Japanese were impressed by even so outdated a book. *Vide* Shimmura, *Zoku Namban Kōki*, p. 120.

24. *Tokugawa Jikki*, vol. 46, p. 292.

25. It has often been stated since Ōtsuki's *Rangaku Kaitei* (1783) that Aoki actually visited Nagasaki, but Shimmura (pp. 21–4) shows convincingly that this was not the case.

26. *Oranda Honsō Wage.*

Chapter Two

THE RISE OF BARBARIAN LEARNING

COMPARATIVELY few people in eighteenth-century Japan ever saw a foreigner. Those who lived in Nagasaki might occasionally have come across Chinese merchants and sailors, and those who lived along the road to Edo might even have caught a glimpse of a Dutchman in his palanquin being hurried off on the annual mission to the capital, but most Japanese thought of foreigners (and particularly Europeans) as of a special variety of goblin who shared only superficial resemblance with normal human beings.

The usual name given to the Dutch was *kōmō* or 'red-hairs', a name more intended to suggest a demonic being than to describe the actual colouring of the foreigners' hair.[1] The Portuguese had also at one time been declared by the shogunate to possess 'cat's-eyes, huge noses, red hair and shrike's-tongues',[2] but the words 'red-hairs' by themselves came to mean only the Dutch, and they were thus always portrayed by Japanese artists with suitably tinted locks. One might imagine that personal observation would have persuaded the Japanese that the foreigners were actually not so terrifying to behold, but one visitor to a Dutch ship reported, 'When we went aboard, the captain and many others took off their hats to salute us. They have dark sallow faces, yellow hair and green eyes. They seem to appear from nowhere, and are just like goblins and demons. Who would not run away from them in fright?'3

As time went on, however, more sophisticated people attempted to disprove the fanciful descriptions of the Dutch which were in common circulation. 'People say that the Dutch have no heels, have eyes like animals and are giants,' related one man, 'but the fact is that people of every country differ somewhat, and just because the Dutch do not resemble us, we must not say that they are like animals. We are all products of the same Creator.' This writer felt that it was not worth the effort to deny the rumour that when Dutchmen urinate they raise one leg like dogs.4

Not only in the matter of personal appearance were the Dutch considered to be very strange creatures; the fact that they were unacquainted with traditional Chinese teachings caused some educated men to classify them as animals on those grounds alone. A daimyo once asked Honda Toshiaki how it was that the Dutch, whose ignorance of the writings of the sages clearly marked them as animals, were nevertheless able to produce such fine articles. Honda answered wryly that even animals are capable of surprising skills.5 Shiba Kōkan, another leading student of Western learning, replied to a similar query, 'If what you say is true, human beings are not as clever as beasts.'6

People like Honda or Shiba, with enlightened ideas about the Dutch, were by far the minority. For most, Oranda (the Japanese rendering of Holland) stood for all that was new and outlandish. When the poet and novelist Saikaku began to write verses in a vein which seemed eccentric to his contemporaries, they referred to them as being in his 'Oranda' style, thus branding their irrationality. 'Oranda' was sometimes also used in an agreeable sense to describe things which were the last word in fashion, but most frequently the term simply meant nonsense. Even the children of Nagasaki at their games cried, 'That's the Dutch way!' when something was done wrongly.7

The few people like the official interpreters who came in direct contact with the Dutch do not appear to have made the most of their opportunities. Their attitude was one of extreme inquisitiveness mixed with a fondness for the exotic. One would like to call this attitude one of 'intellectual curiosity', but a glance at any of the books of interviews with the Dutch reveals the haphazard nature of their questions. 'Who is the commanding general in Holland?' 'Do you have false teeth in your country?' 'Are there big rivers in Holland?' 'What is meant by "mummies"?'8 Such was a typical series of questions, and however carefully answered, virtually the same things would be asked of the next group of Dutch to be examined.

It was Japanese love of the exotic which led to the collection of all manner of European curiosities, ranging from watches to strange animals. Dutch books and scientific instruments were bought at high prices by wealthy amateurs, not for their intrinsic interest, but as oddities. The scholar Ōtsuki Gentaku (1743–1813), justifying trade with the Dutch, gave a long list of useful objects imported from Holland,9 but in practice only Dutch medicines and cloth were widely known or used in Japan. Economists complained that the importation of Dutch goods led to extravagance. One man drew up a table of degrees of increasing luxury in dress: the parvenu went from cotton to pongee, to silk, to brocade, to Chinese embroidered cloth and, finally, to Dutch woollens, considered the most unusual and therefore most desirable of all.10

The Nagasaki interpreters shared in the general fondness for foreign things. They were delighted, for example, to attend a Dutch New Year dinner, finding every dish fascinating if not exactly to their taste.11 Some of the interpreters were proud to have a foreign-style room in their

瑠璃燈

Shiba's drawing of the factory
(from Shiba,

director's room on Deshima

Kōkan Saiyū Nikki, 1815)
Collection Professor C. R. Boxer

houses. When Shiba Kōkan visited Nagasaki in 1788 he ate Chinese moon-cakes in a Dutch room, a happy blend of exoticisms. Shiba, however, was much less enthusiastic about Dutch interior decoration than the interpreters. He recorded a visit to the factory director's room: 'There was a row of chairs next to each of which was a silver spittoon standing about two feet high, looking like a flower-vase. On the floor-matting was a rug with a flowered pattern, and a glass chandelier hung from the ceiling.' While Shiba was contemplating the room with faint distaste, the director came in, a long pipe in his hand, and greeted the Japanese. 'Isn't this a splendid place?' he exclaimed self-contentedly. Shiba replied, 'I am dazzled', but to himself remarked that the Dutch seemed to think that the Japanese were very primitive not to go in for such decorations.[12]

Only a few of the interpreters attempted to make scholarly use of their contacts with the Europeans. In 1763 an interpreter named Kitajima Kenshin completed a work called *Explanations of the Dutch Celestial and Terrestrial Maps*, based on Dutch originals of 1700. Kitajima was not content, however, with translating Dutch cartographical theories, but advanced one of his own, that Japan formed a special section of the globe, together with Ezo, Tartary, Corea, the Loochoos, Formosa, Luzon, Java, etc.[13] This region, which he named *Fortis Jamato*, bears a distinct resemblance to the Greater East Asia Co-Prosperity Sphere, although Kitajima's influence is not apparent in the latter concept.

Kitajima was aided in the preparation of his work by the interpreter Nishi Zenzaburō, one of the most gifted Dutch scholars of the time. In 1767 Nishi undertook the ambitious project of single-handedly compiling a Dutch–Japanese dictionary. Had this laudable effort been completed, the study of Dutch would certainly have been greatly facilitated, but Nishi died in the following year, having progressed no farther than the letter B.[14]

Nishi is also known as the man who discouraged the two

Sugita Gempaku

(from Sugita, *Rangaku Kotohajime*, 1869 edition)

physicians Maeno Ryōtaku (1723–1803) and Sugita Gempaku (1733–1817) when they informed him of their desire to learn Dutch. It is clear that some of the interpreters jealously guarded the study of Dutch as a family secret, and this factor may have been behind Nishi's declaration of the virtual impossibility of learning the language. Maeno, who had already had some instruction from Aoki Konyō in Dutch, without making much headway, resolved nevertheless to go to Nagasaki to learn what he could. He made the trip about 1770 and returned with a number of Dutch books and a phrase-book containing a few hundred words. As yet he was unable to do much more than to spell out the words in the learned books he now possessed.

Sugita, who had been so discouraged by Nishi's advice that he had entirely abandoned the idea of studying Dutch, found his interest in Western medicine aroused anew in 1771 when he was shown two textbooks of anatomy. The owner indicated that he was willing to sell, and Sugita examined the books closely. 'I couldn't read a word, of course, but the drawings of the viscera, bones and muscles were quite unlike anything I had previously seen, and I realised that they must have been drawn from life. I wished with all my heart that I might somehow acquire this book . . . but at the time I was so poor that it was entirely beyond my means.'[15] Sugita's clan-leaders came to his rescue and bought him one of the books.

The work Sugita acquired was the *Tafel Anatomia*, written in 1647 by J. A. Kulmus, a German.[16] Once in possession of the book, Sugita was anxious to test its validity with actual experiments, but at the time, the only persons in Japan who performed dissections were the *eta*, or pariah class. These unfortunate people served as butchers, tanners and furriers, occupations felt to lie beneath the dignity of normal citizens, and dissections were considered to be their proper task. Doctors occasionally hired the services of an *eta* for this purpose; some years before Sugita's time two court physicians had written a study based on eight dissections that they had witnessed, in which they attempted to reconcile the discrepancies between the anatomical drawings in Chinese texts with their actual observations. This they did by declaring that on deep reflexion they had come to the conclusion that there must be physiological differences between Chinese and Japanese.[17]

As good luck would have it, a friend wrote to Sugita one day in April, 1771, that a certain doctor was to have a dissection performed on the day following. The scene was the execution ground at Kotsugahara, and the subject was a fifty-year-old woman nicknamed 'Old Mother Green Tea', who had been put to death for some great crime. Sugita asked some of his friends, including Maeno Ryōtaku, to be present. When the latter appeared the next day, he was also carrying a copy of the *Tafel Anatomia*, one of the books he had obtained during his stay in Nagasaki. Sugita's description of what followed deserves to be quoted at length:

We all went to the place in Kotsugahara prepared for the anatomy lesson. The dissection itself was to be performed by an *eta* named Toramatsu, who was reputed to be skilled in this art and who had promised to come. On the day of the dissection, however, he suddenly took ill, and an old man of ninety years, said to be his grandfather, appeared to take his place. He was a robust old man, and told us that he had been performing dissections since his youth and had cut up a good many people in his time.

The dissections which had taken place up to this time had been left to the *eta*, who would point to a certain part he had cut and inform the spectators that it was the lungs, or that another part was the kidneys. Those who had witnessed these performances would go away convinced that they had seen all there was to be seen. Since, of course, the name of the organ was not written on it, the spectator would have to content himself with whatever the *eta* told him. On this day, too, the old *eta* pointed at this and that, giving them names, but there were certain parts for which he had no names, although he had always found such things in the same place in every corpse that he had ever cut up. He also remarked that none of the doctors who had previously witnessed his dissections had ever wondered what these parts were.

When Ryōtaku and I compared what we saw with the illustrations in the Dutch book, we discovered that everything was exactly as depicted. The six lobes and two ears of the lungs, and the three lobes on the right and four lobes on the left of the kidneys, such as were always described in the old Chinese books of medicine, were not so found. The position and shape of the intestines and stomach were also quite unlike the old descriptions.[18]

Sugita and Maeno were by now convined of the superiority of the Dutch anatomy text, and decided to translate it. The only aids to translations which they possessed, however, were the crude vocabularies Maeno had been given in Nagasaki. The two men, together with a colleague named Nakagawa Junan, spent the next four years working on the translation, often spending many hours attempting to determine the meaning of a single word. There was not only the difficulty of discovering what a Dutch term meant, but also of finding a suitable Japanese equivalent for it. Sometimes they used the old words, such as were found in Chinese books of medicine; at other times they were forced to invent new expressions because the Chinese terms did not designate precisely the same things as the Dutch ones. Eventually, however, the translation was completed, and it was decided to publish it. Sugita and Maeno knew that a rather trivial book entitled *Tales of Holland*,[19] published in 1767, had been confiscated and the blocks destroyed because the Dutch alphabet had been reproduced in its illustrations. To smooth the way for their new book, therefore, they had copies presented in advance both to the court of the shogun in Edo and to the imperial palace in Kyoto. Then, when they were assured that there was no objection from any quarter, they released the book to the public, the first work to be translated from the Dutch and openly circulated.

The importance of the *Tafel Anatomia* is not to be measured merely in terms of whatever advance it made possible in Japanese medicine. It started a great wave of interest in Dutch learning of every description, although medicine continued to be the chief subject of study. Most fortunately, this sudden increase of interest in Western learning coincided with the term as factory doctor of C. P. Thunberg, whose stay in Japan has already been mentioned. When the Japanese discovered that Thunberg was far more learned than any of his recent predecessors, they plied him incessantly with questions, both at Nagasaki and at Edo, when he visited the capital. Thunberg recorded how the Japanese looked up to him 'as an oracle, whom they suppose capable of giving them information upon every subject',[20] but at last the inquisitiveness which had so characterised earlier dealings with the Dutch had been given a direction. Although questions on scientific matters did not preclude the possibility of enquiries on trivialities, some useful purpose was now served by the interrogations.

Thunberg was much impressed by the zeal and determination of the Japanese physicians who visited him in Edo, but had a low opinion of their professional skill. He declared that they had so poor a knowledge of internal medicine that it was only by chance that they ever cured anyone. It is amusing to read how, for example, the Japanese doctors would spend a full quarter of an hour feeling the pulse in each wrist of a patient, but Thunberg's insistence on the virtues of bleeding as a cure in a 'host of circumstances' makes one realise that Western medicine had not yet reached its apogee either. But for the Japanese believers in the new Western science there was little room for doubt, and the physicians went ahead with phlebotomies, albeit with trembling fingers.[21]

It was about this time that the Japanese name for foreign studies came to be *rangaku* (the *ran* being extracted from 'Oranda') in place of the old *bangaku* or 'barbarian learning', indicating the new dignity in which they were held. Numerous aspiring young men went to study with Maeno and Sugita. By this time Maeno had become very skilled in Dutch, and had written several books to aid beginners, but the most important textbook was the *Ladder to Dutch Studies*[22] written in 1783 by Maeno's pupil, Ōtsuki Gentaku. In this work Ōtsuki gave only a brief survey of Dutch grammar and pronunciation which, valuable though it was, took second place to the real purpose of the book, the defence of Dutch studies *per se*. The new *rangaku* for the first time was declared to be as worthy of the superior man's attention as traditional Chinese philosophy.

The clash between *rangaku* and Confucianism which first occurred at this time, when Dutch studies were assuming prominence, lasted for many years without a clear victory for either side. Earlier men such as Aoki and Noro were by training Confucianists, and Sugita himself had written that *rangaku's* rise would have been impossible had it not been preceded by Chinese studies, but the Confucianists were quick to attack when they thought they saw a dangerous rival. Ōtsuki defended Dutch studies:

Ever since in recent years Dutch learning has risen, there has been a tendency for Confucian scholars to reject it, declaring that barbarian theories should not be adopted. What is the meaning of such criticism? Dutch learning is not perfect, but if we choose the good points and follow them, what harm could come of that? What is more ridiculous than to refuse to discuss its merits and to cling to one's forte without changing?[23]

Ōtsuki's attitude appears sensible enough to us, and the reader may wonder why the same man could not both study Dutch science and preserve the traditional virtues of filial piety, benevolence, decorum and the rest. However, behind the question of the value of Dutch studies as such lay the key issue of Chinese intellectual supremacy. The established formula for Tokugawa Japan had been the combination of Chinese learning with Japanese 'spirit'. Most of the numerous Japanese Confucianists of the time attempted to demonstrate that the intellectual attainments of China were balanced by the superior Japanese spiritual virtues, and that perfection in both would make the best of all possible men. *Rangaku* had no place in this scheme of things; whatever Japan lacked in the way of learning was to be supplied by China. In other words, the Japanese had to choose between Chinese and Western knowledge as the complement of their own spiritual heritage; it was not possible simply to add *rangaku* to what already existed without profoundly disturbing the prevailing mode of thought.

The first counterblow by the partisans of Dutch learning to the criticisms of the Confucianists took the form of an attack on China itself, not because of any hostility to Confucian morality or towards the Chinese people, but because it was felt that there was room for only one learning. Ōtsuki used the new geographical knowledge to attack China's claims as the centre of civilisation:

Hide-bound Confucianists and run-of-the-mill doctors have no conception of the immensity of the world. They allow themselves to be dazzled by Chinese ideas, and, in imitation of Chinese practice, laud the Middle Kingdom, or speak of the Way of the Middle Flowery Land. This is an erroneous view; the world is a great sphere on the surface of which are disposed the various nations. Although boundaries are determined by nature, each people gives honorific names to the place where they themselves live. China is called the Middle Land, the Middle Plain, the Middle Flower, the Middle Kingdom, or else the Flowery Capital, the Divine Continent. Similarly, Holland calls Germany, her motherland, 'Middelland', and our country proclaims itself to be 'Nakatsukuni'—'The Land in the Middle'. England uses the location of her capital as the starting point in counting degrees of longitude, and must also have a corresponding manner of naming her country.

Speaking from the size of the country, Egypt, a territory of Africa, should be termed the centre of the world. This would mean that China and Japan are at the eastern end of the world, and Holland and the other European nations at the northwest. But what excuse is there for us to adopt the proud usage of China and speak of the Middle Flowery Land, or of Flowery People, Flowery Ships, Flowery Things, etc.? For long years we have been imitating them, senselessly delighting in their ways without thinking of anything else. This has led to our excessive stupidity with respect to geography, and to a limitation on the knowledge we have gained with our eyes and ears. Thus it is that there are people who know only the names of China and India, and some extreme cases who think that Holland is a Chinese possession. Or, they consider every foreigner, apart from the Chinese, to be a barbarian unworthy of comment. How crude and how narrow such learning is![24]

Variations on the same themes are found in the prefaces to the *Ladder to Dutch Studies* which were written by Ōtsuki's friends.[25] 'Our former sovereigns had commerce with all countries, seeking out the best things in each place. They did not choose between "Chinese" and "barbarian", and that is why both Confucianism and Buddhism are found in Japan.' The same writer (Kuchiki Ryūkyō) noted that the compilers of the *Chronicles of Japan* referred to the Chinese as 'barbarians', and that they were thus classed in the first Japanese census. Another preface-writer, Ogino Kyūkoku, declared that Chinese learning was dead, and that its best traditions were now maintained by the Dutch. Dutch learning, which was based on actual facts and not on empty theories, must therefore be studied by Japanese. In these prefaces, then, the method of attack is already shifting from the imputation that Chinese are not better than other people to the more positive statement that they are not as good as the Japanese or Dutch.

The emergence of this attitude is of the greatest significance in the history of Japanese thought. From the beginnings of civilisation in Japan, the model had always been China, directly or indirectly. There had inevitably occurred considerable modifications of Chinese ideas in Japan, and some Japanese aesthetic and spiritual concepts were never vitally affected by Chinese example, but, by and large, China was admitted to be the fount of all wisdom, and such Japanese claims for recognition as existed generally took the form of 'Even though we are a small country, we are just as good as China in many ways.' With the *rangaku* movement, however, the unique claims of China to distinction were denied: 'the sun and moon shine on every place alike.' Japanese scholars began to doubt the value of all that had been believed for more than a thousand years.

The protest against Chinese learning assumed a different form among the advocates of *kokugaku*, or native learning, whose rise to prominence roughly paralleled that of the Dutch scholars, and who were much influenced by them. It was the attempt of the devotees of *kokugaku* to discover in the native literature of Japan and in the Shinto religion a complete culture, and thus to free Japan of all dependence on China. The lengths to which such men went to prove their thesis were sometimes comical, notably in their efforts to demonstrate that the Japanese possessed writing before the introduction of Chinese ideographs, but equally in their fanciful etymologies. A school founded on so insecure a basis was naturally eager to gather to itself whatever outside support there might be, and thus the *kokugaku* scholars quickly adopted the anti-Chinese arguments of Ōtsuki and others. It was even announced that *rangaku* itself was a necessary element in the training of the scholars of Japanese learning. The students of *rangaku* for their part neither welcomed nor rejected their strange allies; in general, their attitude was vaguely respectful towards Shinto, but they knew enough about the rest of the world to realise that Japan was neither the leading nor the most cultured nation.

The Confucianists, who were the common target of the partisans of Japanese and Dutch learning alike, responded acrimoniously, and were perhaps driven further than they intended in the direction of uncompromising orthodoxy. Towards the end of the eighteenth century the government was persuaded by the court scholars to forbid the teaching of any but the strict Chu Hsi school of Confucian philosophy, and though in the nineteenth century the importance of Western learning became increasingly evident, the restrictions on it grew even more severe.

It would be unfair, however, to suggest that all Confucianists were uncompromising enemies of progress. Ōtsuki himself quoted with approval the remarks of Shibano Ritsuzan (1734–1807), an orthodox Confucian scholar who nevertheless saw some value in Western learning. He stated that even barbarians incapable of reading Chinese books might possess the ability to make deductions from their personal observations which were valid for all mankind.[26] This rather grudging admission of the possible merit of foreign learning referred primarily to European medicine, the one branch of *rangaku* which escaped official wrath in the difficult days of the early nineteenth century. The study of Dutch medicine was in any case the object of most of the men who turned to *rangaku*, but when it became dangerous to dabble in other types of foreign learning, some men became doctors in spite of themselves so as to continue their Dutch studies with impunity. Only gradually did Western science gain supremacy in all fields. By this time Confucianism and the old Japanese 'spirit' had drawn together, and the new dichotomy of 'Eastern morality and Western techniques' was made by innumerable Japanese writers.

In the eighteenth century, with which we are primarily concerned in this study, however, there was greater freedom for the students of Western learning. Ōtsuki, who had begun as a doctor, became so proficient in Dutch that he decided to devote himself chiefly to the language. In 1789 he opened the first Dutch Language School in Japan, the Shirandō in Edo. Between 1789 and 1826 the school had ninety-four pupils, chiefly men interested in medicine, but including men of other professions.[27] Similar schools were later founded in other parts of the country. The total number of people who learned Dutch both at these schools and in other ways is impossible to ascertain, but it is true to say that most of the interesting, if not of the influential, men of late eighteenth-century Japan were attracted by the new learning, some only as a curiosity, others with deep conviction. As Sugita wrote in 1815, at the age of eighty-two, when looking back on the development of the studies which he had done so much to promote:

They say that one drop of oil cast into a wide pond will spread out to cover the entire surface, and this may well be so. In the beginning, there were just the three of us— Maeno Ryōtaku, Nakagawa Junan and myself—who came together to make plans for our studies. Now, when close to fifty years have elapsed, this learning has reached out to every corner of the land, and each year new translations seem to be brought out. This is a case of one dog barking at something only to be echoed by 10,000 dogs barking at nothing.[28]

NOTES

1. It is difficult to say precisely what was meant by 'red-hairs'. The Chinese were the first to call Westerners by this name, probably because the Europeans' hair was so much lighter than their own as to suggest the red-haired demons of Buddhist paintings. The Japanese adopted the Chinese term, although individual writers who actually had seen Dutchmen sometimes said that their hair was yellow or brown, certainly much more likely colours.

2. *Tokugawa Kinrei-kō*, vol. 6, p. 572.

3. Hirazawa, *Keiho Gūhitsu*, pp. 2–3.

4. *Cf.* Ōtsuki, *Ransetsu-ben*, p. 494.

5. Honda, *Seiiki Monogatari* (henceforth abbreviated *SM*), pp. 126–7.

6. Quoted in Muraoka, *Shisei no Tetsujin Shiba Kōkan*, p. 32.

7. Shiba, *Kōkan Saiyū Nikki*, p. 92.

8. *Vide Oranda Mondō* (1724), pp. 3–7.

9. Ōtsuki, *Rangaku Kaitei* (henceforth abbreviated *RKA*), p. 221. His list included watches, telescopes, saffron, ivory, powdered sugar, cloves, pepper, velvet and various types of medicine and cloth.

10. Amenomori, *Tawaregusa*, p. 11.

11. Morishima, *Kōmō Zatsuwa*, p. 454.

12. Shiba, *Kōkan Saiyū Nikki*, pp. 100–6.

13. Shimmura, *Zoku Namban Kōki*, pp. 2–5.

14. Itazawa, *Rangaku no Hattatsu*, p. 30.

15. Sugita, *Rangaku Kotohajime* (henceforth abbreviated *RKO*), p. 46.

16. Kulmus' work was more properly called *Tabulae Anatomicae*, but here as elsewhere Sugita's memory apparently betrayed him. The other book that he was offered, the *Anatomia* of Kasparus Bartholius, seems to have entered his collection at a later date. Sugita consulted it and various other textbooks of anatomy in making his translation of the *Tafel Anatomia* known as the *Kaitai Shinsho*.

17. *RKO*, p. 52.

18. *RKO*, pp. 51–2.

19. This work is called in Japanese either *Oranda-banashi* or *Kōmō-dan*.

20. Thunberg, *Travels*, vol. 3, p. 256.

21. *Ibid.*, p. 201.

22. *Rangaku Kaitei*.

23. *RKA*, p. 226.

24. *RKA*, p. 226.

25. *RKA*, pp. 215–7.

26. *RKA*, p. 226.

27. Itazawa, *Rangaku no Hattatsu*, p. 53.

28. *RKO*, p. 86.

Chapter Three

STRANGE TALES FROM MUSCOVY

Rangaku might have remained a purely academic discipline, the stepping-stone to greater knowledge of European science, had it not been for the threats to Japan's peaceful isolation which caused some Japanese to turn to Dutch learning for guidance as well as information. These men were interested not so much in Dutch medicine or astronomy as in discovering how European example could help keep Japan safe from invasion by making the nation strong and economically sound. In the writings of such men as Honda Toshiaki one finds numerous references to the chief outside stimuli to Japan in the late eighteenth century, the letters sent by Baron von Benyowsky, and the return to Japan of the castaway Kōdayū. A discussion of these two figures and their importance is essential to the study of Japan's awakening to the West.

I. THE ADVENTURER'S WARNING

Few more curious personages are to be found in the pages of modern history than Baron Moritz Aladar von Benyowsky, whose career led him from Hungary, the land of his birth, across Asia to exile in Kamchatka, to the coasts of

Japan and China in a stolen vessel, to Europe and America where great dignitaries lent support to his chimerical projects, and finally to death in Madagascar after an attempt to establish himself as 'Ruler of all Rulers'. His lies and intrigues seem to have had little other motivation than a desire to create mischief, and this he did in all quarters of the globe, from the frozen north to the sultry swamps of Madagascar, and from Baltimore to the shogun's palace in Edo.

In his lengthy memoirs, Benyowsky's fertile imagination clothed his adventures in a profusion of picturesque detail. We are told not only of his capture in battle by the Russians, of his terrible journey in chains across the wilds of Siberia, and of his life in Kamchatka during the winter of 1770–1, but of beauteous damsels who could not resist his manly charms, and of the high honours which bravery and ability won for him. Interesting though a full account of his career would be, we need concern ourselves here only with Benyowsky's brief visit to Japan and the incidents immediately surrounding it.

It was in May of 1771 that Benyowsky, weary of his exile, engineered a revolt among the convicts of Kamchatka, and managed to gain control of a small vessel lying in the harbour. Typically enough, he proclaimed the purpose of his actions to be the overthrow of the 'usurper Catherine II', thus seeking to impart greater dignity to what must have been a rather sordid uprising. But this ambitious project was driven from Benyowsky's mind by more pressing considerations; his badly-equipped vessel was soon short of provisions, and it seemed doubtful that the crew would survive the journey back to Europe, much less have the energy to restore the rightful prince to the Czardom of All the Russias.

Fortunately for Benyowsky, land was sighted on 8 July 1771, or about two months after the escape from Kamchatka. The adventurer had much to say concerning his experiences in Japan at the 'Bay of Usilpatchar', as he fancifully called it.

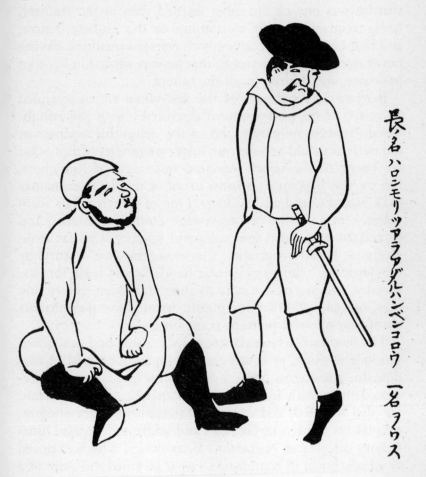

長名 ハロンモリッツアラアゲルハンベンコロウ 一名ヲワス

Benyowsky and his servant

(from Kondō, *Henyō Bunkai Zukō*, 1804)

There he was royally received by the great 'Ulikamhy', of whom he was informed 'that he was King of the province, and had married one of the daughters of the Emperor; that he was one of the most learned men in the country, being acquainted with astronomy in the highest degree, and that his soul was endued with celestial qualities, having never done harm to any one; that he was adored in his own province, and desired in all the others.'[1]

Benyowsky's account of the festivities which attended his visit, of his philosophical discourses with the enlightened Japanese monarch, and of the delightful manners of the natives would arouse our suspicions merely from what we know of the usual Japanese treatment of foreigners, but we also happen to possess proof of the fictitious nature of 'Ulikamhy' and all his court. One of Benyowsky's shipmates kept a record of the voyage from Kamchatka, and he related in a much less colourful manner, that far from receiving lavish hospitality, the strangers were warned by the Japanese 'who passed their hands across their throats, thereby wishing to intimate to their unbidden guests that they, one and all, hosts and guests, would have their throats cut if they allowed them to come on shore.'[2]

The harbour where Benyowsky's ship had anchored was one in Awa, in south-eastern Japan. The lord of that domain, anxious to get rid of his unwanted visitors, presented them with liberal amounts of rice, water and salt. He also accepted, and eventually passed on to the shogun, two letters written in German and addressed to the Dutch factory director in Nagasaki.[3] Benyowsky, who had posed as a Frenchman in Kamchatka,[4] now assumed the guise of a commander in the Navy of Her Imperial Roman Majesty, that is, the Empress of Austria, and claimed the help of the Dutch as an ally and friend of the 'high-mighty and illustrious states of Holland'. He apparently hoped that Dutch intercession with the Emperor of Japan would enable him to remain in the country long enough to conclude some profitable trading. But four days after his arrival in Awa, Benyowsky yielded to the menacing gestures of the natives and departed. After a brief stay at nearby Tosa, he next anchored at Ōshima off the southern tip of Kyushu.

While in Ōshima Benyowsky sent the factory director four more letters, three of them to express his gratitude for the provisions which the Japanese had given him at Awa and Ōshima. The last of the letters was by far the most important and gained great celebrity in Japan as 'Benyowsky's Warning'. It has aptly been called the 'first piece of national defence literature' in Japan, and is significant enough to be quoted here in full.

Highly Illustrious, High and Well-born Gentlemen, Officers of the Highly Esteemed Republic of Holland
Unkind fate, which has for some time been driving me here and there on the sea, has brought me for a second time into Japanese waters. I have come ashore here in the hope I might possibly meet with your high excellencies, and thus obtain help. It has been a great misfortune for me not to have had the opportunity of speaking to you personally, for I have important information to disclose. I have deemed it necessary because of my general respect for your illustrious states to inform you in this letter of the fact that this year, in accordance with a Russian order, two galliots and a frigate from Kamchatka sailed around Japan and set down all their findings in a plan, in which an attack on Matsma [Hokkaidō] and the neighbouring islands lying under 41° 38′ N. Lat. has been fixed for next year. For this purpose a fortress has been built on the Kurile island nearest to Kamchatka, and ammunition, artillery and a magazine have been readied.

If I could speak to you personally, I might reveal more than writing permits. Your high illustriousnesses may make such preparation as you please, but my advice, as an ardent well-wisher of your illustrious republic and a co-religionist, would be that you have a cruiser ready if you can. With this I further commend myself and am as subscribed, your most obedient servant

Baron Aladar von Bengoro[5]
Army Commander in Captivity.

20 July 1771 on the island Usma.

When I went ashore I left there a map of Kamchatka which may be of use to you.

We may wonder what reason Benyowsky had for sending such false tidings to the Dutch. Of their untruthfulness there can be no doubt. Far from planning aggressive moves against Japan, the Russians had all they could do to hold together their Pacific empire, which had never consisted of much more than a wretched colony in Kamchatka (where vodka was the most plentiful commodity), a handful of traders in the Kuriles and a string of tiny outposts in America, sometimes marked by such revealing names as Massacre Bay. Benyowsky was certainly aware of these facts, but a passion for the truth was never one of his attributes. Perhaps he hoped to ingratiate himself with the Dutch by disclosing the supposed Russian plot, but it is difficult to see what he expected thereby to gain.

In any case, Benyowsky's departure from Japan a month before even his first letter had reached the Dutch deprived him of the pleasure of witnessing the confusion he had aroused. The Japanese, unable to read Benyowsky's German, turned his letters over to the Dutch factory officials for translation. To aid in the identification of the mysterious foreigners, they also produced a pair of trousers and a shirt which had been bartered by some of Benyowsky's crew at Tosa, but the Dutchmen remained baffled as to the nationality of the pretended officer of the Holy Roman Empire. It was eventually suggested that the ship might have been a Spanish galleon on the way to Mexico from the Philippines, the only European vessel known to be near Japanese waters.

For many years afterwards, the meaning of Benyowsky's letters was discussed by earnest Japanese and, indeed, they started a new type of thinking about the problems of war. Apart from the two abortive attempts by the Mongols to invade the country in the thirteenth century, Japan had never known the fear of an attack from abroad, and military defence planning had been confined to problems that might arise in such internal warfare as had beset Japan previously to the establishment of peace in 1600. The sudden revelation of an external threat to Japan's security necessitated a great change in strategy, and led to a serious agitation in favour of increased military preparations.

The group of national defence enthusiasts who drew inspiration from Benyowsky's warning was at first limited in size by the secrecy with which his letters were surrounded. It was impossible, however, to prevent the interpreters and Dutchmen who had taken part in the translation from confiding the contents of the messages to interested visitors. Hirazawa Kyokuzan (1733–91), who journeyed to Nagasaki in 1774 as a member of a daimyo's entourage, left the earliest Japanese account of the foreign ship which several years before had touched at Awa. He was told that the letters revealed the captain of the ship to be a Russian under orders from his country to survey the waters of Japan in preparation for a Russian attack. It was gratitude for the provisions and firewood received at Awa which had prompted the captain to make his startling confession. 'Then he set sail and nobody knows where he went.'[6]

Three years after his return to the capital, Hirazawa set off for Hokkaidō, apparently to ascertain the truth of the rumours he had heard of Russian infiltration. It was not often that men of letters journeyed to the lonely northern island; not only did reports of its dismal climate discourage visitors, but suspiciousness and even hostility towards outsiders were well-known traits of the Matsumae clan which ruled the island. Hirazawa received surprisingly friendly treatment, however, presumably because it was clear that his visit was in the nature of a literary excursion and not an official tour of inspection. He related to the clan leaders the terrible warning of Benyowsky, and urged them to adopt new defence-measures, but his alarm was not shared by his hosts, who were doubtless confident that the bravery of the Japanese warrior was still a fair match for foreign guns.[7]

Another visitor to Nagasaki who was stirred by Benyowsky's letters was Kudō Heisuke (1734–1800), a doctor who visited the city in 1780 in order to study Dutch medicine. While he was there he became friendly with the interpreters, and eventually with the factory director himself, who confided many state secrets to him. Kudō learned, for example, that the Dutch considered Japanese policies to be highly inept in that they had permitted the Russians to extend their grasp to one after another of the Kurile Islands. Kudō was nevertheless inclined to discount reports of Russian designs on Japan, declaring that he believed them to have been invented by the Dutch traders in order to preserve their trade monopoly. In discussing an encounter between Russian traders and Matsumae clan officials of several years before he also wrote, 'I cannot believe that Russia intends to wage war on us. No importance could have been placed by the Russian government on the incident which took place in Ezo. I think it must rather be that the Russians have heard of the abundance of precious metals in Japan and wish to trade with us.'[8]

But Kudō could not be entirely tranquil; the news of Benyowsky's visit had upset him greatly. He wrote, 'We do not know what Benyowsky had in mind when he sailed around Japan surveying our coastline, but we must not ignore the fact that he did so. A detailed enquiry should be made into what happened.'9 This sugestion, together with his other findings, was included in Kudō's book *A Study of Red Ainu Reports* (by 'Red Ainu' he meant 'Russian'), completed in 1781. The work was later brought to the attention of Tanuma Okitsugu, then virtual dictator of Japan, who was so impressed by it that he ordered the Matsumae clan to submit a report on the situation in the north. The clan leaders responded in vague and mystifying terms, hoping thus to satisfy the government without revealing their military weakness, but Tanuma rejected their report and directed that a small expedition be sent to Ezo, Karafuto and the Kuriles to obtain first-hand information.

The mission of 1785-6 was described in the *Ezo Miscellany*,10 a short, factual work which, far from confirming Kudō and other enthusiasts who had vaunted the wealth of Ezo, related in detail the actual hardships of life in that desolate region. The members of the expedition were also able to confirm rumours of Russian activity in the Kuriles, but only in the most negative way. On the island of Urup they came across one miserable party of 'Red Ainu' who had been living there for six years. The contrast between the condition of these lonely men and the stories that the Japanese had heard of the fearsome Russian threat to Ezo made one of the party ask the Russians about what had happened to Benyowsky. 'Oh,' replied a trapper, 'he sailed off to America to teach the natives about Russian customs and astronomy.'

By the time that the mission to the north had returned to Edo, Tanuma was out of power, and his successor showed himself to be without interest in the explorers' information. The *Ezo Miscellany*, like so many other useful books written about this time, was consigned to oblivion in the government archives. But the repercussions of Benyowsky's visit were far from ceasing at this point; the most important product of his stimulus to Japan, the *Kaikoku Heidan*

(*Military Talks for a Maritime Nation*) by Hayashi Shihei (1738–93) did not appear until 1791.

Of all the late-eighteenth-century students of the West, Hayashi was the one who gained the greatest fame during his lifetime, both because of the intrinsic interest of his work and because of the sensational aspects of his career. For readers of today, however, the *rangaku* scholars who devoted themselves to the study of European arts or history are likely to appear the most congenial, and Hayashi's almost exclusive preoccupation with military science counts in his disfavour. He was, however, a person of exceptional significance in Japan's discovery of the West, and one well worth our careful study.

Hayashi came from the north of Japan, the home of many of the most intransigent of Japanese thinkers. Although his interest in things European was at first restricted to Dutch horsemanship, to study which he visited Nagasaki in 1775, he soon moved on to a more general consideration of European ways, possibly under the influence of his friend Kudō Heisuke.[11] After two more trips to Nagasaki he was filled with new ideas, and his impatience at the intellectual isolation in which Japan was living grew ever more intense. His visit of 1782 resulted in the compilation of his first major work, a geography of Corea, the Loochoos and Ezo. He chose this subject because he believed that all Japanese, regardless of their wealth or education, should be acquainted with the geography of these countries. The work contains some interesting things, but it is now commonly treated as a preliminary study for the epoch-making *Kaikoku Heidan*, which begins:

What is meant by a maritime nation? It is a country not connected by land to any other, but which is bordered on all sides by the sea. There are defence preparations which are suited to a maritime nation, and which differ in kind from those prescribed in Chinese military works, as well as from those which have traditionally been taught in Japan by the various schools. . . .

Military preparation for Japan means a knowledge of the way to repel foreign invaders, a vital consideration at present. The way to do this is by naval warfare; the essential factor in naval warfare is cannons. To be well prepared in these two respects is the true requisite of Japanese defence, unlike the military policies appropriate to such continental countries as China and Tartary. Only when naval warfare has been mastered should land warfare be considered.[12]

It may only seem too obvious to the reader that Japan, an island nation, had to possess a navy, but at the time that Hayashi wrote the above lines, Japan did not have a single warship nor, for that matter, a single vessel of any great size or pretensions. Military science meant only the art of civil warfare in the mountains and valleys of Japan, and the tactics which were studied were chiefly those found in such ancient Chinese texts as the celebrated *Art of War* by Sun Tzu. These works had not dealt with the problems of an invasion by enemy ships because China's chief worry had always been the violation of her land-frontiers by hordes of savage tribesmen; the respect for Chinese precedent was so great in Japan that no one since the half-forgotten days of the Mongol invasions had stopped to consider the military implications of the fact that Japan is surrounded by water.[13]

To combat this reliance on Chinese example, Hayashi felt it necessary to discredit China in the eyes of the Japanese. This he attempted to do by depicting the Chinese as potential enemies to Japanese independence rather than as bringers of enlightenment, their traditional role. The Manchu Dynasty, he asserted, had corrupted the good ways of the Chinese people. 'I believe that it is not improbable that some future Manchu ruler, profiting by a period of internal peace, will engage in rash foreign ventures, hoping to emulate the old achievements of the Mongols. If this happens, the Chinese will be moved chiefly by greed, and the benevolence of the Japanese government will not suffice to subdue them. Nor will they be intimidated by Japanese military prowess, for their attacking armies will be enormous.'[14]

It is hard to say how seriously Hayashi meant this argument to be taken; probably it was intended as no more than a warning that Japan must not assume complacently that the Chinese could be counted on to behave themselves like gentlemen. The real threat to Japan, as Hayashi often relates, was Russia.

Russia in recent years has become the mightiest of the nations of Europe. Her armies have extended their conquests to the distant territories of Tartary, to the land of Siberia, and even so far as Kamchatka. To the east of Kamchatka, however, there is no territory worth taking, and that is why there are indications that Russia has turned her attention towards the Kurile Islands. Already in 1771 an adventurer named Baron Moritz Aladar von Benyowsky was sent from Muscovy to Kamchatka, and from there to Japan, where he visited various harbours. He sailed halfway around Japan, sounding the depths of the different ports. Especially of note was his stay in the province of Tosa, where he left a letter for the Dutch director resident in Nagasaki. His motives for coming here are to be hated and feared.[15]

Hayashi's apprehensions of the possibility of a Russian attack were intensified by the high opinion he had formed of European military techniques. Unlike the Chinese, who relied most heavily on elaborate stratagems, or the Japanese, who placed their confidence in native courage and proficiency in close fighting, the Europeans considered fire-power to be the most important element in warfare. They had invented many unusual weapons including the air ship, which was designed primarily to terrorise the enemy soldiers.[16] The Westerners excelled particularly in naval warfare, and built ships of surpassingly fine construction. Hayashi had been informed that Benyowsky's vessel was 'powerfully built, like a small fortress',[17] rather excessive praise, we may feel, for the small galley Benyowsky commanded. Hayashi believed that European ships were so much superior to Chinese ones that Japan could not possibly find guidance in naval matters except from the West.

Behind the greatness of the European nations, Hayashi saw their wonderful laws, which kept them peaceful and orderly. 'Nations sometimes do invade each other's territories and attempt for many years to hold their conquests, but it never happens that soldiers of the same country fight among themselves. This is a point to which Japan and China have yet to attain.'[18]

It was also by virtue of the wonderful laws that so many Europeans had been inspired with the ambition to conquer distant lands. The great European tradition of learning (dating back perhaps 6,000 years) and the general familiarity with the sciences of astronomy and geography made this ambition easy to satisfy even without recourse to arms. Japan must not comfort herself with the thought that the Europeans were so far away that it was unlikely they could invade her. If Western armies did not themselves come to Japan, there was always the possibility that the Chinese and Manchus, who had become increasingly friendly towards the Europeans, might also adopt the wonderful laws and then experience the same desire for territorial expansion. Then the overwhelming military power of China could easily be brought against complacent, indifferent Japan.[19]

What remedy existed, then, against attack either by Europeans or by European-inspired Chinese? Japan must build her defences. Every part of the coastline of Japan should be fortified with naval batteries such as already were found in Nagasaki. This might seem an impossibly difficult task, but it could be completed in fifty years. 'A frontierless sea-road leads from the Nihon Bridge in Edo to China and Holland. Why is it that there are defence installations only in Nagasaki?'[20]

Before any more positive military steps might be taken, however, the samurai had to be re-educated. As a result of the protracted period of peace, the samurai had forgotten about the art of war and had surrendered themselves to debilitating luxuries. Schools must be established for instruction in both military and cultural subjects, for without literary attainments a soldier is no better than a barbarian. Such institutions would eventually produce men versed in both disciplines, rare though they have been in the course of history. Many Japanese generals had become famous, but with only two exceptions they had all lacked the necessary cultural abilities to make of them truly great men: these were the legendary Emperor Jimmu and Tokugawa Ieyasu. China could boast of a few such men, but the greatest of those endowed with both literary and martial talents was the Empress Catherine of Russia who had 'spread her virtue and extended her power'.[21]

The *Kaikoku Heidan*, Hayashi's contribution to the solution of Japan's military problems, cost the author a great deal of trouble. He apparently sold maps and even prints of his drawing of a Dutch ship in order to raise funds with which to pay the printer.[22] The first volume was published in 1787 in his native city of Sendai, but difficulties held up the rest of the work, and only four years later did the whole appear. No more than thirty-eight copies were actually bound into book form, but one of them fell into the hands of an enemy. Hayashi was denounced as a disseminator of false reports and as a danger to the state; eight months after the publication of his book he was arrested and sent to Edo where he was imprisoned. This unhappy turn of events can hardly have come as a great surprise to Hayashi, who had self-consciously written in the preface to the *Kaikoku Heidan*:

The teachers of military science for many generations past have all based their doctrines on Chinese textbooks, which naturally has meant that they have fallen into Chinese ways and have been ignorant of the proper defences for a maritime nation. I am the first person to have discussed this matter which has excited my deep concern. My extensive investigations into the subject have yielded the information incorporated in this book. But I know that no ordinary citizen is permitted to disclose such facts even if he possesses them; this silence is taken as a mark of circumspection. As I am a single man who likes to act when he is convinced of something, I have not given a second thought to the possibility of incurring the displeasure of the authorities. I have therefore listed without ornamentation those factors which have made it easy for any invader from Benyowsky on to attack Japan. My purpose in compiling this book has been to inform the people what is the essential defence for a maritime nation. This is why I have undertaken so grave a problem in spite of the humbleness of my position and the smallness of my virtue. I realise that I have gone far beyond my station and that I shall not escape punishment. But it is his words and not the author which matter.[23]

Hayashi was arrested by order of Matsudaira Sadanobu, chief of the state councillors, on the grounds that he had published a book which dealt with affairs of state, and which advocated the violation of existing laws. On being informed of his arrest, he recited a poetical epigram, the first of several famous ones composed towards the end of his life: 'Will this head fly or won't it? Spring will soon be here.'[24] Hayashi remained for almost six months in an Edo prison before this question was answered for him. During this time he received messages of sympathy and even promising offers of escape, but he stoically declined to shirk his punishment. The counsel ultimately prevailing that Hayashi was an ignorant person whom it would be pointless further to interrogate, an order was given that he be returned to Sendai for confinement. The blocks of the *Kaikoku Heidan* were also ordered to be destroyed.

After his return to Sendai, Hayashi was allowed to live in relative comfort in his brother's house, but he had fallen into a melancholic state and took no pleasure in anything. He gave himself the soubriquet of 'The Hut of the Six Withouts' (*Rokumuan*) from a poem he composed at this time: 'I have no parents, no wife, no child, no printing-blocks, no money, and nothing to be happy about.'[25] He lived for another year in this state of depression before he expired of chagrin.

Hayashi's crime in the eyes of the shogunate did not consist in his having ventured to criticise the government, but in his having published views considered inimical to the internal security of the state.[26] As Kaempfer, the learned German, had put it a century before, 'Liberty of Conscience, so far as it doth not interfere with the Interest of the secular Government, or affect the peace and tranquillity of the Empire, hath been at all times allow'd in Japan, as it is in most other Countries of Asia.'[27] Honda Toshiaki, for instance, had profited by the 'Liberty of Conscience' to write criticism of the government far more severe than Hayashi's, but was prudent enough not to publish his manuscripts. Matsudaira Sadanobu was actually not opposed to Hayashi's principal ideas, as is demonstrated by the fact that he afterwards ordered a strengthening of shore defences and himself made a tour of inspection of the eastern coasts[28]; he simply could not tolerate the insubordination Hayashi had shown in appealing publicly to the nation for support of his cause. The punishment that Hayashi received does not appear to us to have been very severe, but Matsudaira thereby succeeded in discouraging other independently-minded persons from publishing their opinions (and, incidentally, gave to Hayashi a measure of fame denied to more cautious contemporaries).

It cannot be pretended that the *Kaikoku Heidan* was inspired entirely by Benyowsky's visit and letters, but the essential points of the book—the danger from abroad and the need for sea defence—had their origins in Hayashi's speculations on the meaning of the adventurer's mysterious voyage. A European counterpart to the *Kaikoku Heidan* may perhaps be found in the memoir written in July 1776 by the French diplomat Jean-Benoit Scherer and presented to the French foreign ministry.[29] According to this strange document, word had leaked out from the Russian embassy in London of an English plan for a joint Anglo-Russian attack on the Japanese Empire. The combined fleets of the two countries would be placed under the command of Captain Cook, who would rendezvous with the Russians at Kamchatka under pretext of searching for a northern passage. Russia, Scherer's document went on, had promised to help the British with the prosecution of the American Revolutionary War if the campaign in Japan were successful, and England in turn agreed to help Russia by 'amusing Germany by a war that she would have her allies make' if this were necessary. Japan would be helpless to resist the Anglo-Russian invaders because, Scherer had learned, almost all weapons in the country had been melted down to make building-material. The only way of forestalling this attack would be to send a French fleet under Bougainville to supply the Emperor of Japan with arms with which to repel the foreigners.

The reader may perhaps already have guessed the source of Scherer's strange information. It was none other than Benyowsky who, not content with having upset Japan with his prophecy of an impending Russian onslaught, sought to hoodwink the great statesmen of Europe with an elaborated version of the same story. Scherer acknowledged his debt to Benyowsky, and suggested that Bougainville's fleet pick up the adventurer in Madagascar on its way to Japan, so that it might profit by his profound knowledge of the island empire. But the French foreign minister, the Comte de Vergennes, was sceptical about the reliability of the memoir, and the student of history was thus robbed of the pleasure of reading of a French fleet sailing into Edo Harbour with arms for the astonished Japanese. That would have been a spectacle worthy of Benyowsky.

2. THE RETURN OF THE CASTAWAYS

In 1637 it was decreed that no Japanese subject might leave the country or, having left it, return[30]: thus it was attempted to keep Japanese from learning of the outside world except as directed by the government. Before this edict there had been flourishing Japanese colonies in the Philippines and such distant places as Siam and Java, while Japanese mercenary troops were widely used both by Asiatic monarchs and by the new European rulers of the East. But with the prohibition on overseas ventures and on the construction of ocean-going ships, only isolated groups of Japanese Christians were left outside the country, and the Japanese soon lost their mastery of seamanship.

It should not be thought, however, that there was no longer any shipping within the confines of the Japanese Empire. According to Honda, ninety ships carrying rice alone entered Edo Harbour every day, and many more were constantly navigating inshore waters with cargoes of produce from the farming provinces on their way to Osaka and Edo. Such ships were small, poorly constructed and inexpertly handled, for the skippers no longer knew the old lore of the sea, and had not yet learnt the new science of navigation. When typhoons occurred it was inevitable that some ships should be lost at sea and others wrecked on distant coasts. Honda described the helplessness of such vessels when they were carried out to sea by a storm.

Even when the weather improves, the crew is at a loss to tell in which direction to head, and the ship floats about helplessly. As a last resort they cut off their hair and make vows to Buddha and the gods. Then they take out pieces of paper on which have been written the names of the twelve directions, roll them up into balls, and put them into a basket with a hole in its lid. (This they call *o-kuji*, chance.) The captain and crew, in tears, fervently call on Buddha and the gods of heaven and earth to indicate the direction. They grasp the basket in their hands and strike the lid. Then, when one of the pellets jumps out, they pick it up, their eyes blinded by tears of joy, and cry that it is the direction vouchsafed by Buddha and the gods. They then set their course by it, and go completely astray.[31]

Japanese ships were sometimes carried northwards by the Black Current to Kamchatka or the Aleutian Islands, and even to the western coast of North America. Other ships were driven by tropical storms as far south as Annam. From time to time castaways from shipwrecked vessels were returned to Japan, as in 1685, when the Portuguese brought to Nagasaki twelve Japanese who had been shipwrecked near Macao, thus attempting to restore friendly relations with Japan. The authorities were naturally suspicious of Portuguese motives, but after examining the ship and finding no religious articles or commercial wares aboard, accepted the castaways, and rewarded the Portuguese for their efforts with thirty sacks of rice. The old distrust of Catholicism persisting, the Portuguese were ordered never to visit Japan again, and the attempt to renew trade relations thus failed.[32] The Chinese and Dutch, who still enjoyed this privilege, also occasionally returned shipwrecked Japanese sailors, probably in the hope of ingratiating themselves thereby with the government.

Most of the castaways, however, never saw their native land again, either perishing under the attacks of hostile natives, or else intermarrying with them and thus losing their Japanese identity. Of such happenings we have, of course, no record, but from the end of the seventeenth century there had been a series of Japanese shipwrecked in Kamchatka, some of whom later gained considerable fame. It was in 1697 that Vladimir Atlassov, the conqueror of Kamchatka, came across a Japanese sailor named Dembei who was living in a native village. Presumably because of difficulties in communication, Atlassov did not at first learn the stranger's nationality. He related:

. . . that a Prisoner, who came over Sea in the Bussi (*a kind of whaling vessel*), had a peculiar Language; he wore small Whiskers, and had black Hair, and by his Visage did not look unlike a Greek. He said farther, that this Stranger wept as soon as he saw an Image among the Russians, by which he gave them to understand that they had the like in his Country. Wolodimir had this Man two years with him, in which Time he had learn'd something of the Russian Tongue; And having been two Years, before Wolodimir's Arrival, among the Koroeiki, he spoke at first in that Tongue, by an Interpreter; He said he was an Indian, and that in their Country there was a great deal of Gold, and whole Houses of China: Their Kings liv'd in Silver and gilt Palaces. Wolodimir had, likewise, taken a Piece of Silver-Coin from the Koroeiki, about one Sixth of an Ounce in Weight, which this Stranger affirm'd to be his Country-Coin. He said, that they used no Sables, no other Furs, for Linings, in India; But that their Cloaths were made of all Sorts of Stuffs, quilted with Cotton. Atlassow said, that that this Stranger travell'd with him, 6 Days Journy, from Anadirskoi to Liski, where he fell sick, and his Legs swell'd, for which Reason, he was brought back to Anadirskoi Simovia. He gave him the Character of a Man of good Sense and Breeding.[33]

Dembei's true identity was eventually discovered, and he was taken to St. Petersburg where he was presented to Peter the Great in January of 1702. The czar made various enquiries about Japan and later ordered that Dembei be sufficiently instructed in the Russian language to permit him to explain the grammar of Japanese to 'four or five adolescents'.[34] Three years later was founded the Japanese Language School, which lasted in spite of many vicissitudes until 1816, when it became impossible to find anyone willing to study Japanese.[35]

Since it was obvious that the newly-organised school could not survive the death of Dembei unless replacements for him were discovered, it was decreed that if any Japanese were shipwrecked on the coast of Kamchatka, one of them should be sent to St. Petersburg. During the following century or more, wrecks occurred with sufficient frequency to keep the school provided with a teacher most of the time. The castaway-professors were generally trained for a few years in the Russian language, baptised, given Russian names and wives, and then installed in their academic duties.

It may be imagined with what consternation the Japanese government learned (in 1781) that a school had been established in Russia for the purpose of teaching the Japanese language. 'Japan's secrets are being revealed to the foreigners!' was the general cry. There was little justification for such alarm; the school was certainly one of the most ineffectual ever created. When Kōdayū, the most famous of the castaways, was asked to correct a dictionary compiled by one of his predecessors, he was surprised to find that most of the words were in patois and of a coarse nature.[36] The students, discouraged by the ineptness of the instruction, had to be offered special inducements to stay on, but nothing could make them learn usable Japanese. On the few occasions when their services were required the graduate interpreters were totally unintelligible in their adopted language, as one might expect when a Russian attempted to speak an illiterate Japanese fisherman's tongue. The lowest point of the school was reached near its end, when it was discovered that two Russians who had been studying Japanese for nineteen years were still unfamiliar with the elements of the language.

The reason for the existence of the language school was not, as it was feared, in order to facilitate an invasion of Japan. It was rather an expression of the eighteenth-century passion for exploration which caused governments and individuals to allot great sums of money for the purpose of voyages of discovery. When, for example, Captain Broughton sailed round the island of Ezo and along the eastern coast of Japan (thereby causing much commotion among the inhabitants), it was not in order to acquire new colonial possessions for England, but because Broughton was 'a navigator who was zealous to extend the bounds of geography, and who was well aware that little was to be done in any other part of the Pacific Ocean.'[37] This disinterested predilection for geographical knowledge was difficult for Japanese to understand, but it was before long to give way to the nineteenth-century ideas of Captain Krusenstern, who wrote after his voyage of 1803–4:

With regard to taking possession of Aniwa, this could be done without the smallest danger, as the Japanese, owing to their total want of weapons of every description, would scarcely think of resistance. . . . I am convinced that this conquest would not cost a single drop of blood.[38]

When Kōdayū appeared at the court of St. Petersburg in 1791, Russian interest in Japan had dwindled almost to the vanishing point. The last major Russian-sponsored voyage of discovery in the area of Japan had been Captain Spanberg's of 1738–9. He had been instructed to overcome the 'inveterate Asiatic unsociableness' of the Japanese by returning any castaways who happened to be in Kamchatka, and by other demonstrations of amity, but his brief contacts with Japanese officials did not come to anything.39 In the years that followed Spanberg's expedition occasional flashes of interest in Japan had saved from extinction the moribund language school, but by the time of Catherine the Great, neither the desire to improve existing maps nor the hope of commercial advantage drew people's attention towards the island empire. Territorial aggrandisement, such as Captain Krusenstern was to suggest, does not appear to have been widely considered.

The most important event in Russo-Japanese relationships up to the end of the eighteenth century was the visit to Russia and return to his native country of Kōdayū, the ship-captain from Ise, whose career will be described below. The earlier Japanese castaways in Russia of whom we have record were pathetic but colourless sailors, at first bewildered by the unfamiliar society which they had accidentally entered, and then swallowed up by it, almost without a trace. Kōdayū, however, was a lively and intelligent person, able to hold his own and more in the strange circumstances in which he found himself. Consider the description of him by M. de Lesseps, a French traveller who met Kōdayū in Kamchatka in 1788:

His figure has nothing in it singular, and is even agreeable; his eyes do not project like those of the Chinese; his nose is long, and he has a beard which he frequently shaves. He is about five feet in stature, and is tolerably well made.

His superiority over his countrymen was calculated to make him be distinguished; but this circumstance has less weight than the vivacity of his temper and the mildness of his disposition. . . . The freedom with which he enters the house of the governor and other persons, would among us be thought insolent, or at least rude. He immediately fixes himself as much at his ease as possible, and takes the first chair that offers; he asks for whatever he wants, or helps himself, if it be within his reach. . . .

He is possessed of great penetration, and apprehends with admirable readiness every thing you are desirous to communicate. He has much curiosity, and is an accurate observer. I was assured he kept a minute journal of everything he saw, and all that happened to him. . . . His repartees are in general sprightly and natural. He employs no concealment or reserve, but tells with the utmost frankness what he thinks of every one.[40]

Lesseps also informs us of the veneration in which Kōdayū was held by his men. We can only imagine that he was a source of great strength to them during the trials they had already endured. In January of 1783, Kōdayū's ship, the *Shinshō Maru*, had set sail from his native port of Ise for Edo with a cargo of rice.[41] The first night out the ship was caught by a severe storm, and was driven far off its course. For seven months the small vessel wandered about the ocean, and it must have seemed to the crew that they were fated never to see land again, when one day, the fog suddenly lifting, a lookout descried the island of Amchitka in the Aleutians. The overjoyed men made all speed to get ashore, little realising that this bleak island with its perpetual fog and cold was to be a worse prison than ever was the *Shinshō Maru*.

Four years passed on Amchitka. As companions in their loneliness the Japanese had two Russian fur-trappers as well as a number of Aleut natives. When at length a sealing vessel came to transport the furs to Kamchatka, it was decided to take along the surviving Japanese. Of an original sixteen men only nine were left.

Kamchatka did not prove to be a great improvement over Amchitka. The Japanese led a wretched existence there, hungry most of the time if not suffering worse calamities. This Russian possession was then one of the dreariest places in the world, having fallen into such disrepute that 'even its name is hardly pronounced without a mixture of horror and disgust; it is looked upon as a country in which hunger, cold, poverty, in short every species of misery is concentrated.'[42] Three more Japanese died in Kamchatka before they were removed to Irkutsk in Siberia, since 1753 the location of the Japanese Language School.

It seems likely that had it not been for the energy of Kōdayū the surviving Japanese would have spent the rest of their days in Siberia. Three times Kōdayū requested permission to return to Japan, with only one reply: he was informed that it was the will of the empress that the Japanese settle in Russia and become merchants; she herself would give them money for this purpose. Kōdayū was still not daunted. He became friendly with Erik Laxman, a Finnish scholar living in Irkutsk, and interested him in the plight of the Japanese. Laxman agreed to accompany the five remaining castaways to St. Petersburg, there to petition the empress for authorisation to leave Russia. The Japanese were delighted at this turn of events, but just then two of them were taken so seriously ill that they could not make the journey. Thinking they were on the point of death, they both adopted the Russian faith. As Kōdayū explained:

When people die in Russia who have not received the teachings of the Church, they are not buried in holy soil, but are treated much like dead animals. For this reason, when Shinzō was very ill and thought he was certain to die, he was converted to the Russian faith. Then, to his surprise, he recovered, and he bitterly regretted not being able to return to Japan with me.[43]

Kōdayū, his two companions, and Laxman set out from Irkutsk in January of 1791 and travelled day and night at the greatest possible speed to St. Petersburg. But the unhappy castaways were doomed to still another delay: three days after their arrival Laxman fell gravely ill, and was forced to remain in bed for three months. Kōdayū's affection for his benefactor made him devote all his energies to tending him—'and thus it was I thought no more about our petition'.

It was not until October of that year that Kōdayū was granted an audience with the empress, but already he was well known to the fashionable world of St. Petersburg. Invitations and presents poured in from all quarters; everyone was desirous of meeting a Japanese, especially so engaging a one. Kōdayū bore these attentions with dignity and amiability, fully living up to his new role of a 'noble savage'. Certain court officials of a more practical nature began also to consider the benefits that might accrue from trade with Japan, but Catherine herself at first remained very sceptical on this subject. Only after meeting Kōdayū and hearing in detail Laxman's arguments on the great commercial opportunity which repatriating the Japanese might afford, did she change her views.44 In 1792 she issued an edict to the Governor of Siberia directing him to return Kōdayū and his two companions to Japan in the manner outlined by Laxman's memorial. She ordered him further to select certain merchants to go along on the journey, and enumerated presents which the governor was to offer to the Japanese authorities in his own name. Possibly it was the fear of a rebuff from the Japanese which caused the empress deliberately to divorce herself from direct connexion with the mission and to insist that it be placed under the command of an official of minor rank.

The ship *Ekaterina*, under the command of Lieutenant Adam Laxman, the son of Kōdayū's friend, sailed from Siberian waters on 13 September 1792, with the three castaways aboard. The port of Nemuro in Ezo was reached on 17 October, and Laxman sent ashore letters in Russian and Japanese announcing the reason for his visit. The local authorities in Ezo were thrown into great confusion by the arrival of these unexpected guests, and advice was frantically sought from Edo. In the meantime, Laxman was hospitably received and even invited to use the governor's bath.

When Laxman's letters were delivered to Matsudaira Sadanobu, he was perplexed as to what he should do.[45] The meaning of the Japanese message was clear in spite of certain faults of orthography: the Russians intended to proceed to Edo and negotiate for trade. Matsudaira, good Confucianist that he was, looked to precedent for guidance. The last attempts by European nations to secure trading privileges in Japan were made by England in 1674 and by Portugal in 1685. Both nations had been refused, the English because their queen was Portuguese, and the Portuguese because they were of that nation detested as the source of the Christian heresy.[46] In the case of the Russians, however, there could be no question of a Portuguese alliance, and their variety of Christianity was apparently harmless. Matsudaira moreover appreciated the Russian kindness in having returned the castaways, and felt that their behaviour in the affair had been exemplary. He asked the opinions of three advisers, who variously responded: (1) the castaways should be accepted and the Russians then ordered to leave at once; (2) the Russians should be asked to negotiate in Nagasaki; and (3) Ezo should be opened for trade.[47]

In the end, Matsudaira fell back on another precedent. In 1727, the King of Cambodia had sent presents to the shogun, asking for trade. The presents had been refused, but the Cambodians were issued with a permit to enter Nagasaki Harbour.[48] Matsudaira felt that the Russian request was analogous enough to invoke this precedent, and thus he could treat them legally and with the proper etiquette. If the Russians, like the Cambodians, failed to pursue their trade efforts, they at least would not have been insulted by a refusal. If they did seek trade in Nagasaki there would be time to reconsider when they came. Laxman was accordingly informed that he would have to make his request for trade at Nagasaki, the normal place for dealings with foreigners. The Russian envoy was issued with a document permitting him to call at that harbour and, although he was warned that no favourable response could be promised, it seems likely that had he sailed immediately to Nagasaki, an agreement might have been reached. Laxman, however, considered that he had performed all that lay within his authorisation, and decided to return to Russia for further instructions.[49]

All, during the course of these negotiations, the three Japanese castaways had disconsolately waited for the day when they might be allowed to go back to their homes. Laxman steadfastly refused to part with them, however, because of his avowed intention of proceeding to Edo for their transference. He consented to release the castaways only when the shogunate had made it perfectly clear that unless Laxman yielded them on the spot he would have to take them back to Russia with him. By this time, however, one of the three Japanese had died of scurvy.

The Russian ship departed, and Kōdayū, restored to his native land, was again very much a centre of attention. He was summoned before the shogun, who examined the books and presents he had brought back, and interrogated the former castaway about his life in Russia. His questions were asked at random, and often suggest that the shogun was more interested in displaying his own knowledge of Russia than in learning new things from Kōdayū. The interrogation sometimes took the form: 'There is a great clock in the castle-tower of Moscow. Have you seen it?' Similar enquiries about the statue of Peter the Great and a famous Muscovian cannon were followed by, 'Have you ever seen a camel?'[50]

The scribe of the interview between the shogun and Kōdayū was Katsuragawa Hoshū, a physician of considerable attainments who at one time had been given instruction by Thunberg, the Swedish scientist. Dissatisfied with the fragmentary interrogation he had witnessed, Katsuragawa resolved to make fuller use of the knowledge that Kōdayū had gained in the West. Day after day he questioned the former ship's captain about every detail of his experiences in Russia. The ninth volume of his report, for example, contains articles on sleighs, sedan-chairs, boats, military equipment, swords, musical instruments, silverware, lacquer, books and printing, hour-glasses, compasses, billiards, umbrellas, chess, tiles, glass, soap and many other subjects.[51]

Certain information that Kōdayū could probably have furnished does not appear in Katsuragawa's book. News of the French Revolution, for instance, must certainly have reached Kōdayū's ears while he waited in St. Petersburg for his audience with the empress, but no mention of it is made, either because it did not occur to Katsuragawa to ask about such matters, or else because he was unwilling to include potentially dangerous thoughts in his work.

Within the limitations he imposed upon himself, however, Katsuragawa did a magnificent job of drawing out from Kōdayū's recollections the most comprehensive picture of a European nation yet obtained in Japan. Our respect for Kōdayū's powers of observation is also increased; little of interest in Russia appears to have escaped his eyes. But once he had told his story and demonstrated for the benefit of print-makers his proficiency in writing Russian script, there seemed to be little left for him to do. People were of course curious about his experiences, but he was not the social lion in Edo that he had been in St. Petersburg, and before long he all but disappeared from public attention. This turn of events did not disturb Kōdayū much; he married and took employment in the herbary of the shogun, where he spent the years until his death in 1814 (at the age of 72) quietly cultivating his garden.[52]

In the isolated world of Japan the return of one of her citizens from abroad was an event notable enough to merit discussion for many years. Kōdayū's stories caused the fears over Russian southward expansion to be joined (though not replaced) by an intense admiration for Catherine the Great and her rule. Matsudaira and other important men in Japan waited with impatience for Laxman's ship to appear in Nagasaki Harbour. It seemed as though a new era might soon commence, one in which Japan would be emerging from her isolation of long standing. Why, the Japanese wondered as the years went by, didn't the Russians come back? They could only suppose that the question of trade between the two countries was as important a consideration to the Russians as it was to themselves. The court of St. Petersburg, however, did not entertain very high hopes of commercial profits from Japan, and besides there were urgent matters closer to home which demanded their attention. The repercussions of the French Revolution and of the rise of Napoleon were so keenly felt in Russia that little attention could be spared for the minor matter of trade with Japan.

Not until 1804 did the Russians make use of the permit that Laxman had received. In October of that year, Captain Krusenstern's ship, the *Nadezhda*, bearing Ambassador Rezanov, sailed into Nagasaki Harbour to ask for trade. For six months the Russian ambassador was kept waiting while leading figures in the capital debated over the policy to be adopted. Matsudaira Sadanobu, now out of power, attempted to persuade the government to deal with the Russians, and his opinions were shared by most of the enlightened men of the day. It was only after months of uncertainty that the reactionary leadership of the shogunate was able to decide to send the Russians away. This action aroused sharp outcries: some writers declared that the treatment of the foreign ambassador had been disgraceful, and even inhuman. 'The Russians must think that we are animals!' declared Shiba Kōkan.[53]

*

It is difficult to estimate precisely the lasting results of the two major outside stimuli to Japan of the late eighteenth century—Benyowsky's warning and the return of Kōdayū. The country remained closed to the foreigners even after these events, and official policy became if anything more reactionary. Though there would thus seem to have been little positive effect, there were certain political changes brought about, and thought within the nation was intensely stimulated. Among the changes we may note the assumption of direct control over Ezo by the shogunate, beginning in 1799, and the establishment of a magistracy (*bugyo*) at Hakodate. Two northern clans were ordered to defend Ezo, the Kuriles and Karafuto, and exploration parties were sent out by the government to survey these domains.

The *rangaku* movement had led Japanese chiefly towards the scientific achievements of the West. Contact with Russia made Japan aware that her isolation might soon be broken, and gave new impetus to the movement to make the nation technically and militarily the equal of Europe. However, the powerful conservatism of the leaders of the government resisted the pleadings for change by the men of the new learning. This does not mean that the latter were of no importance, but only that no group of individuals, however great their prestige or learning might be, was strong enough to shake the rigid Confucian structure of Tokugawa Japan. To achieve this, greater and even compelling pressure from outside Japan had to come.

NOTES

1. Benyowsky, *Memoirs and Travels*, vol. 1, p. 398.
2. Kropf (in *Notes and Queries* for 27 April 1895) quoted this account by Stepanov, a man who sailed with Benyowsky from Kamchatka (p. 324).
3. Copies of Benyowsky's six letters are preserved in document 40/11488 in the Rijksarchief at The Hague. Document 11710 (part of the Deshima *Dagregister*) contains the account of the Dutch reaction

to the letters. I have quoted below from these two documents. Kondō Morishige (in *Henyō Bunkai Zukō*, p. 70) gave a translation of the warning letter which is approximately correct in outline, but considerably altered from the original.

4. Lesseps, *Travels in Kamtschatka*, vol. 1, p. 156, related his surprise at the cool reception he was accorded by the Kamchatka officials when he first arrived. He discovered that this treatment resulted from 'the disadvantageous impression which they had imbibed of the character and genius of our [French] nation, originating in the perfidy and cruelty exhibited in the person of the famous Beniowsky in this part of the peninsula. This slave called himself a Frenchman, and acted like a true Vandal.'

5. Benyowsky, in his guise of an Austrian officer, adopted this Germanic version of his name in writing to the Dutch, and he was thus known also to the Japanese. Benyowsky's name was more properly Benyovszky, but it was by the former spelling that he was known in England.

6. Hirazawa, *Keiho Gūhitsu*, p. 8.

7. Shimmura, *Zoku Namban Kōki*, pp. 29–33.

8. Quoted in Kōno, *Aka-Ezo Fūsetsu-kō no Chosha Kudō Heisuke*, p. 605.

9. *Ibid.*, p. 601.

10. *Ezo Shūi* (Cambridge University Library MS, Siebold 300). This copy is stated to be the work of Satō Genrokurō, but the book is sometimes credited to other members of the expedition.

11. Hayashi, *Kaikoku Heidan*, p. 261 (biographical notes by Muraoka Tsunetsugu). The surname Hayashi is pronounced 'Rin' by some writers, i.e. Rin Shihei.

12. Hayashi, p. 7.

13. I mean, of course, defensively. Before the country was closed, armed Japanese ships had ranged about the East. The inferiority of the Japanese Navy had worried Hideyoshi, and indeed had been one of the causes of the failure of his Corean campaign. But Japanese military thinkers never considered the possibility that foreign ships might attack Japan.

14. Hayashi, p. 9.

15. *Ibid.*, p. 9.

16. *Ibid.*, p. 45. Hayashi includes a drawing of a *luchtschip* which he had seen in a *Kriegsboek*, presumably some Dutch military work. He declared his intention of making an airship and testing it, when he had the time.

17. *Ibid.*, p. 19.

18. *Ibid.*, p. 11. What exactly he meant by 'wonderful laws' (*myōhō*) is not clear; quite possibly it was Christianity.

19. *Ibid.*, pp. 24–5.

20. *Ibid.*, p. 18.

21. *Ibid.*, p. 242.

22. Boxer, *Rin Shihei and his Picture of a Dutch East-India Ship*, p. 53.

23. Hayashi, pp. 11–12.

24. Komiyama, *Fūken Gūki*, pp. 125–6. In the original, 'Kono kōbe, tobu ka tobanu ka? Ake no haru'. Since Hayashi was arrested at the end of the year, it was the 'eve of spring'; in the lunar calendar spring begins with the first day of the first moon.

25. This famous poem is known in two versions. The one quoted is 'Chichi haha mo naku, tsuma naku ko naku, hangi naku, zeni mo nakereba, mata omoshiro mo nashi'. The other version substitutes for the last three words, 'shinitaku mo nashi'—'I don't want to die either'.

26. Sansom (in *The Western World and Japan*, p. 226) states that another reason for Hayashi's arrest was his crime in having 'confided his views to certain Court nobles who were known to be hostile to the shogun's government'.

27. Kaempfer, *History*, vol. 2, p. 1.

28. *Cf.* Matsudaira, *Uge no Hitogoto*, pp. 167–9, for his views on sea defence.

29. Scherer's memoir is printed in full in Lefèvre-Pontalis, *Un Projet de Conquête du Japon par l'Angleterre et la Russie en 1776*, pp. 440–3.

30. *Tokugawa Kinrei-kō*, vol. 6, pp. 568–9.

31. Honda, *Chōki-ron* (in *Honda Toshiaki-shū*), pp. 211–12.

32. *Tokugawa Kinrei-kō*, vol. 6, pp. 594–8.

33. Strahlenberg, *An Historico-Geographical Description, etc.*, p. 462.

34. Barthold, *La Découverte de l'Asie*, p. 229.

35. Harima, *Rokoku ni okeru Nihongo Gakkō no Enkaku*, pp. 791 ff. Harima's account is the most complete. *Cf.* Lensen, *Early Russo-Japanese Relations*, p. 9.

36. Katsuragawa, *Hokusa Bunryaku*, pp. 259–60.

37. Broughton, *A Voyage of Discovery to the North Pacific Ocean*, p. v.

38. Krusenstern, *Voyage*, vol. 2, pp. 67–8. Aniwa is a cape and bay at the southeast end of Saghalien.

39. Golder, *Russian Expansion on the Pacific 1641–1850*, pp. 220–1.

40. Lesseps, vol. 1, pp. 211–15.

41. The voyage is described in Hayashi, *Tsūkō Ichiran*, vol. 8, pp. 134 ff.

42. Krusenstern, vol. 2, p. 219.

43. Katsuragawa, p. 254. Shinzō was given the name of Nicolai Kolotygin, and was so known to Klaproth who consulted him in 1805 about problems of translation. (Klaproth, *San Kokf Tsou Ran To Sets*, p. ii.)

44. A full account of Laxman's part in the return of Kōdayū, and the text of Catherine's edict may be found in Lagus, *Erik Laxman*, pp. 227–35. A Japanese translation of the edict is in Harima, *Rokoku Saisho no Kennichi Shisetsu Rakusuman*.

45. Matsudaira, pp. 164–7, contains his account of the incident.

46. Kaempfer, vol. 3, pp. 341–60, contains the 'Japan Diary' of the 1674 English ship.

47. Inobe, *Matsudaira Sadanobu to Ezo-chi Kaikō*, p. 1367.

48. *Ibid.*, p. 1369.

49. A translation of Adam Laxman's diary may be found in Harima, *Rokoku Saisho no Kennichi Shisetsu Adamu Rakusuman Nisshi*. Japanese scholars differ very considerably as to the degree of success of Adam Laxman's mission. Some believe that he all but opened Japan to Russian trade; others declare that the permit to visit Nagasaki was only a polite face to the unalterable conservatism of the shogunate. Laxman himself was pleased with his accomplishments, and the Empress Catherine II permitted him to include a Japanese sword in the family coat of arms.

50. Ramming, *Russland-Berichte schiffbrüchiger Japaner*, pp. 37–9. The shogun's questions were apparently based on an account by the factory director Hemmij, translated by Katsuragawa as *Roshiya-shi*. (In *Nihon Bunko*, vol. 5.)

51. Katsuragawa's book was entitled *Hokusa Bunryaku*.

52. Shimmura, *Shiden Sōkō*, p. 291.

53. Shiba, *Shumparo Hikki*, p. 472.

Chapter Four

HONDA TOSHIAKI AND THE
DISCOVERY OF EUROPE

I. HONDA'S CAREER

THE biographical information we possess
about Honda Toshiaki (1744–1821) is disappointingly
limited even for an age as reticent about the details
of individual lives as was his. Our chief source is a
short account in the nature of an encomium written
by Uno Yasusada, one of his pupils, in 1816, while
Honda was still alive.[1] Uno bestowed on his teacher
the usual items of praise of virtuous Japanese: Honda
had simple tastes, wore thin clothing in winter, and
slept only four hours a night. Uno failed, however, to
discuss matters which interest us far more, such as
the circumstances of the composition of Honda's chief
works, or the relation of Honda to other figures of his
time.

We are told that Honda was born in the north-western
province of Echigo, where his father, a samurai, had taken
refuge after killing a man. The geographical factor in
Honda's life was important, for his interest in the northerly
regions was first inspired by stories he heard from people
of his province who had visited Hokkaidō or who had

farmed there during the summer. In a memorial written in 1792, Honda stated:

I was born in northern Echigo, and when I grew up I used to mix with sailors, even occasionally going to sea with them. I became well acquainted with the geography of Ezo and with the customs and nature of the Ainu. From that time until the present, when I am fifty years of age, I have never ceased day or night to think of ways of developing the region.[2]

As a second son, Honda was under less obligation than the eldest to remain in Echigo with his family and to carry on its line. He appears to have had early ambitions of engaging in public affairs, and to this end decided to go to the capital. At the age of eighteen he arrived in Edo, and soon afterwards began the study of mathematics under Imai Kanenobu, heir to the school of Seki Kōwa, greatest of all Japanese mathematicians. He also studied astronomy and fencing. By the age of twenty-three he had become so proficient as to be able to open a school of his own in the district of Otowa. The subjects he taught were mathematics, astronomy, geography and surveying.[3]

Honda, along with his pupil Sakabe Kōhan, is often credited with having founded the studies of astronomy and navigation in Japan on a scientific basis, and also holds a place in the history of Japanese mathematics.[4] But he seems to have lost interest in these sciences and, entrusting the work of teaching at his school to Sakabe, devoted himself almost entirely to political studies. He travelled widely throughout Japan, examining geographical and social conditions, supply problems in various regions, and the general situation in the country. Personally coming into contact with bandits and highwaymen, he learned of the circumstances which force men to turn to such pursuits, and evolved plans both for preventing loss at their hands and, more important, for the elimination of the causes of banditry itself. Everywhere he found poverty and misery, with their attendant evil of infanticide. The one solution which suggested itself to him was that of trade, not only trade within the country, but with the nations of the entire world.

The first step towards achieving the kind of trade that Honda sought was a knowledge of navigation. To improve his ability in this science, he studied Dutch, becoming proficient enough in the language to be able to read and translate a work on navigation. In his books Honda referred constantly to Dutch learning, but we do not know how much he actually knew of the language. None of his longer translations survives, but certain mistakes in Dutch that he made in his other works suggest that his grasp of the language was not very secure. In any case, he was presumably capable of handling the short descriptions linking navigational tables. His advice to would-be students of Dutch was perhaps revealing of his own limitations; he said that it was best to begin with mathematical texts, for then one could always make some sense of the numbers at least.

Honda does not appear to have had any close friends among the *rangaku* advocates. His correspondence is directed instead to two liberal Confucian scholars of Mito, Tachihara Suiken (1744–1823) and Komiyama Fūken (1764–1840).[5] In his letters to them Honda expounded his views on the problems which concerned him most, and in return received their criticism. Tachihara, the more distinguished of the two friends, was the general supervisor of the Mito historical bureau, which was then compiling the *Dai-Nihonshi*, a monumental history of Japan. Honda and his friends also exchanged books, Tachihara apparently having sent him even prohibited Christian works which had been preserved in Mito. In 1799, at their request, Honda secretly made a journey to Hitachi, where he drew up a programme for increasing local prosperity.[6]

In 1801 Honda went to sea as captain of the *Ryōfū Maru* on a tour of the north. This may not have been his first journey to this region. Apart from such jaunts as he took as a young man, he may have gone as far as Kamchatka in 1784, as his biographer, Uno, claimed.7 In 1785 he persuaded the shogunate expedition to the northern islands to take him along, but at the last moment he fell ill, and Mogami Tokunai took his place. In any case, his enthusiasm for the north, which was so great as to earn for him the pen-name of Hokui—'northern barbarian'—seems to have abated considerably after his voyage on the *Ryōfū Maru*. The account of his journey, which we should have expected to be filled with descriptions of the wonders of the north, is little more than a ship's log. This sudden change of feelings, if indeed there was one, may have stemmed from his disillusionment after the actual sight of the bleak islands he had so often praised. In 1808, when it was suggested that he make another trip to the north, Honda requested that Mogami again go in his stead, pleading his advanced years.

Honda entered the service of the Lord of Kaga in 1809 in the capacity of adviser on foreign affairs. Among other duties, Honda built warship models which he displayed and operated on a theatrical stage within the castle enclosure. The Lord of Kaga was apparently much interested in Honda's ideas and continued to support him until 1816 although Honda actually left his service after only six months. Many samurai from Kaga went to study with Honda in Edo, of whom the most famous was Zeniya Gohei (1771–1852). He became an outstanding advocate of foreign trade and, less prudent than his teacher, died in prison for his pains.8

Little was recorded concerning Honda's personal life. Nothing, not even her name, is known of his wife. He had a daughter, Tetsu, who was proficient in Confucian studies (unlike her father) and showed special talent for music.9

Honda died in Edo in 1821. A century after his death, on 11 February 1924, Honda's merits were at last recognised by the Japanese court as a result of the favourable attention his writings were beginning to attract at that time, and he was posthumously granted a junior fourth rank.

During his lifetime and for many years afterwards, Honda's chief writings were known only to a small group of friends and students. He was thus able to permit himself the greatest liberties in them. Honda also wrote a few memorials to Matsudaira Sadanobu in which he outlined his views on the development of Ezo and other problems, but these naturally had no wider circulation than the manuscripts of his other works. Thus it was that Honda's name was little known, and one comes across few references to him in nineteenth-century accounts. In 1888 a version of his *Tales of the West* (*Seiiki Monogatari*) was published as a supplement to a Tokyo newspaper,[10] and three years later the first printed edition of his *A Secret Plan for Managing the Country* (*Keisei Hisaku*) appeared. Others of Honda's manuscripts have been printed in recent years, but a complete edition of his writings does not exist.

The first critical essay on Honda did not appear until 1911,[11] and it has only been since about 1930 that his name has figured regularly in histories of the Tokugawa period. Although it is probably safe to say that very few Japanese of the present day have heard much more of Honda than his name, his admirers have attempted to win greater celebrity for him by styling him 'the Japanese Malthus' or 'the Japanese Benjamin Franklin', with some justification at least, and it seems likely that his obscurity will soon be replaced by a better understanding of the man. The first requirement is the preparation of a suitable edition of his works. Honda's style is extremely difficult to follow; he often shows a complete contempt for normal grammatical usage. To make matters worse, he was given to digressions which interrupt the sequence of his ideas, as well as to repetitions, often word-for-word, of illustrative anecdotes, thus destroying whatever interest such stories intrinsically possess. Only a very generous and patient reader would read through a whole volume of Honda's writings, though he would be amply rewarded for his pains. It will be the duty of an intelligent editor to bring order out of the present chaos of Honda's works, and thus restore to Japan one of her most original thinkers.

The dating of Honda's writings is sometimes difficult because, as has been mentioned, they were not printed during his lifetime. Most of them fall within the decade 1790–1800, with his two chief works both having been completed in 1798. The following is a list of his most important works: they are found in the collection *Honda Toshiaki-shū*, edited by Honjō Eijirō.

Ezo Miscellany (*Ezo Shūi*), 1789.

Views on the Development of Ezo (*Ezo Tochi Kaihatsu Guson no Taigai*), 1791.

Memorial on the Development of Ezo (*Ezo Kaihatsu ni kansuru Jōsho*), 1792.

Explanation of Natural Government (*Shizen Jidō no Ben*), 1795.

Tales of the West (*Seiiki Monogatari*), 1798.

A Secret Plan for Managing the Country (*Keisei Hisaku*), 1798.

Statement on Government (*Keizai Hōgen*), c. 1800.

Waterways (*Kadō*), 1800.

On Ships (*Chōkiron*), 1801.

2. THE CALL OF THE WEST

For Honda Toshiaki and some of his contemporaries, Europe was that part of the world whose long years of civilisation had taught the nations the folly of war, whose people lived in splendid houses free alike from the dangers of fire and robbery, and whose rulers devoted themselves entirely to benevolent plans for the welfare of their subjects. This portrait of life in eighteenth-century Europe may make us smile—it would certainly have made Voltaire smile—but it was not much further removed from reality than contemporary European descriptions of wise Persians or Chinese. The purpose of such fanciful accounts of distant countries was in both cases the same: to call attention to deficiencies at home by praising the superior ways of little-known foreigners, and thus to create desire for reform and progress.

The early *rangaku* scholars had demonstrated that Dutch learning was of value. Later men had disputed China's claims of being the centre of the world, and by Honda's time there were some who elevated Europe to the position of Japan's model in all things. But before an examination of the intrinsic superiority of Western achievements might be undertaken, it was necessary for the friends of European civilisation to prove the great pedigree of the Western nations. In so doing they afforded an interesting parallel to those of their European equivalents who wrote admiringly of the timeless antiquity of China. Timelessness, however, was not the point emphasised by these lovers of European science and precision; most sought to state exactly how much older Europe actually was. 'Which of the nations of the world was first to become civilised?' asked Honda, and himself replied that it was Egypt, whose civilisation dated back over 6,000 years. China, he added, was only about 3,800 years old, while Japan could boast of a mere 1,500 years since the Emperor Jimmu founded the country.[12] He therefore concluded that it was only to be expected that young nations like China and Japan failed to exhibit the same perfection in their institutions that Europe had long ago attained.

The foundation of Holland was most precisely dated by Japanese writers who, unacquainted with the Christian significance of Western chronology, imagined that 1787, or whatever the year happened to be, marked the number of years since that event.[13] Honda, though second to none in his admiration for Holland, did not believe the country was quite so old; the Western date, he asserted, was based on the year of birth of a compassionate and efficient Roman emperor named Alexander, who had formed the calendar, among other notable achievements.

Regardless of the dates employed by the pro-European scholars to prove their theories, the effort was always to demonstrate that the greater antiquity of the West meant that it was in every way superior to the East. Shiba Kōkan declared that Germany was the oldest of all nations, adding, 'The foundation of Japan has been a matter of very recent times. That is why learning here is so shallow, and thinking so lacking in profundity.'[14] Honda complained that although six thousand years' experience had gone into the making of every European institution, Japan nevertheless chose to ignore the ways of the West in favour of less highly evolved Chinese usage. Japan was 'an isolated island', a small country of no great age or learning. Now was the time to adopt the practices of the 'parent nations' of Europe.

The argument that 'with age comes wisdom' was a clever one, although rather specious in this instance. A more pertinent general argument in favour of Western usages was that of utility. Western writing (or architecture or calendars) was pronounced to be more efficient and convenient than the Japanese equivalents, and therefore more desirable. Or, the claim might be advanced that some Western custom appeared to contribute to the prosperity of the European nations, and therefore ought to be adopted in Japan. But although such arguments possessed greater plausibility than the one based on the comparative ages of civilisations, they were not incontrovertible, and, as a last resort, the six thousand years of European civilisation could always be invoked.

The battle over the merits of Western learning was carried into almost every imaginable field by the *rangaku* scholars and their associates. Some of the major topics considered by them will be given below together with the discussions that arose from these.

(a) Painting

Nowhere was the new attitude towards the West more strikingly exhibited than in the field of painting. During the days of the Portuguese there had been a certain amount of painting in the Western style done in Japan, chiefly of religious subjects, but little permanent influence had resulted from it, and the main techniques had to be learned afresh in the eighteenth century. *Ukie*, a Japanese adaptation of Western perspective, was first used by the print-makers, notably Okumura Masanobu (1686–1764), but for reasons of design rather than to achieve greater realism, later the chief desideratum. In the middle of the eighteenth century Maruyama Ōkyo (1732–95) founded a school of painting which also borrowed certain European techniques, but neither the innovations of Masanobu nor those of Ōkyo sufficed to make them Western-style painters; an untrained critic would be hard put to find anything specifically un-Japanese in their works.

The first artist to have painted in a thoroughly European manner was Hiraga Gennai (1729–80), a talented eccentric with a penchant for writing books with indecent titles. Hiraga visited Nagasaki in 1753 in order to study Western painting, but soon extended his interests far beyond this field. Shiba Kōkan recorded how Hiraga, fascinated by a Dutch zoology-book in the collection of one of the Nagasaki interpreters, sold all of his household possessions, including his bed-clothes, in order to purchase the volume.[15] In addition to being a noted zoologist and botanist, Hiraga was one of the first in Japan to understand the workings of

Hiraga Gennai
(portrait attributed to Katsuragawa Hoshū)

electricity, and was first (in 1764) to produce asbestos in the country. Playwright, novelist, scientist, mining expert, potter, political-writer by turns, Hiraga's greatest contributions were probably in the field of painting, not so much in the works he himself produced, but in the great influence he exerted on younger men.

Hiraga's first successes as a teacher of painting were in Akita, where he had been invited in 1773 to investigate mining possibilities. Hiraga did not confine himself to prospecting, but gave lessons in Western-style painting to some of the local samurai. When his first pupil, Odano Naotake (1750–80) appeared for a lesson, Hiraga asked him to draw a flour-dumpling from above. When he had finished his sketch, Hiraga rejected it, declaring, 'You can't tell whether it's a tray or a cart-wheel', and thereupon taught Odano the principles of shading. Odano learned how to delineate objects by lightness and darkness of colour, rather than by line alone, as was customary in Japanese painting. The skill which Odano eventually acquired is apparent in the illustrations which he drew for Sugita's translation of the *Tafel Anatomia*, but his early death prevented him from developing into a major artist.[16]

The daimyo of Akita, Satake Yoshiatsu (1748–85), noting the progress made by Odano in Western art, asked Hiraga for lessons. Satake became one of the outstanding painters in the European style. He proclaimed his view of art, 'For painting to be of any use whatever, it must resemble the object it portrays. If one paints a tiger in such a way that it looks like a dog, the lack of resemblance becomes comical. Those lofty spirits who claim that one should paint conceptions and not mere forms lose sight of the practical uses of painting.'[17] This was an attack on the traditional schools of painting which regarded the close depiction of real forms as 'artisan's work', and insisted that the 'spirit' of the subject must be portrayed. But, Satake argued, such a view of art was not practical, not at all what Westerners meant by the term.

Honda, though no artist, was interested in Western painting for its practical value.

'Why is it that European painting differs from Chinese and Japanese painting?' someone asked.

I replied, 'European paintings are executed in great detail with the intention of having them resemble exactly the objects portrayed so that they will serve some useful function. There are rules of painting which enable one to achieve this effect. The Europeans observe the division of sunlight into light and shade, and also what are called the rules of perspective. For example, if one wished to draw a person's nose from the front, there would be no way in Japanese art to represent the central line of the nose. In the European style, shading is used on the sides of the nose and one may thereby realise its height.'[18]

Ōtsuki Gentaku was more lyrical in his praise of a flower picture by the Dutch artist Willem van Ruyven, painted in 1725:

In the shapes of the flowers, the forms of the fruits, and in the design of the birds and insects, there is such realism in the colours, such precision in the positions, such brilliance, that one feels exactly as if one were seated in some celebrated garden whose exquisite perfumes scented one's sleeves. Ah, the skill with which life has been copied may indeed be called robbing the art of the Creator.[19]

The most important exponent of Western painting in the late eighteenth century was Shiba Kōkan (1738–1818). Shiba's name has already been mentioned in numerous connections, but at this point greater attention must be paid to the details of his career. In *A Record of Kōkan's Repentances*, he tells us:

From my boyhood days I used to plan how I might satisfy my ambition of winning a name for myself by my special artistic ability. My desire to leave a reputation behind even after my death led me at first to think of sword-making, for swords are passed on to later generations as a soldier's most important weapon. I planned thus to enjoy renown with posterity, but the country is now at peace, and though famous old swords are still used by the samurai for ornamental purposes, nobody wants new swords. Besides, the sword is an instrument for killing people and is thus wicked. That is why I repented of that career.[20]

Shiba traced his later employment as a maker of dagger-hilts, as an apprentice painter, and finally as a highly successful forger of prints of the *ukiyoe* artist Suzuki Harunobu. Perhaps 'forger' is too strong a word, for the composition of the pictures, if not the style or signature, was Shiba's own. But he was not content with these easily-won laurels, and turned to the study of Chinese painting, in which he quickly achieved proficiency. Then as now the Chinese style required the mastery of certain conventions; leaves might not be drawn as an artist saw them, but as described in textbooks of painting. Similarly, every element in a landscape was prescribed, from the 'dragon's spine' of the mountains to the number of strokes of the brush to be used in depicting the figure of a traveller crossing a tiny bridge.

Shiba had no trouble with these conventions, and before long was teaching the secrets of Chinese painting to others, notably the chief officials of the Lord of Sendai. After Shiba had given an illustrated lecture on Chinese techniques, which had quite dazzled his audience, he was summoned before the lord himself, and created a great impression by drawing in the Chinese style a Japanese man and woman. He was kept painting for twelve hours by the delighted spectators, and a brilliant future was freely predicted for him.[21] All these events took place before Shiba was thirty.

In the meantime Shiba had also met Hiraga Gennai (in 1763) and from him began to learn of Western oil-painting. The first subjects he attempted in the European style were landscapes, especially Mount Fuji. Thus, even while his fame as an artist in the Japanese and Chinese styles was reaching its height, he was already devoting himself increasingly to Western painting. His original preference for these new techniques apparently arose from his love of Fuji, and his desire to paint the celebrated mountain in all its aspects. The Chinese-style painters would have nothing to do with so Japanese a mountain as Fuji, and filled their pictures instead with nameless Chinese mountains copied from old masters or from textbooks. The traditional Japanese schools of painting were also incapable of portraying Fuji as it actually looked, preferring a vague and misty 'delineation of the spirit' of the mountain. For such Japanese artists Shiba had nothing but contempt—'People talk of Japanese painting, but it is derived entirely from China, and even when its exponents are drawing Fuji, Japan's celebrated mountain, the methods they employ are Chinese. Nothing whatever has been invented in Japan.'[22]

Shiba noted that cheap prints of Fuji sold at the way-stations to Edo were very popular with members of the Dutch embassies to the capital, and from this concluded that the mountain must be peerless in the world. This justified him in his determination to do greater justice to the true beauty of the peak than any previous artist. What he sought in his pictures was not to illustrate the grandeur of nature and the smallness of man, nor to demonstrate any of the other spiritual lessons that might be gained by an artist from the sight of Fuji, but to depict as exactly as possible the mountain's appearance. He gave his theory of art:

What is remarkable in painting is that it enables one to see clearly something which is actually not there. If a painting does not truly portray a thing, it is devoid of the wonderful power of the art. Fuji-san is a mountain unique in the world, and foreigners who wish to look upon it can do so only in pictures. However, if one follows only the orthodox Chinese methods of painting, one's picture will not resemble Fuji, and there will be none of the magical quality in it which painting possesses. The way to depict Fuji accurately is by means of Dutch painting.[23]

Western oil painting, he added, was not a polite accomplishment of dilettanti, like Chinese calligraphy, but was 'an instrument in the service of the nation'.

This remark suggests another use which its admirers discovered in Western art—its educational value. Many Japanese, including the Shogun Yoshimune and Matsudaira Sadanobu, had been impressed by the detailed illustrations found in Dutch botanical and zoological works. In such books it was obviously essential that an object's true appearance be shown, rather than its 'spirit'. Shiba and Honda were also struck by the pedagogic use made of symbols in Western art. Shiba related how the Dutch taught morality with their symbols (*zinnebeelden*), and Honda was at great pains to unravel the symbolism of a Russian map. 'There are human figures on this Russian map. The woman is the Empress Ekaterina. There is also a letter E with plants sprouting from it like an aureole. This must mean that the light of virtue is cast on the four continents from the E. The four nude figures each represents a continent, and this means that all the continents will in the future belong to Russia. To have presented a map with this significance to the Japanese officials was a bold Russian plan to test whether they could conquer Japan.'[24] This was certainly extracting the full meaning of each symbol!

Painting thus became for such men a practical means to an end rather than 'art for art's sake'. This didactic view of the purpose of art was closer to the views of the Confucian moralists than to those of eighteenth-century

European painters (who were enchanted with the decorative Chinese art), but Honda and Shiba would have been pained to be told so. Chinese painting had become for Shiba no more than a set of artistic clichés, and he felt that only Dutch art possessed the vitality which brought it close to the lives of the people. Honda went a step further in pronouncing it to be the best medium for popular instruction, contrasting Dutch books of information illustrated by explanatory diagrams with the Chinese and Japanese tradition of esoteric learning passed down from teacher to pupil.

One of the works to which Honda referred was the *New and Complete Dictionary of the Arts and Sciences* (1769)[25] of Egbert Buys, a book which was very important in Shiba's career. When, about 1780, he began the study of Dutch, at first with Maeno Ryōtaku and later with Ōtsuki Gentaku, he went over those parts of Buys' encyclopaedic dictionary which dealt with the arts.[26] It was thus that in 1783 he rediscovered the art of engraving, lost in Japan since the days of the Jesuit missionaries. Although Shiba's engravings (which were chiefly maps) possessed the merit of being pioneer experiments, they were judged to be far inferior to Dutch ones. Matsudaira Sadanobu accordingly sent a protégé to Nagasaki in 1799 to learn the art directly from the Dutch. This man was so successful in his maps of the world that Matsudaira gave him the soubriquet of Aōdō—'Hall of Asia and Europe'—and it is by the name of Denzen Aōdō that this first great Japanese engraver has since been known.[27]

Shiba used often to visit the Dutch embassy while it was staying in Edo. On one of these occasions the factory director Isaac Titsingh, who contributed so much to the development of scientific interest in Japan, gave Shiba a copy of the *Great Painter's Book*[28] by Gerard de Lairesse, and a perusal of its pages caused him to plunge deeply into the study of oil-painting. Apart from the help Shiba received from Hiraga Gennai, it is not clear just what training he underwent. Another writer described the training of a Dutch painter:

The Red-Hairs are extremely proficient in painting. Everyone who learns this art first studies carefully the anatomies of men and women, and learns to draw naked people. Later they draw clothed people as well.[29]

This may have been the procedure Shiba adopted. In any case, he decided in 1788 to visit Nagasaki in the hope of improving his knowledge of Western painting. He visited a group of Japanese artists who were experimenting with oils and pronounced their work to be very poor.[30] After he had returned to Edo, he described his journey in a diary illustrated with delightful little drawings in the Japanese style, as if Shiba felt that his first manner was more suited to the informal narrative than the painstaking accuracy of the Dutch style.

Shiba continued to paint until the end of his life although his main interest shifted first to science and then to philosophy. His reputation as a painter is today very high, and his pictures are proudly displayed by museums. The dispassionate observer might find his works interesting rather than beautiful, but his technical skill is quite evident. Shiba's work is also important because of his influence on many later Japanese artists including Hokusai (who in turn influenced the French impressionists to make the circle of borrowing complete). Whatever one may think of contemporary Japanese painting in the Western style, it is clearly the descendant of Shiba's experiments and of his passion for usefulness and truth.

(b) Writing

During the period 1592–1614 the Jesuit Mission Press had issued a number of Japanese books printed in Roman letters, for the most part religious tracts. Like much else

that had come with the Portuguese, however, the Western
alphabet had faded from the memory of the Japanese by
the late eighteenth century. It is true that Arai Hakuseki,
in one of his accounts of interviews with the Italian priest
Sidotti, had written in 1713 of the simplicity and excellence
of the alphabet,[31] but it was only with the growth of Dutch
studies that Western writing became a matter of great interest to Japanese intellectuals. The pioneer work was the
Tales of Holland (1765) by Gotō Rishun, in which the alphabet was given in normal print, script and in Gothic letters,
together with a brief description.[32] The ease with which the
alphabet might be learned was extolled in Ōtsuki's *Ladder
to Dutch Studies* (1783), and in the *Kōmō Zatsuwa* (1787) by
Morishima Chūryō was found an attack on the use of
Chinese characters as a method of reproducing the sounds
of Japanese. This took the form of a relation of how foolish
the Dutch thought the Japanese system of writing to be,
a consideration of importance to the increasingly self-
conscious Japanese.

In a Dutch book which describes the customs of all
countries, the use of Chinese characters is ridiculed thus:
'In China a character is used for every object and thing.
Some characters have only one meaning, while others are
used to express ten or twenty ideas. There are probably
tens of thousands of them. Thus, though the natives of
China study them day and night, so earnestly that they forget about sleeping and eating, they are unable to learn in
the course of their lifetimes all the elements in their country's writing. Thus it is that there are few people who can
read easily books written in their own tongue. This is the
height of the ridiculous. In Europe, twenty-five letters are
not considered inadequate.'

Chūryō believes that in the olden days writing was
simple, and no characters were ever used. In later times,
Chinese characters were borrowed to indicate the fifty

sounds of Japanese. In subsequent generations Chinese characters came to be used for meaning as well as sound, and the national custom of using only a few easy characters was abandoned in favour of the complicated and troublesome Chinese system. Why was this?[33]

The distinction drawn by Morishima between the spoken sounds of Japanese and the symbols used to represent them is a fundamental one in the history of the language. As he stated, Japanese sounds were first written by using Chinese characters phonetically. From these phonetic signs was evolved the Japanese syllabary, or *kana*, but the use of characters to express both native and Chinese words is very old. A rough analogy may be made between the use of Roman letters to represent the sounds of old English, and the increasing adoption of words from the Latin language to make modern English. Just as some English scholars chose to display their learning by the use of difficult Latin expressions and allusions, so Japanese scholars did with corresponding Chinese terms. Similarly, there were both Englishmen and Japanese who wrote their serious works in the classical language, finding the native tongue incapable of all the desired nuances. This analogy is far from perfect, for the system employed in writing Japanese is infinitely more complex than the English one, but there is at least a rough parallel.

The attack on the use of Chinese characters in part reflected the generally anti-Chinese sentiments of the advocates of European learning. Honda, for example, decried those scholars whose reputation for learning was based entirely on their ability to read Chinese characters. He said that the amount of time required to learn the tens of thousands of characters could be put to better use—'Instead of attempting to win a name as a scholar by one's mastery of Chinese characters, it is more sensible to use our Japanese *kana* and to concentrate on the meaning.'[34]

The Japanese party of exploration which visited the Kuriles in 1786 was much impressed by the ease with which the Russian alphabet could be taught to the natives, and the advantages of an alphabet for pedagogic purposes was often mentioned by progressively-minded persons. Shiba felt that the restrictions on learning imposed by the necessity of first mastering the complicated (and, for Japanese, superfluous) Chinese characters had prevented the development of science in Japan.

Human beings from the age of two can say 'Papa' and 'Mama'. As they grow up, they naturally acquire familiarity with many words. No one has to study how to pronounce the sounds of *tenchi*, but no one can read the characters for the word without learning them. Chinese characters are used in both China and Japan, and without studying them it is impossible to read books or to understand the teachings in the classics. However, in Japan the pronunciation which is employed is basically the native one. Ordinary conversations are invariably in native words, and there are no characters for many of the expressions. The Western nations, instead of characters, use signs which merely indicate the pronunciation. Is it not a waste of time to read books first without understanding the meaning and only then to ask a teacher about it? Since in the West they use the sounds of their own language in writing, they have but to look at a book if they want to learn about the principles of heaven and earth. It is like reading Japanese *kana*. There is never a distinction made between elegant and common language. Thus one can learn all the fundamental principles without having need of a teacher.35

Shiba showed his acquaintance not only with Western script but with the Corean, Manchurian and Indian alphabets. It was apparently his view that each nation should have an alphabet (or syllabary) of its own. For the Chinese, the use of characters might be most practical, but for

Japanese the native *kana* was greatly to be preferred in that it suited the words of ordinary speech much better than any other system. Honda Toshiaki, who also advocated the use of *kana* in preference to Chinese characters, felt that the Western alphabet was still better. The *kana* signs in the first place were twice as numerous as the letters of the alphabet, which made them less convenient. The *kana* was also unable to represent all possible sounds, unlike the versatile alphabet. Most important, the alphabet was used by almost all the countries of the world, and was thus better suited to the needs of a nation with international trade than any more localised system.

For Honda the system of writing employed in Japan was, like the painting, an invitation to dilettantism instead of a practical tool. He wrote:

If a careful study is made of their system of writing and ours, it will become apparent which one is correct and which false. Because of the deficiencies in our system, people spend most of their time in idle and elegant pursuits, the number of which constantly increases. They are forgetful of themselves, and when they reach old age it is too late for them to repent. It was fortunate for the Westerners that they foresaw this eventuality and took steps to avoid a system of writing so profitless to the nation.[36]

The struggle to eliminate the use of Chinese characters is still going on today, 150 years after the pleas of Honda and Shiba were first written, with not much greater chance of success than before. The chief obstacle in the path of pure *kana* or romanised script would appear to be the enormous number of homonyms originally borrowed from the Chinese, but which are now as much a part of normal Japanese as, for example, 'electrical' or 'moment' are of English. The advocates of native learning attempted to purify the language of Chinese-derived words and thus remove this obstacle, but the results are as startling as if the

English words above given were to be replaced by 'amber-crafty' or 'eye-blink', words of a purely native character.

At the end of the eighteenth century the use of Western script was restricted to a small number of enthusiasts. Shiba was fond of signing his paintings 'K. Shiba', in the Western manner, while other artists used Dutch words, and sometimes meaningless phrases, as decorative elements in their works. Ordinary people regarded Western writing as something outlandish and utterly bewildering. Captain Golownin, a Russian who was captured by the Japanese in 1811, recorded:

They considered a specimen of Russian writing as great a curiosity as an inscription in Japanese would be looked upon in Europe, and shewed us a fan upon which were inscribed four lines of a popular Russian song, signed by a person named Babikoff, who, it appeared, had visited Japan along with Laxman. Though these lines must have been written twenty years before we saw them, yet the fan was as clean and fresh as if perfectly new. The owner kept it wrapped up in a sheet of paper, and set so much value upon it, that he would scarcely suffer it to be opened.37

Thus the practical Western script managed to furnish yet another amusement for the Japanese dilettanti!

(c) Books

It is not very surprising that there are but few references to European belles-lettres in the writings of Honda, Shiba and others of their time. Dutch novels or plays would have been far too difficult for the average *rangaku* scholar to understand. Besides, the emphasis was always on the practical value of Western learning, and this might have been difficult to establish in the case of light fiction. Honda had even denied that such books existed:

Since it is the custom in Europe to consider above all whether a thing is of use to the nation, there is an academy which examines all books before they are printed in order to ensure that none of a frivolous or indecent nature appears.[38]

Shiba, however, was familiar with one work of Western literature, *Aesop's Fables*. This famous book had first appeared in a Jesuit-sponsored translation of 1593 but, like other publications of the Portuguese period, was no longer known in the eighteenth century when Shiba discovered a copy in the Lord of Kii's library. He translated a few of the fables into Chinese and made up others in Aesop's manner.[39] The particular appeal of the fables for Shiba—he said, but we may not believe him—lay in their didactic value, their use as 'symbols'. Thus he managed to salvage something practical from an otherwise merely entertaining book.

Part of another Western literary work was known to Hirazawa Kyokuzan, who heard the following tale while he was in Nagasaki.

Some ten years ago a ship was stranded on an island, and two men of the crew went ashore to look for water. There they encountered a giant over ten feet tall with one eye in the middle of his forehead. The giant was glad to find the two men. He seized them and took them off with him to a rocky cavern. The giant sealed the entrance to the cave with a huge boulder. Inside there was another giant, the mate of the first one. The cave was spacious, with cracks in the rock serving as windows. There were many beasts inside.

One of the giants went out and the opening was shut as before. The other giant caught the two men and fixedly regarded them for a long time. Suddenly he seized one of them and began to eat him from the head downwards. The other man looked on in terror and astonishment as though he were watching demons in a nightmare. He could not think how he might escape. While the giant was

devouring half of the first man, the other covered his face
and could not bear to look. The giant then fell into a
drunken sleep, snoring like thunder.

The man pondered how he might safely escape. Finally
he made up his mind and gouged out the giant's eye with his
dagger. The giant let out a great cry and ran wildly about
in his rage. He groped around for the man who was, however, lying flat on the floor of the cave. The giant, for all
his ferocity, was unable to find the man because of his
blindness. Then he opened the entrance to the cave a little
and drove out the animals. One by one he let them out,
apparently resolved thus to catch and kill the man. The man
was trapped, but he quickly caught hold under the belly
of a huge boar. The giant let the animal out, not realising
the trick that had been played him. The man was thus able
to escape to his ship, which at once set sail.[40]

Hirazawa was related this bit of the *Odyssey* as the actual
experiences of a certain man, but he was not wholly inclined
to believe the tale. According to Western atlases which he
had consulted, there was indeed a land of giants, but no
mention of their being cannibals as well.

It is interesting to speculate how Homer's story found its
way to Nagasaki in 1774. Most probably it was told to the
Japanese by one of the more literate Dutch factory em-
ployees, but perhaps it had arrived in a more complicated
way across the breadth of Asia. Hirazawa claimed not only to
have heard this version of the Polyphemus episode, but also
to have read less elaborate variants of it in books of travels
and strange tales. It was the most likely type of European
literature to be rendered into Japanese; one of the first
translations (published in 1859) of a European novel was
the *Record of Wanderings* 'written by an Englishman, Robin-
son Crusoe'.

With but few exceptions, however, the books imported
to Japan up to the end of the eighteenth century were all

of an obviously practical nature. Among the most popular works were the dictionary of Buys above mentioned, and the Chomel *Encyclopaedia*, a copy of which Titsingh gave to one of the interpreters. In later years Sugita Gempaku and other outstanding *rangaku* scholars began a translation of Chomel's work, but after thirty-five years of hard work, the project was finally abandoned.[41]

The principal interest was in Western scientific books. This fact is evidenced by an incident which occurred in 1762, when the interpreter Nishi Zenzaburō, together with some of his colleagues, attended an auction of the effects of a Dutch merchant. Although they bought a number of souvenirs, they failed to acquire any of the auctioned books, even though these included a sea-atlas, dictionaries, law books, Kaempfer's *History of Japan*, and various other works.[42] Apparently the only books which Japanese desired at the time were works of medicine, natural history, astronomy and physics. By the end of the century there were quite good collections of scientific European works in different parts of Japan, including one which Matsudaira Sadanobu had with some qualms begun:

I began about 1792 or 1793 to collect Dutch books. The barbarian nations are skilled in the sciences, and considerable profit may be derived from their works of astronomy and geography, as well as from their military weapons and their methods of internal and external medicine. However, their books may serve to encourage idle curiosity or may express harmful ideas. It might thus seem advisable to ban them, but prohibiting these books would not prevent people from reading them. There is, moreover, profit to be derived from them. Such books and other foreign things should therefore not be allowed to pass in large quantities into the hands of irresponsible people, but it is desirable, on the other hand, to have them deposited in a government library. If there is no one to read them,

however, they will merely become nests for insects. I informed
the Governor of Nagasaki that if such works were acquired
by the government, they would not be dispersed in the
country, and could thus be consulted if there were any
official need of them. Thus it came about that foreign books
were purchased.43

Other libraries were in the possession of individual Nagasaki interpreters, one of whom, Shizuki Tadao (1758–1806),
made what was probably the most remarkable translation
of the eighteenth century. This was his *Rekishō Shinsho* of
1798–1802, a textbook of physics and astronomy derived
from an English work of a century before. Although
Shizuki disclaimed being anything more than a 'tongue-
man', his work was no mere translation, but a fresh study
of all the available material on the subject, especially designed for Japanese readers. In addition to works by Keill,
the author of the original of the *Rekishō Shinsho*, Shizuki
read studies by Newton and Napier, as well as Chinese
versions of other European works. Ōtsuki Gentaku declared Shizuki to have been the most skilled of the interpreters, and the excellence of the *Rekishō Shinsho* would
confirm his opinion.

Shizuki distinguished himself also with his translation of
part of Kaempfer's *History of Japan*. This section in Kaempfer's text was entitled 'An Enquiry, whether it be conducive
for the good of the Japanese Empire to keep it shut up,
as it now is, and not to suffer its inhabitants to have any
Commerce, with foreign nations, either at home or abroad.'44
Shizuki's rendering was more simply entitled *On the Closure
of the Country*, and its purpose was to show that a celebrated
European believed it wisest for Japan to continue her policy
of isolation. This was perhaps the sole example of a Western
book being cited to prove that the traditional Japanese
ways were best. It was more commonly assumed that
European writers on returning to their countries from

Japan wrote accounts ridiculing the backward ways of the Japanese.

It may seem strange that Shizuki, an outstanding scholar of Western science, was at the same time an advocate of national isolation, but no necessary contradiction was involved. Ōtsuki Gentaku, for example, believed that the Japanese must master Dutch learning, but once this had been accomplished, no further traffic with the West would be required. Honda's admiration for the West was always tempered by his fear that the foreigners might learn too much about Japan, and he thus also showed himself more partial to isolationism than we would expect of so progressive a man. Shizuki must have shared with these two men the belief that it was essential to preserve Japan's free option as to what she would borrow from the West; opening the country would necessitate the admittance of undesirable foreign ideas as well as useful scientific learning.

Shizuki's contributions as a translator were not equalled by any of the other *rangaku* scholars, and indeed, the seeming absence of translations in an age of great curiosity about the West is quite remarkable. Apart from the *Tafel Anatomia* and a few officially requested renderings of short geographical and historical works, the eighteenth century did not produce any significant translations. This may be attributed in part to a feeling that all persons seriously interested in the West would learn Dutch, in part to the fear that once the laborious work of translation had been accomplished it would be impossible to have it printed because of strict government censorship. We know that some translations were circulated privately. Honda, for instance, was so proud of his translation of a Dutch textbook of navigation that he intended to present it to all Japanese ships' captains. He wrote, 'It ought to prove the most valuable thing on the ship.'[45] But neither this nor any other of Honda's translations enjoyed any wider renown than among the circle of his friends, and such must also have been the fate of Dutch books done into Japanese by other scholars. It is perhaps as well for the reputation of some of the *rangaku* advocates that such works have not been preserved; many of the curious misapprehensions of foreign history and geography current in the eighteenth century must have had their origin in mistakes of translation or interpreting.

The period of haphazard translation was brought to a close in 1803, when the shogunate established an office at the Edo observatory for the translation of Dutch astronomical and surveying works, followed in 1811 by the creation of a similar office with more general translation duties.[46] From this time on scientific books were regularly acquired and rendered into Japanese.

A word may be said at this point concerning the knowledge of European languages other than Dutch in eighteenth-century Japan. By the middle of the century there were no longer any Portuguese interpreters at the Deshima factory, and whatever interest in European languages existed was channelled into the study of Dutch. In 1779, however, when the Shogun Ieharu ordered Maeno Ryōtaku to translate the inscriptions on a set of engravings in his collection, Maeno discovered to his dismay that they were in Latin.

The great lord ordered me to translate the inscriptions on the Western pictures, and I have respectfully undertaken the task. They were made in France, but the text is in Latin, the language from which French was derived. It is both elegant and concise, and capable of expressing profound meanings. Therefore, no one who is not learned, be he French or Dutch, is familiar with it, much less people in Nagasaki.[47]

Maeno conscientiously went ahead with his task although he had few other aids than a Latin-Japanese dictionary some 150 years old. Having no knowledge of Latin grammar, his interpretations of the quatrains describing each of the pictures left something to be desired. For example, the Latin word *est* was rendered as 'animal food' with the imaginable consequences to the sense of the poem. Maeno bravely struggled on, translating the inscriptions both into Japanese and into classical Chinese, with which language he thus identified the high cultural level of Latin.

The return of Kōdayū in 1792 meant that there was at least one Japanese quite familiar with the Russian language. He brought with him a number of books, and may have translated some, but of this we have no record. In 1811 Captain Golownin spoke with a 'learned academician' who 'employed himself in translating from the Russian a work on arithmetic, published at Petersburgh for the use of the public schools, and which had been brought to Japan by Kodia [Kōdayū]'.[48] But even before Kōdayū's time there were Japanese in the Kuriles who knew a little Russian, learnt from trappers in the region, or perhaps in Kamchatka. Later, when Captain Broughton visited Ezo in 1796, he was questioned by Japanese, one of whom claimed to have been at Petersburg.[49]

Organised instruction in other European languages began in 1808 when the factory director Doeff gave lessons in French to six pupils. In the following year a group of Japanese began the study of Russian and English, and from that time on these languages were regularly studied.[50] In 1826, when Kondō Morishige compiled a list of foreign books in Japan, he enumerated many grammars and dictionaries of English and other non-Dutch European languages, as well as such works of science, history and literature as had been accumulating in the country during the preceding half-century.[51] The list is an impressive one and demonstrates again how grossly Japanese knowledge of the West before Perry's arrival has been underestimated by most historians.

(d) Religion and Philosophy

If there was one point on which virtually all Japanese intellectuals of the late eighteenth century were agreed, it was the uselessness of Buddhism and the degeneracy of the Buddhist clergy. This attitude is surprising in view of the fact that every person was required by law to be associated with a Buddhist temple, and a man who had spent his life denouncing every aspect of the religion (like Honda Toshiaki) was almost certain to be interred after his death within temple grounds.

There were different reasons why such diverse groups as the Confucianists, *rangaku* and native-learning scholars each found Buddhism so detestable, but common to all was the view that the Buddhist monks were ignorant and lawless. The large numbers of temples and priests might seem to demonstrate that the religion was in a flourishing state, but, it was claimed, not one in a hundred of those who took the vows did so from a sincere desire to espouse the principles of the Buddha.[52] Believers in the supremacy of the native Japanese learning asserted that the foreign character of Buddhism itself made it inevitable that the monks should lead unworthy lives; other scholars felt that the priests' sorry state resulted from their abandonment of the true intent of basically good Buddhist laws. Shiba Kōkan began one of his numerous diatribes on the latter theme, 'Monks nowadays are the idlers of the nation, and do not practise the calling of true priests.'[53]

When we examine the variety of Shiba's views on Buddhism, they may strike us as a confused *potpourri* of everyone's criticisms, probably because his habit of grouping together short essays written at different times makes it impossible to follow the chronological development of his ideas. It is interesting nevertheless to observe the tortuous line of his opinions, from careful suggestions for restoring Buddhism's dignity to violent attacks on the religion. Of the former views we may cite his statement that

A self-portrait of Shiba Kōkan
(from Shiba, *Kopperu Temmon Zukai*, 1808)
Collection Professor C. R. Boxer

a proper understanding of Buddha's teachings could benefit the nation greatly. Learning, he said, was the essential requirement of a priest. 'He who wishes to become a true minister of Buddha's faith needs only to have the proper mental qualifications. He need not enter a temple or shave his head.'[54] The enlightened priest would not read the sutras for their literal meanings, but as symbols of higher truths. This was very demanding, but if priests were recruited among mature, educated men instead of among farm youths, before long there might be great religious leaders who could penetrate to the inner truths and thus redeem Buddhism in the eyes of the nation.

From this view, found in several of his essays, we move on to stronger criticism:

Confucianism and Buddhism may briefly be character-ised as follows. The former lays down the principles of benevolence, righteousness, decorum, wisdom and sin-cerity to guide man in daily living, enjoining him to obey them during his life. The latter religion views man's life as a brief dream, and teaches him not to worry about a mere phantasy.[55]

Stronger still:

Everyone, high and low alike, should study the Way of the Sages. One should read the *Analects* and the *Great Learning* over and over. People should not study Buddhism. It is a false teaching. The origin of the various Buddhist sects is to be found in the Christianity of the West. This was the foundation for Sakyamuni's teachings.[56]

And to make the confusion complete:

There should be in our divine land no other creed but that of the Great Goddess of Ise. Buddhism is a heterodox Indian religion, and a teaching foreign to us. It is not the proper one for the Land of the Gods, and the nation has been too long in prohibiting it.[57]

There is hardly a statement on religion by Shiba but has its contradiction in his writings. In the convolutions of his thought we can trace the spiritual confusion of a sensitive man who had been deeply influenced by the new foreign learning. Shiba was perfectly willing to admit the superiority of Western science—'China and Japan have no science' —and castigated the Japanese for their emotional 'womanish' preference of the trappings of religion to the bare truths of science. Yet, however great his admiration for European learning, and we must remember that Shiba was not only a painter but an outstanding populariser of science, he felt that there was something spiritually unsatisfying in its teachings. He managed in some way to obtain information about the Christian religion, thinking that it might form the complement to the scientific knowledge of the West, but Christianity's superficial resemblances to Buddhism persuaded him that it was essentially the same religion, later adopted by Sakyamuni and transmitted to the nations of the East.[58] For a while he considered the possibility that Buddhism, in spite of its ludicrous errors of fact as found in its religious writings, aimed at higher truths not expressed. In the end he abandoned this idea, summarily rejecting Buddhism and Christianity alike as foreign. Confucianism and Shinto also attracted him for a time, but the behaviour of professional Confucianists alienated him from that philosophy, and his reason made him see through the primitive nature of Shinto.

After all these unsuccessful attempts at finding a religion or philosophy which could satisfy his spiritual side as Dutch learning did his mind, Shiba fell into a kind of misanthropy which made one Japanese writer liken him to Schopenhauer.[59] He is more apt to remind us of Heraclitus or one of the other early Greek thinkers in the specific tenets of his philosophy, and it is quite possible that he read about their theories in some Dutch work. Shiba believed that fire was the primordial principle, and that from it had come water. The primal nature of fire had caused the Shintoists to make of the sun their chief goddess, and the Buddhists also identified their central deity, Dainichi, with the sun. In the world formed by the interaction of fire and water, man cut but a poor figure. 'It is entirely a matter of personal preference that man considers himself to be the most excellent of creatures.'[60] Shiba even contrasted the meanness of man with the co-operation and fairness exhibited by the ants, but man's scientific achievements, which enabled him to measure the grandeur of the universe, distinguished him above other creatures.

Heaven and earth were formed by the energy of fire and water. These two principles fill space and give life to all things, and all things live in them. Compared with the vastness of the heavens, man does not seem even so great as a tiny insect. Man may imagine that he enjoys long life, but the swiftness with which his life ends may be likened to that of the autumn cicada that knows not the spring, or the mushroom born in the morning that withers by nightfall.

And yet, man is the marvel of creation in that he knows the immensity of the heavens, has measured earth's limits and travelled to its most distant shores, never ceasing in his running, leaping, moving. Everywhere on the globe grows the insect called man, and his numbers are beyond reckoning. Each of these creatures has eyes, a nose, and a mouth, similar to all others but different, and possesses aspirations of his own . . . There is no such thing as friends of the same mind. Though we may laugh together over such a book of idle words as this one, we will soon diverge in our desires. Though we are alike, we are unalike.[61]

At the end of his life Shiba lost interest in all the things which had formerly given him pleasure, and turned to the nihilistic teachings of Taoism. On his deathbed he is reported to have said, 'Even if someone wanted a painting,

I would not draw it. If a prince summoned me, I would not go. I am weary of Dutch learning, astronomy, and thinking up new inventions. Only Lao Tzu and Chuang Tzu give me any pleasure.'[62]

Shiba was typical not only of the more sensitive thinkers of his time, but of similar men in the days following the Meiji Restoration of 1868, when the first flush of enthusiasm for the West had given way to disillusion and dissatisfaction. Men in such a state are likely to turn first, as Shiba did, to old beliefs, and to attempt to salvage from them the wisdom they need in their time of trouble. Shiba was passionately devoted to the new learning, and was a great pioneer on its behalf, but though science taught him the potentialities and limitations of man, it did not satisfy his religious and ethical preoccupations. Rejecting one set of beliefs after another, he finally found comfort in the Way which could not be named.

In sharp contrast with Shiba's twists and turnings, we have the direct and positive views of Honda Toshiaki on the subject of religion. He applied to it his universal test: 'What use does it have?' In the case of Buddhism there was no doubt in his mind. Japan, already at a disadvantage because civilisation had been slow in spreading eastward from its source in Egypt, had suffered from the impact of this religion.

Since Japan was then a young country, practical learning had not yet been developed here, and this outside interference came to hamper further the growth of knowledge. Buddhism usually has the effect of causing people to waste their time in utter ignorance.[63]

Although Honda was particularly severe towards Buddhism, he showed little sympathy for the other religious teachings followed in Japan, always because of their lack of practical value for the nation.

There are indeed Confucian books of wisdom, but the

scholars derive no use from them. Buddhists read their scriptures, but as it is their practice to chant them in the original Sanskrit, they sound rather like the croaking of frogs. As for Shinto, it is the rule to speak of its profound mysteries, but these do not appear to be of any help to the ordinary people.[64]

Honda's wholesale rejection of traditional Japanese beliefs came from his basic conviction that the existing conditions in Japan had to be changed. All things which contributed to these conditions must therefore be eliminated, and their place taken by the institutions of more successful countries.

In general, one may say that Japan is at a standstill, while Russia is moving ahead. Because of our tendency towards ineptitude in all things, Russia has become master of standstill Japan's Kamchatka. The reason why the barbarians of islands east, south and west of Kamchatka all seem to be attracted like ants to the sweetness of the Russian order is that the Russians have made capital out of their experiences of struggle and toil during the past 1,500 years.[65]

The only religion which escaped severe criticism at Honda's hands was Christianity. It is true that he sometimes waved the bloody shirt of the forbidden religion in order to win support for certain proposals, such as his desire to have a clearly-defined frontier established between Japan and Russia, but on the whole he was friendly to the Christian religion. He had been informed that important Chinese had adopted Christianity, finding it a religion far preferable to Buddhism, and wondered if that were not the secret of the prosperity of China's port cities.[66] If such were the case, Christianity would be the one religion with a really practical value.

Honda, while deploring the supposed Portuguese plots to invade Japan, revealed great admiration for the Catholic priests who had visited the country. He related the history of one of them at some length. 'He had been selected by the Emperor of Rome to sail to Japan and to give instruction in the Catholic religion as well as in the principles of natural government. It was not his mission to prepare the people for a conquest of the country, as the Portuguese had done, but to transmit the benevolent and merciful institutions of the Roman emperor.'[67] The shogunate had unfortunately refused to heed the priest's words, and after forty years of imprisonment in Japan, the virtuous foreigner died without having accomplished anything. Honda believed that the 'principles of natural government' which the priest had sought to convey to the Japanese might yet serve as a remedy for the otherwise hopeless situation which prevailed. 'Whoever puts it into effect will leave a name for all generations to come as a great leader. The benevolent and merciful system of the Emperor of Rome will naturally be founded. If this happens, the two nations will enjoy friendly relations, ships will go back and forth between them, and considerable profits will accrue to both countries.' Honda concluded his account with the words, 'It was unfortunate and unkind that this person, who could have helped the nation, was cruelly neglected during the forty years he lived in Japan.'[68]

As may be judged from the above extracts, Honda's admiration for Christianity was not based on any detailed knowledge of its theology, but rather on the fact that it appeared to be the faith of prosperous and well-governed foreign nations. The only Christian work he quoted was the *Seven Conquests* by Didacus de Pantoja (1571–1618), an anecdotal account written in Chinese about virtuous persons who conquered the seven sins and wicked ones who did not. From this book Honda apparently learned little more than that in the West no man, not even an emperor, might have a concubine; this, he felt, was eugenically most desirable.[69] But neither Honda nor any of the other scholars of foreign learning was really much interested in Christian doctrine.

It remained for the Shinto propagandists, especially Hirata Atsutane (1776–1843), to employ the theological resources of Christianity in the general attack on Buddhism. The Shinto religion had for many centuries been under the domination of Buddhism, and whatever its importance as a popular cult, it could not boast of any independent philosophical foundation. In the eighteenth century attempts were made to reconstruct pure Shinto, divorced from the later Buddhist accretions, in the old historical and poetical texts. The religion that emerged from these researches was not at all impressive, and Hirata turned to Western books for help in bolstering his faith. He obtained copies of works by Matteo Ricci written in Peking two hundred years earlier, and translated with few alterations two dialogues between Ricci and a Confucian scholar, merely substituting his own name for Ricci's. Thus we have Hirata uttering such statements as, 'Blessed are they that suffer for the cause of righteousness, for theirs is the Kingdom of Heaven and they shall not die. How could this utmost mystery of Shinto be measured in human terms?'[70]

Hirata entirely remodelled the amorphous Shinto religion along Christian lines, affirming his belief in a central divinity who ruled over all creation, rather than in countless gods of approximately equal powers, the usual Shinto view. The immortality of the soul, the existence of the devil, the reward in heaven or punishment in hell for deeds done on earth, and many other Christian concepts were taken over by Hirata. When existing Shinto beliefs approached Christian ones, the link was immediately established; thus, Izanagi and Izanami, the first man and woman, were likened to Adam and Eve.[71]

Once he had created a solid basis for Shinto, Hirata proceeded to attack Buddhism and Confucianism, particularly the former, with bitterness and crudity. As an example of his methods, his attempt to discredit the person of Buddha may be mentioned. Hirata declared that Gautama Buddha came from the region of Colombo, which he in Japanese fashion pronounced *kurombō*, an uncomplimentary term for a dark-skinned person,[72] thus appealing to the prejudices of his readers.

Hirata denounced Buddhism and Confucianism as foreign doctrines, but was entirely cordial towards the equally-foreign Western learning. He praised the European nations as splendid places 'which have established the limits of human knowledge and recognise the grandeur of God.'[73] In this fact, he believed, was to be found the true meaning of Western learning, and not in scientific achievements. This view was not shared by most of the enthusiasts for Dutch learning, however, who turned to the West for practical information rather than transcendent truths.

(e) *Science*

The early interest in Dutch medicine had lesser counterparts in the Japanese studies of botany, zoology, physics and other European sciences. Some of these have already been discussed; others are not of particular relevance in a study devoted chiefly to Honda Toshiaki. Two, however, must be treated more fully at this point—astronomy and geography.

The most important development in Japanese astronomy of the late eighteenth century was the introduction of the Copernican theory. As early as 1778 the philosopher Miura Baien (1723–89) was informed by one of the Nagasaki interpreters of the theory adopted in the West 'that the sun does not move and the earth is not stationary', and in 1788 Shiba learned the same thing on a visit to Nagasaki.[74] Five years later he published a popular account of the Copernican theory which was developed in successive works until the *Explanations of Copernican Astronomy*[75] of

1808. In a preface to the work, Shiba's friend Hayashi Yoshikage wrote of the distrust with which the Copernican theory was at first received in Japan, and of Shiba's part in persuading intellectuals of its validity.[76] Honda mentioned how, when he saw Shiba's first description of the Copernican theory, he was reluctant for a time to accept the new idea, but after consulting older works of astronomy perceived its correctness. Once having entered the circle of believers, Honda poured scorn on those who still clung to the traditional astronomical conceptions.

Everyone in Europe now knows about this theory, which was first given to the world some 280 years ago, but Chinese and Japanese do not even dream of such things. It is understandable that people think that the sun causes the day and the night, but some are of the opinion that every day a new sun is created, travels from east to west, and then disappears . . .

In recent years, however, European astronomy has been introduced to Japan, and everyone has been astonished at the theory that the earth is actually whirling about. No one is prepared to accept it as the truth. Thus it is that in Japan great scholars, astonished at the idea, have declared, 'If the earth were spinning about, my rice bowl and water bottle would turn over, and my home and store-house would be broken to bits. How can such a theory be true?'

It is entirely to be expected that disbelievers are far in the majority. Even in Europe the Copernican theory was not at first believed, and only after generations of progressively-minded men was everyone finally converted to it.[77]

The opposition to Copernican astronomy came principally from reactionaries who were against any new ideas, particularly foreign ones, and from Buddhists, some of whom continued to write anti-Copernican treatises until late in the nineteenth century. Among the scientifically-minded men, however, the Copernican theory found far

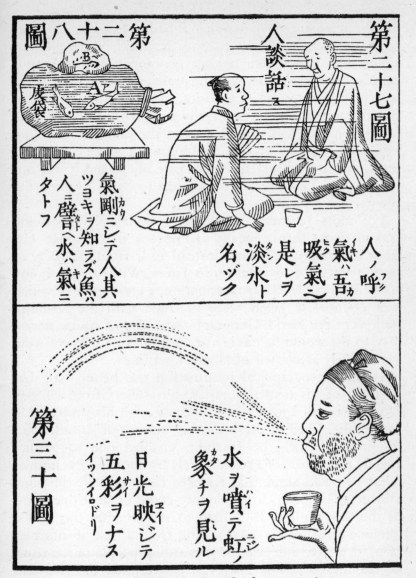

A page of Shiba's scientific demonstrations

'People do not realise how strong the atmosphere is;
air is for men what water is to fish.'
'Spitting out water we can see a rainbow.'

(from *Kopperu Temmon Zukai*, collection Prof. Boxer)

readier acceptance in Japan than it had in Europe. This was partly because, as G. B. Sansom has said, 'the beliefs of China and Japan were neither geocentric nor anthropocentric,'[78] and partly because the prestige of Western science was such that any of its theories, however strange or distasteful, was certain to find ready acceptance among all the leading intellectuals. By 1811 even the officials in remote Hokkaidō with whom Captain Golownin spoke considered the Copernican theory to be the true one,[79] and it was not long before Japanese were claiming to have invented the theory themselves.[80]

For most Japanese, as Honda complained, astronomy was no more than a means to improve the calendar. His great interest in the science instead arose from his desire to perfect the art of navigation in Japan. Without astronomy it was impossible to learn navigation, a knowledge of which was essential if Japan were to trade with the far-flung nations of the world. Geography was also of course necessary to the would-be navigator, and the two sciences were very closely associated in Honda's writings.

Honda's geographical information was better than that of most of his contemporaries, but suffers from curious weaknesses, all apparently connected with his propaganda for empire. Chief of these was his 'science of latitudes and longitudes' which, he thought, enabled one to predict exactly the climate of a place merely by knowing its latitude. Thus he could argue that Kamchatka must have the same climate as England, and therefore could be developed into as thriving a place. It is hard to say whether this was a genuine error on his part arising from a lack of information, or merely a device for persuading people of the truth of his thesis. Honda also vastly overrated the size and desirability of certain islands which he had marked for Japanese expansion; this seems more clearly attributable to his propagandistic efforts.

In general, if we can believe the writings of Honda and

his fellow opponents of vulgar errors, people in Japan at the end of the eighteenth century had only the vaguest notions of geography. It was still almost universally believed that the earth was flat. China and Corea were regarded as actual though distant countries; Russia lay on the borders of reality, somehow threatening Japan to the north, while such countries as India and Holland were like the 'Island of Devils' of the Japanese story-tellers. The information about European countries which was likely to filter down to the ordinary people was of such nature as to confirm their belief in the fantastic character of those remote lands. Hirazawa Kyokuzan was told and believed that in England the dead were not buried, but stored in mountain caves 'where they do not rot even after a thousand years, so that their descendants can recognise them.' He also heard (a distortion of the story of St. Patrick and the snakes of Ireland?) that there were no rats in England; those that came ashore from ships died as soon as they touched English soil.[81]

Against a background of such tales, whatever their origin, Honda's geographical knowledge appears quite respectable. We do not know all the sources of his information, but he was certainly familiar with the *Geographie* by Johann Huebner, a famous eighteenth-century work which had gone through many editions in Europe. What he knew of the Kuriles and other northerly regions, on the other hand, was learned either from his own experiences or those of his friends, and thus of greater significance in the history of geography in Japan. Mamiya Rinzō (1780–1844), the famous explorer of the north, acknowledged his debt to Honda. At a time when several European expeditions had failed to determine whether Saghalien was an island or connected to the north with the mainland of Asia, Japanese explorers discovered the channel which makes Saghalien an island. Maps by Japanese cartographers were eagerly sought by Europeans when such expeditions as Captain

Broughton's called at Hokkaidō. Gradually, under the leadership of such *rangaku* enthusiasts as Honda, geography developed from a collection of strange stories about faraway lands to a science which could command the respect of Europeans.

(f) The Western Way of Life

The incessant and apparently directionless questions to which European visitors to Japan were subjected represented desperate attempts to establish an image of the almost inconceivably different life led in the West. Whether the Dutch practised tattooing, or the number of windows in the czar's palace, do not strike us as vital knowledge, but the Japanese clung to such bits of information as elements of factual reality in their picture of an otherwise incomprehensible world. It was seldom attempted to evolve any general view of European ways; most writers contented themselves with observing that Westerners had red hair, green eyes and white skins, and with a few remarks on European curiosities.

Honda showed no such hesitation to describe Western life. Beginning with his basic assumption of the great antiquity of European civilisation, Honda went on to portray the splendid life which such a tradition had made possible. He had heard, for example, of London Bridge, and attributed to it all the splendour he could imagine. He continued:

The magnificence of the stone embankment along the river and of the construction of the bridge itself is such that one doubts that it was accomplished by human labour. When it comes to grand edifices, no country in the world can approach England.

There is also no country comparable to England in the manufacture of very delicate things. Among the articles which have been imported into Japan by the Dutch, none have been more precious than the watches. Some of them are so exquisite that hairs are split to make them. London is considered to produce the finest such workmanship in the world, followed by Paris in France and Amsterdam in Holland. In these three capitals live people virtually without peers in the world, who are the handsomest of men. The houses in their towns and cities, even in the outskirts, are built of stone. They are from two to five storeys tall and surpassingly beautiful.

Why is it that the people of these three cities, who are human beings like everyone else, have attained such excellence? It is because many centuries have elapsed since they were civilised, and because their political institutions are founded on the principles of natural government.[82]

The rulers of the European nations were responsible for the excellence of the political system. They governed 'not by military force but entirely by virtue', because they knew that the people would resent laws which were imposed on them by force. In their relations with foreign nations, they exhibited perfect amiability and courtesy; when envoys arrived from distant countries whose languages could not be understood, the court treated them with silent and polite attentions. Honda described a picture he had seen of the Spanish envoy to the King of Holland bowing and kissing the monarch's hand. 'This may indeed be termed true courtesy, but isolated island kingdoms understand nothing of such demonstrations of politeness.'[83]

In Europe, Honda continued, the sciences are officially encouraged, particularly those like astronomy and geography which are necessary to ocean trade. The sovereigns and their ministers devote themselves to these studies with such good effect that 'the precious metals, treasures, unusual products and valuable manufactures of the whole world are all drawn to Europe.' The common people also participate in the great intellectual activity—'In European countries it is the practice to investigate thoroughly the laws, institutions and arts of the whole world: this is the chief pursuit of everyone from childhood.'[84] Scholars travel freely from country to country and are able to bring to bear the experience gained when they criticise their own governments. Since, moreover, the merit system is practised in the great capitals, persons from every part of Europe flock to them, and it is as a result of the concerted efforts of such men that London, Paris and Amsterdam stand unique in the world. The governments of Europe, particularly that of France, also show themselves most compassionate towards those persons who, contrary to the general rule, are not highly prosperous. Honda heard of French charitable institutions, and believed that if France were not so distant there would be a great migration there of Japanese who wished to take advantage of such benefits utterly lacking in their own nation.[85]

Of course, insisted Honda, one must not think that the admirable way of life of the Europeans was reached without struggle. Houses were built of stone with copper roofs only when the susceptibility of wooden houses to fire and robbery had become apparent. The advantages of peaceful trading relations with other countries instead of warfare were learned slowly. 'The Europeans must have adopted the natural method of government only in the light of mistakes they had previously made because of inexperience during the 6,000 years of their history.'[86]

Since Japan had the model of European life to imitate, it would not be necessary for her to go through 6,000 years of history in order to reach the same high level. Honda, on the basis of his knowledge of Western institutions, had evolved a programme of action for the nation which would bring about the great prosperity that all men desired; this will be discussed in the following section, which treats Honda's economic theories.

3. HONDA'S ECONOMIC THEORIES

The economic thought of Honda Toshiaki forms the most important part of his work in spite of the magnitude of his achievements in the field of science. Unlike his contributions to mathematics and navigation, however, Honda's economic writings remained unknown for many years and thus exercised no immediate influence on his time. His ideas were perhaps of too great originality for them to have won favour in any event, but they did not spring into being without antecedents. Rather, we must look into the history of economic ideas of the Tokugawa Period in order to appreciate Honda's particular contributions.

The two factors which dominated all others in the economic and social life of Honda's time were the persistence of peace and the closure of the country. The first of these created the peculiar problems of the era; the second prevented them from being solved. The numerous economic writers of the time (including Honda) never failed to pay tribute to the wisdom of Tokugawa Ieyasu in having established the foundations of a peace of over 200 years, but however pleasing this situation might appear, it brought with it serious problems. It was paradoxical that Tokugawa Japan, founded as a military state, should have experienced one of the longest periods of uninterrupted peace that any country has ever known. The paradox was extended by the maintenance of an idle and decadent military class, the samurai, for the protection of the people from non-existent perils of war. The division of the nation into four classes— samurai, farmers, artisans and merchants—(in descending order of importance) had officially been recognised. The samurai were accorded their pride of place because of their importance in defending the country, but after so long a period of peace, this had come to seem an almost meaningless function.

Scholars attributed to the samurai various other duties,

including the instruction and guidance of the commoners, whose ignorance was at first assumed and later encouraged. They were to serve as models to the entire nation in their virtuous and frugal ways. But as time went on, the samurai proved themselves unworthy of their high responsibilities. They did not devote themselves in time of peace to the study of the literary arts but, as they were compelled to spend much of their time in Edo, indulged in all the pleasures which the capital could afford. They showed few qualms about leaving the farmers behind on their country estates to get along as well as they could without their models of proper conduct. The samurai not only thus forfeited their moral leadership of the nation, but their extravagant habits frequently caused them to run up heavy debts with the city merchants. If, after he had converted into cash his stipend of rice, a daimyo[87] was still short of funds, his usual procedure was to extract more taxes from the already-suffering farmers in his domain. This sometimes led to uprisings, especially in the closing years of the Tokugawa period, but on the whole the Japanese farmers were docile and lived in quiet misery.

Most of the samurai could see no way out of the predicament in which they found themselves. They were not schooled in the practical realities of business life, but were taught to despise everything which savoured of trade as a low seeking after profit. Thus, though they might be so heavily in debt to merchants as to be at their complete mercy, and though they might feel it necessary to address the merchants they met in the street in terms of great politeness (instead of the brusque tones of the superior), by training the samurai were convinced that all their difficulties were the result of the business men's striving after profit, and that if only the whole people would follow their own example of placing righteousness before other considerations, all problems would soon be solved. This attitude might be described as being properly Confucian, but to a realistically-minded person like Honda, it was absolutely infuriating.

The incapability of the samurai cost them their position of leadership in all but name. Pre-eminence among the four classes naturally did not devolve on the farmers, traditionally considered the second highest class. Although the farmers were always lauded as 'the foundation of the nation', the source of life-essential food and clothing, in practice they were treated far worse than the artisans and merchants who ranked below them. The farmer was the sole regular taxpayer in Japan, and new measures were constantly being devised to increase the amounts he paid. Such measures usually assumed the guise of (and may actually have been intended as) benevolent laws to relieve the plight of the suffering tillers of the soil, but their condition thereby grew only the worse. They were exhorted to work harder and produce more, but if ever they did enjoy a bumper harvest, the value of the rice was likely to be so low as to cancel out most of the profit, and increased taxation would take care of the rest. In addition to their normal woes, the generation 1770–90 saw an unprecedented series of natural disasters—volcanic eruptions, floods, epidemics, drought—which brought about severe famine conditions.

Yet in the midst of their misery the farmers were incessantly enjoined to abandon their ways of extravagance and self-indulgence. Such admonitions were made in part because of official resentment over any improvement in the standard of living of the farmers, however slight. The discovery that farmers now had mats on their floors drew forth the same cries of horror from eighteenth-century Japanese economists as the unrestrained drinking of tea by farmers did from their English contemporaries.[88] A second cause for complaint about the farmers' extravagance stemmed from the fact that some of them, finding it impossible to make a living on the soil, had gone to the cities for employment. This was laid to their love of luxury rather than to necessity, but already a century before, Kumazawa Banzan (1619–91), one of the most intelligent of the Confucian scholars, had noted, 'If there happen to be one or two rich families among fifty or a hundred poor ones, people are sure to say that the farmers are well-off and extravagant . . . There are so many farmers that even if one or two come from each village and are seen in the cities, they appear to be numerous.'[89]

The general discussions by philosophers and economists of the unhappy lot of the farmers did not go beyond the exhibition towards them of a kind of pity, and the recitation of Confucian platitudes about benevolence and righteousness. Honda realised how sterile such discussions were, and attempted to discover some formula for national prosperity more feasible than the old 'Work harder, spend less.' There was perhaps nothing wrong with this time-tested dictum, but except in the rare instances of capable management of domains by enlightened men, no amount of hard work or thrift on the part of the farmers seemed to improve their lot: improvement itself was not necessarily considered desirable.

The third of the classes, the artisans, was the least important and least discussed. The artisans were classed with the merchants as 'townsmen' (chōnin), and most of the attacks on the merchants were thus levelled in part at the artisans as well. There was, however, the general feeling that since the latter actually produced something, they were not quite so culpable as the profit-grabbing merchants. The agitation against extravagance was nonetheless directed against the livelihood of the artisans for, apart from certain imported wares, most luxury goods were produced by this class. This fact was realised by a few writers who protested against the sumptuary measures of the shogunate (which were, practically speaking, the only economic policies recognised by the Confucian-minded rulers). These men believed that the money spent on objects of luxury went into the hands of craftsmen and was thus not thrown away.

The government has ordered that there be no more gold- or silver-leaf made. It has also decreed that the manufacture of especially beautiful toys and dolls be discontinued. Although I speak with trepidation, I believe that this is an inept policy and presently will usher in a decline in Japan. If I may be permitted to conjecture the government's reasons for such action, I imagine it is their deep-seated judgement that luxury in society in the cause of misery, and that to use foil on useless articles such as children's toys is to waste gold and silver. But the persons who are willing to pay high prices for such articles are not poor people, but always great or wealthy ones, and thus it amounts to putting money into circulation.[90]

The modern reader may find little to choose between the proponents of sumptuary laws and those who believed in the public benefits of private extravagance. Honda's attitude was characteristically independent: he felt that it was desirable for a ruler to be liberal in his patronage of the artisans, not merely because this circulated money, but because it encouraged the production of fine articles which could serve as suitable material for export.

The merchants, whose position was officially the lowest, and who were the target of attack of virtually every law-giver and philosopher, had managed by the late eighteenth century to rise nevertheless to the position of greatest power. In vain were sumptuary laws levied against them; if they were forbidden to wear silk, they would line their cotton garments all the more gorgeously. The books, theatre and art of the time were all designed to please their tastes. A special philosophy for businessmen was evolved, the so-called 'teachings of the heart' (*shingaku*), which preached that it *was* possible for merchants to show benevolence and to shun excessive profit-grabbing.[91] This

philosophy did not have any noticeable influence on the
ways of most of the merchants, and the criticisms to which
they were subjected grew all the more bitter in the late
eighteenth century. Hayashi Shihei declared, 'Townsmen
have no other function than to siphon away the stipends
of the samurai,' and another writer called them the 'weevils
of the state'.[92] This was a new view of the businessmen;
previously they had been thought contemptible because
they ran after gain, but not useless or worse.

Although all writers deplored the avarice and general
baseness of the merchants, few of them offered any specific
solution to the problem. Some were of the opinion that the
samurai should assume the functions of the merchants, be-
lieving that the innate probity and righteousness of the
warrior-class would protect it against falling into the evil
ways of tradesmen. Honda was in favour of this rather
naïve proposal, but extended it to mean operation of vital
services not merely by virtuous samurai in place of wicked
businessmen, but by the government itself. Only the government, he felt, was qualified to perform such functions. His
may not have been an entirely practical answer to the
question of what was to be done with the merchants, but it
impresses us as being more sensible than the moral diatribes of other eighteenth-century writers.

In spite of its faults and inadequacies, the organisation of
Japan into four social classes was favoured by writers of
every shade of political belief, from the most conservative
Confucianist to dissidents like Honda. Schemes were often
brought forward to ensure the maintenance of society along
the rigid lines of samurai, farmers, artisans and merchants,
but in point of fact, there was a constant mixing of the
classes which it was impossible to prevent. Farmers drifted
into the towns to become artisans and merchants, while the
samurai mended their difficult financial positions either by
contracting marriage-alliances with the merchants or by
setting up in trade for themselves. This mobility of the

classes was made possible by the fact that the class-system was a political expedient and not an article of religious belief. It was possible, though extremely difficult, for the son of the humblest farmer's family to rise to high position, while the fall from glory of many samurai was a feature of Tokugawa history.

Above the four classes stood the government, feudal in origin and still preserving many feudal customs, but essentially a modern centralised state. In the early part of the eighteenth century, control of the government was still in the hands of the shogun, a member of the Tokugawa family, which had come into power after the Battle of Seki-gahara in 1600. The shogunate exercised varying degrees of authority over the country; in the central part of Japan, close to the seat of its power, there was no question about the finality of its decisions, but in remote regions in the south or north of the country, often only so much obedi-ence was given the shogunate as was in consonance with the plans of the local barons. To control the barons a system known as *sankin kōtai* had been established, under which the various daimyo were required to spend alternate years in Edo, and to leave their families there as hostages. This system had an additional advantage for the shogunate in that it necessitated large expenditures by the daimyo, who were thus forced to maintain establishments both in their provinces and in the capital. These provisions, however, worked greater hardships on the small nobles than on the powerful 'outside lords'.93

By the late eighteenth century political power had left the direct control of the shogun, and had passed into the hands of advisers. The most noteworthy examples of this type of political figure in Honda's time were Tanuma Okitsugu (1719–88) and Matsudaira Sadanobu (1758–1829). It is difficult to make a fair appraisal of Tanuma today. The histories of the period were all written by people who were opposed to him and who were desirous of pleasing his successors. He is inevitably referred to as 'notoriously corrupt', and certain delightfully ingenuous remarks are attributed to him, such as: 'Gold and silver are so precious a treasure that they may scarcely be bought with human lives. If someone is so desirous of serving his government that he will part with even such a treasure, it is clear that his purpose must be loyal. The strength of his purpose may be measured by the size of the present.'[94]

Tanuma's regime has been characterised as a 'government by bribery', and its extravagance is legendary, but it does not actually appear to have been very dissimilar in character to most of the later shogunate administrations. When economic troubles arose, resort was had to the two usual shogunate expedients, sumptuary laws and manipulation of the coinage. The sumptuary laws were quite strict, but had little apparent effect, while the currency debasement only caused inflation. Tanuma, however, was not content with these time-honoured panaceas for economic ills. Marsh-reclamation was begun under his orders, and the settlement of Ezo projected.[95] Tanuma was also interested in how the West might help Japan. He extended his patronage to Hiraga Gennai's European studies. Later, he requested the Dutch to send carpenters from Batavia to instruct Japanese workmen in the building of bigger ships for the Osaka-Nagasaki trade, and it appeared to Isaac Titsingh, factory director at the time, that the country might soon be opened to European ships. Japanese sailors had already received training in the handling of Dutch boats.[96]

But Tanuma's administration was dogged by natural calamities which he was powerless to control. The worst of these was the eruption of Asama-yama in 1783, which was followed by a terrible famine. In 1784 Tanuma's son was assassinated, and it became apparent that his own regime could not last much longer. The suffering due to the famine was blamed on the government, and Tanuam was eventually forced to resign in 1786.

His successor was Matsudaira Sadanobu, of whom there has already been considerable mention. Matsudaira's avowed intention was to go back to the policies of his ancestor, Tokugawa Yoshimune. This entailed a complete repudiation of all of Tanuma's projects, including the obviously constructive ones. Like Tanuma, he issued sumptuary laws, but unlike him, Matsudaira chose to restore the value of the coinage (as Yoshimune had also done). He was so determined to return to the glorious old days that it was a matter of indifference to him if his policies caused widespread depression in the cities. The honesty of his regime was admirable, but wits of the time complained that 'fish don't live in clear water' and there was longing for the old muddiness of Tanuma's day. Matsudaira's policies were not much more successful than Tanuma's in spite of his personal integrity, and he resigned in 1793 after only six years in power.

Matsudaira's failure was not due to any lack of ability on his part. His writings show him to have been a man of great intelligence. His weakness was indicated by Shiba Kōkan, who said of Matsudaira that he was 'very learned and clever but knew next to nothing about geography.'[97] Ignorance of geography kept him from following Tanuma's tentative projects of opening the country and developing Ezo, and thereby made it impossible for Matsudaira to extricate Japan from her economic difficulties. As long as it was forbidden to trade with foreign countries, there was no means of dealing effectively with the alternating problems of famine and surpluses, and as long as transport facilities within the country remained hopelessly inadequate, there would continue to be great inequalities of distribution. Geography, including its adjunct sciences of surveying and navigation, was the key to the solution of both the internal and external problems, as Honda Toshiaki pre-eminently realised.

Trade within and without the country on a large scale

was also the only way to stabilise the price of rice, over-whelmingly the most important crop. Instead of adopting this solution, however, Matsudaira followed the example of Yoshimune and attempted to lower the price by deflation. This policy was successful enough when there were small or moderate crops, but when there was a bumper harvest, deflation contributed to reducing the price of the rice to a dangerously low level. At this point inflationary measures might be taken to force the price upwards, but generally the only persons to profit by these contradictory policies were the merchants (and artisans) who, unlike the samurai and farmers, did not rely on rice for their livelihood.

Another favourite remedy for the rice problem which was often proposed was that of the 'ever-normal granary'.[98] This ancient plan called for the government to purchase rice at high prices in years of plenty, and to store it for lean years, when it would sell the rice at lower prices than pre-vailed. The scheme had an appealing simplicity, but though it was tried from time to time in both China and Japan, it never succeeded in the long run. It could work only if fat and lean years followed each other fairly regularly; a series of bountiful harvests would exhaust the capacity to buy rice, while the storehouses would be emptied by any pro-longed famine. The system also required honest administra-tion, and this was not always available.

The final means to which the government used to have recourse in dealing with high commodity-prices was to command them to fall. Yoshimune issued decrees to this effect in 1724 and 1726, with little practical effect, as might be imagined.[99] Honda clearly showed the futility of such attempts to control prices.

The ineffectualness of all these measures was only sur-passed by the official interpretation of the causes of the economic distress. Everything was attributed to the mer-chants' want of righteousness. One good Confucian hope-fully suggested that if even only ten per cent of the merchants would have consideration for the samurai and farmers, and show their righteousness by selling at lower prices, they would enjoy such popularity that all the other businessmen would be forced to lower their prices too.[100] Kumazawa Banzan, who was wise enough to recognise that it had been the gradual switch from a rice to a money economy which had placed the power in the hands of the merchants, could think of no better solution than the restoration of the old rice standard.[101]

Honda Toshiaki was not immune to the traditional economic ideas that were constantly being brought forth as entirely new programmes. At different points in his writings he advocated both the inflation-deflation and the 'ever-normal granary' plans, but these were rather in the nature of temporary expedients for him. His main economic programme is to be found in the 'four imperative needs' which he enumerated in his *Secret Plan*. These were (1) gunpowder (2) metals (3) shipping and (4) colonisation. The names of these needs in themselves do not fully explain what Honda included under each of them. He was interested in explosives primarily for their use in blasting new channels for rivers, part of his programme of improved transport and flood control, rather than for their military purposes. By metals he meant precious metals which, in mercantilistic fashion, he wished to attract to Japan, and base metals, the use of which he advocated in place of wood in order to reduce loss to rot and fire. Shipping and colonisation were the key-points in his planning, and must be treated at length.

Honda, either independently or under Hayashi Shihei's influence, had become convinced that Japan must live up to her geographical situation as an island nation, and not imitate the continental usages of China. Hayashi had stressed the necessity of a navy and familiarity with naval tactics; Honda placed his emphasis on the benefits that would come from merchant shipping. The examples of the prosperity of Holland and England, both maritime nations, made it clear to him that only through foreign trade could Japan attain lasting prosperity. This trade required ships of sufficient size and strength to withstand long voyages, and a knowledge of navigation which would permit Japanese captains to guide their vessels to any port in the world. By such trade it would become possible for Japan to 'obtain what we lack for that which we have', a familiar phrase of Honda's.

Honda insisted that shipping be government-owned. He felt that it was disgraceful that, under existing conditions, the lives of the citizens were left to the caprices of the merchants; if they so chose, the owners of the rice-ships which daily supplied Edo with its food could starve the city out. The government, on the other hand, would act in the interests of the people, and use its ships to move rice from the growing areas to the cities. Honda noted that it sometimes happened that in one part of Japan there were such surpluses that grain was left to rot on the ground, while in another part of the country there might be a famine. Two reasons for this condition existed: the fewness of navigable rivers (which should be remedied by widening and clearing rocks from streams by means of explosives), and the lack of shipping. The government could eliminate this problem by moving the grain to the areas where it is needed, thus benefiting both the growers, who would otherwise lose the value of the rice, and the starving people in the famine-stricken areas.

Such measures, Honda believed, would do much to help relieve existing conditions, but greater national prosperity would eventually cause an increase in population by removing the reasons for infanticide. Even when every part of the land was brought under cultivation, there would still not be enough food, for though the land is limited in size, the population can grow indefinitely. The only solution to this problem was to expand the territory available for cultivation by overseas expansion, at first to islands close to Japan, later to historically Japanese islands such as the Kuriles and the Bonins, and finally to Kamchatka, the Aleutians and North America. These regions at present might be under Russian or other foreign domination, but since Japan was far better situated geographically for ruling them it ought not to be difficult to regain what carelessness in the past permitted to be taken away. When an empire had been won for Japan, her prosperity would be unequalled. The capital of Japan should then be moved to Kamchatka because of its central location and because it was potentially a richer place than Japan itself. Food and other products from the new dominions would flow into Japan in return for the benefits of civilisation which Japan would extend to the as yet savage natives. Then Japan's position would be such that she would be acclaimed as Mistress of the East, to balance English supremacy in the West.

As this summary of the 'four imperative needs' indicates, Honda's plans for 'managing the country' was of quite a different order from the traditional Confucian advocacy of hard work, frugality and righteousness. He did not, of course, reject all the old conceptions. He declared that it was essential that the four classes of society be maintained. This did not prevent him, however, from insisting that merit and not class be the qualifying factor in appointing persons to official positions. His bitterness towards the merchants did not differ greatly from that of other writers, but he recognised the necessity of trade. The answer Honda gave to the question of what was to be done with unscrupulous businessmen was not that they should be taught benevolence, not that it was desirable to revert to an age when money was unknown, but that the merchants must be kept under strict control by government supervision. For the farmers he showed real sympathy, based on first-hand experiences of their sufferings.

The difference between Honda and other writers on economics of his time was his pragmatic approach. His chief concern was always the practical benefits that might be obtained from any policy. He was by no means indifferent to ethical issues, but it was not enough for him that a ruler be steeped in Confucian lore; he must also be a skilled man of science familiar with the new techniques of civilisation. It was for this reason that he exalted the Empress Catherine of Russia above any of the sage emperors of China or martial heroes of Japan. Honda's impressions of the empress's life were exceedingly garbled, but it is obvious what qualities he thought she possessed. They are illustrated by an anecdote twice related by him. Some twenty years ago, he said, the Empress of Russia heard about a lake in Siberia which used to overflow every August and flood the countryside. She accordingly issued a proclamation asking her people to suggest some means of eliminating this danger. One man stated that he knew of a way, and the empress granted him an audience. When she heard his plan she declared, 'Heaven has sent you to me,' bowed twice to heaven, gave the necessary orders to her ministers, and then retired into her palace.[102]

Here, then, was the model ruler in action. When she was informed of something afflicting her people she at once attempted to discover a remedy by appealing to the entire nation. Thus, capable men among the lower classes might give their suggestions, as well as persons close to the government. Then, when she had heard the wise man's scheme and judged it to be feasible, she did not hesitate to grant all the necessary funds. The Empress Catherine thus implemented her ethical interest in the affairs of her people with the necessary practical steps. No wonder, concluded Honda, that the Russian domains have increased so greatly that they now include Kamchatka and the Kuriles! Half of the world belongs to Russia, and most of it won not by force, but by the wisdom of the Empress Catherine. 'True possessions are gained through acts of virtue; countries which submit to force of arms do not yield in their hearts.'

Honda discussed the ways in which Japan might follow Russia's example under three main headings: foreign trade, population and colonisation.

(a) Foreign Trade

As has been related, at the end of the eighteenth century Japan's foreign trade was restricted to China and Holland. There was no legal reason why ships could not come to Japan from such countries as Siam or Annam, as had happened earlier in the century, but the Japan trade had become steadily less profitable for foreigners. The only export of any consequence was copper; Thunberg described it as the finest known, containing much gold. However, ever since Arai Hakuseki had written the *Short Account of Specie* (about 1708) there had been increasing feeling on the part of Japanese intellectuals against the export of this metal. In his work Arai had given highly-exaggerated figures about the amounts of gold, silver and copper that had been sent abroad, and had lamented this fact, declaring that metals were the 'bones' of a country, which once removed would never grow again.[103] Honda accepted both Arai's figures and his conclusion. By his time the government had severely limited the export of copper, but Honda felt that it was inexcusable that even relatively small amounts of this article of permanent value should be traded for the perishable fripperies brought in by the Chinese and the Dutch.

Apart from his condemnation of the export of copper, Honda did not devote much attention to the Nagasaki trade, nor suggest what functions it might best fulfil, for he regarded it as an entirely negative arrangement. He was convinced that Japan should not be content to let foreign countries bring their wares to her; she should follow European usage and herself seek out trade in all quarters of the globe. The first step in Japan's new and aggressive policy of foreign trade should be the establishment of commercial relations with Russia.

Places should be set aside on Etorofu and Kunashiri where Japanese goods can be traded for Russian ones. In this way there can be peaceful trade, and we shall learn about both the Russian people and their country, knowledge which will certainly prove beneficial.[104]

In his desire to promote trade with Russia, Honda had been anticipated by Kudō Heisuke, who had written:

Trade with Russia will be a good way to help foster the development of Ezo. If Ezo can thus be brought under Japanese control, all of Ezo's products including precious metals will be available to us. Trade with Russia necessarily cannot be confined to Ezo. Nagasaki and all other important ports should also be opened to Russian trade.[105]

Kudō's proposal that the major ports of the empire be thrown open to Russian ships was extraordinarily liberal in its intention, but it was quite contrary to Honda's idea of foreign trade. Honda looked back wistfully to the old days when Japanese ships had sailed to the countries of southeast Asia, and deplored the later edicts which had destroyed the Japanese merchant marine. For him it was essential that trade be carried out on Japanese ships; this was necessary not only as a matter of prestige but also for the profits of carriage by sea. Whether Japan was open or closed to foreign ships was a matter of indifference to him; he was interested only in seeing to it that Japanese ships took advantage of the accessibility of foreign ports.

Honda was aware of the problem of finding suitable Japanese goods for export if copper were not to be sent abroad. His solution took the following form:

As part of a national policy, every effort should be made to promote the production in this country of articles which are of as fine manufacture as possible. If such efforts are made, individual industries will be encouraged, and attempts to improve the quality of Japanese products will follow. In that way many articles famed for their excellence will be produced in this country. This will help us to gain profit when trading with foreign nations.[106]

This statement shows Honda's desire to associate Japan with the advanced, manufacturing countries, rather than with less developed lands which can only offer raw materials for trade with foreign powers. Shiba Kōkan, on the other hand, believed that trade with Russia would be a good way of disposing of Japan's surplus rice at a profit. He quoted a Chinese philosopher to demonstrate the futility of attempting to dispose of rice when there is a glut.

Huai Nan-tzu wrote, 'One does not sell firewood in a forest, and one does not vend fish on a lake. That is because there is more than enough on the spot.'
Since there isn't any Japanese rice in other countries, we should load big ships with it, and sell it in Russia and elsewhere. We could then obtain goods from other lands such as medicines and valuable manufactures that we do not possess here.[107]

Honda differed from Shiba also in the matter of the benefits to be derived from foreign trade. He was not interested so much in the natural products or manufactures of other countries as in their precious metals—their permanent treasures. He described in detail the prosperity of the port of Amsterdam, dwelling especially on the number of ships which come in from abroad (including Japan) each year laden with gold, silver and fine copper. The importance given by Honda to precious metals recalls the mercantilism still popular in the Europe of his time, and it is worthy of note how exactly his theories tallied with the definition of mercantilism as 'a set of doctrinal tendencies which over-emphasised the precious metals, foreign trade, manufacturing, the desirability of a dense population, and state action in economic matters.'[108] One is tempted to suggest a European origin to Honda's programme, but this is not at all likely. His desire to obtain precious metals from other countries, for example, is the counterpart to Arai's fear that Japan was losing her own precious metals in trade with China and Holland. The other points of resemblance to European mercantilism have similar native origins, but they were all brought to their logical conclusions and welded into a system by Honda's original efforts. Mercantilism was an old story to eighteenth-century Europe, but for Japan it was a great discovery.

(b) Population

Honda's theory of population is developed at greatest length in his *Tales of the West*, although it occurs elsewhere in his works. In brief, it was Honda's belief that the natural rate of increase of the population of Japan was 19.75 times in 33 years, and it was only because of deficiencies in the administration of the country that this increase was prevented. If parents were able to feel a reasonable amount of security in the future of children they brought into the world, there would no longer be abortion or infanticide to cut down the population. The increasing population would then outstrip the growth in food supply, and it would be necessary for Japan to acquire foodstuffs from abroad, both by trade and by colonisation. Honda's final picture of Japan, in other words, was of a strong manufacturing country supported by an empire which produced raw materials.

Honda's views on population have earned for him the name of 'the Japanese Malthus'. They also resemble somewhat the theories of Hung Liang-chi, known as 'the Chinese Malthus'. By examining the writings of the Englishman and the Chinese, we may be able to understand Honda's ideas more clearly, and to realise the inapplicability of the nickname which he has been given by well-meaning writers.

Malthus published his first *Essay on Population* in 1798, the same year as Honda's *Tales of the West*. It was his belief 'that population, when unchecked, goes on doubling itself every twenty-five years, or increases in a geometrical ratio' while subsistence increases only arithmetically. The checks of which he wrote were misery and vice; he recognised no others at first, but later admitted a 'preventive check' which 'arises from that distinctive superiority in his [man's] reasoning faculties, which enables him to calculate distant consequences.'[109] In countries like the newly-founded United States of America, where there was little misery or vice, the predicted increase in population had occurred. Eventually, Malthus concluded, the Indians would be 'driven further and further back into the country, till the whole race is ultimately exterminated, and the territory is incapable of further extension.'[110] According to this reasoning, the acquisition and settlement of colonies was no more than a 'slight palliative' to a hopeless problem: even if suitable people were willing to emigrate, instead of the dregs of the nation, even if a callous view were adopted regarding the rights of the natives of the places to be colonised, the normal expansion of the population would soon fill up any territory, leaving the situation more or less as before.

Malthus did not offer any solution to this gloomy state of affairs, except perhaps the hope that the 'preventive check' would be used more often. One thing he stressed was the inadvisability of the government's tampering with the natural checks of misery and vice. Legislation providing support for poor men's children would only tend in the long run to make the problem more acute. Malthus wrote of one such attempt, 'I entirely acquit Mr. Pitt of any sinister intention in that clause of his poor bill which allows a shilling a week to every labourer for each child he has

above three.'[111] Thus he exonerated Pitt of displaying anything worse than crass stupidity in wishing to save the lives
of starving children.

The conclusions of Malthus were bolstered by numerous
examples drawn from the history of many countries. He
took China and Japan as instances of countries which were
already so intensively cultivated that there did not seem
to be any possibility of increasing food production sub-
stantially even over many years. How then, he wondered,
could the huge population of China be sustained? As an
answer he quoted with approval a missionary historian who
had written, 'Notwithstanding the great sobriety and in-
dustry of the inhabitants of China, the prodigious number
of them occasions a great deal of misery.'[112] Thus, the
natural check of misery, combined with the vicious practice of infanticide, kept the population of China from
exceeding too much the limited food supply.

Hung Liang-chi, who based his theory of population-
growth on personal observation, rather than on a reading
of world history, came to approximately the same conclusions as Malthus. His views are contained in an essay,
Peace, written in 1793. As the title of the essay indicates,
Hung associated the dangerous growth of the population
with the prolonged peace. He began:

There has never been a people which did not like peace,
and never a people which did not wish peace to last for a
long time. Now that there has been peace for a hundred
years, it may be said to be of long duration. If we consider
the population, we shall find that it has increased to five
times what it was thirty years ago, and ten times what it
was sixty years ago. When this enquiry is pushed back one
hundred or more years, the increase will be found to be
not less than twenty times.[113]

Hung took the case of a prosperous farmer living alone
in a large house with one hundred acres of land to cultivate.

As his family increases, and servants are added to help care for them, the house will become unbearably crowded, and the produce of the land will support them but inadequately. Hung answered the arguments of those who claimed that there were natural checks to population-increase such as floods, drought and epidemics, by pointing out that only one or two people in ten ever suffer from these disasters. To those who objected that wise princes could cause the opening of new lands on the borders, and thus provide additional food, Hung replied that benevolent measures by rulers, however desirable, were only likely to increase the population still more. He concluded:

To sum up, when there has been protracted peace, heaven and earth cannot but produce people, and the substance produced by heaven and earth for the nourishment of man will never equal his numbers. When there has been protracted peace, the princes and ministers naturally cannot keep people from reproducing, and that which they supply for the livelihood of the people cannot meet their needs.[114]

These views were quite exceptional for China, where a large population had always been considered desirable. Another suggestion of Hung's, that the quality of the people may suffer when each family has too many children, seems of startling modernity. But his short essay naturally did not have the epoch-making significance of Malthus' work; it was more in the nature of a wise observation than a manifesto or a proclamation of the shape of things to come. Hung quietly made his point—the paradox between the ideal of peace and the suffering that may come from it— and then moved on.[115]

Honda's chief statement of his views on population was written five years after Hung's essay, but there is nothing to suggest that he was influenced by the Chinese writer. The background of Honda's views was quite different from that of Malthus' or Hung's. Since the beginning of the eighteenth century the population of Japan had been stable, and temporary increases were usually cancelled by famines or other disasters. The farming population had probably even decreased during the period. Infanticide was so widely practised in the north of Japan that it was customary among the farmers to raise only one or two of the children born to them. The farmers also bore the brunt of famine suffering, and their numbers had been much reduced in the period 1770–90. Over-population would thus not appear to have been the serious problem in Honda's Japan it was threatening to become in China, but it must be remembered that it was the growth in numbers of unproductive samurai and merchants which had so taxed the resources of the farmers as to force upon them drastic birth-control measures. This Honda understood, and it was his hope that the farming population might be enabled by his plans to increase naturally. Only when he had charted in his mind its possible growth did he realise that some day the territory of Japan would not be able to produce enough food for everyone. Far from being dismayed by this prospect, as Malthus had been, it represented for Honda an incentive for overseas expansion and development of an empire.

Honda's point of departure, like Hung's, was in the problems of an extended peace, but the implications were different for him.

Some old Chinese sage once stated that the moral principles have their origin in marriage, but no teaching has been evolved to deal with problems that arise from this relationship. Therefore, whenever there has been a period of continued peace, husbands and wives, fearful lest it become increasingly difficult for them to earn a living, and aware that if they have many children they will not have any property to leave them, confer and decide that, rather than rear children who in later years will have great difficulty in making a decent living, it is better to take precautions before they are born and not add another mouth to feed. If they do have a child, they secretly destroy it, calling the process by the euphemism of 'thinning out'. This practice is most prevalent in the thirteen provinces from the Kantō to Ōu.[116] It is an evil custom which inevitably arises when there has been a protracted peace, and is due also to the lack of any governmental system of guidance.

No more important business of the state exists than finding a solution to this problem. If it is neglected, the longer peace continues, the more the samurai will grow in numbers, and their extravagance will keep pace. The same will be true of the merchants and, carried along by the tendency of increase in these two classes, priests, artisans and idlers will also multiply in numbers. This will mean, of course, that it will be very difficult for the farmers to feed them all. Then, when a point is reached where there is insufficient food for the samurai, artisans, merchants and idlers, there will presumably be nothing better to do than to oppress the farmers, and the farmers will then be in dire straits.

There is a limit to the amount of land that can be farmed. There is also a limit to the amount of rice that can be grown, a limit to the amount of annual levies and taxes that can be paid, and a limit to the rice that will remain when the taxes have been met. It may be attempted to make this limited supply of rice meet the needs of all the people, but the attempt will fail, for the samurai, merchants, artisans, priests and idlers are constantly increasing in numbers.[117]

The immediate solution offered by Honda to the problems besetting the farmers took the form of state subsidy of children. Farmers should be granted two sacks of rice a year for each child until it reaches the age of fifteen, when it can be of use to the nation. Next, various reclamation and development projects (enumerated in the second part of his *Secret Plan*) would bring prosperity to certain depressed regions. Finally, the adoption of his 'four imperative needs' by the government would bring about general prosperity, and the population would increase at the rate of 19.75 times every thirty-three years. This astounding figure was reached by Honda in a simple enough manner. He began with two newly-married couples of which the husbands are fifteen years of age, and the wives thirteen. If they produce a child every two years for thirty-three years, when women can no longer bear children, there will be seventeen boys and and girls in each family. These in turn having married their opposite numbers in the other family will produce forty-five grandchildren to the original couples by the end of thirty-three years. Thus a total of seventy-nine children and grand-children (excluding possible great-grandchildren) have been born to the original four people, an increase of 19.75 times.[118]

It is hard to believe that Honda was sincere in giving these figures as the 'natural increase'. Here, as at certain other points in his work, the propagandist appears to have got the better of the thinker. The same desire to convince which led him to assert that Kamchatka was a splendid country, in spite of all he could have read of the land, also induced him to put forward this extravagant figure as the normal birth-rate. We may contrast Honda's estimate with Malthus's more conservative claim that the population unchecked would double every twenty-five years, a figure arrived at after careful study of census reports. Honda's theory of population was in comparison no more than an intelligent observation, like that of Hung Liang-chi, but he was not satisfied merely with stating it, as Hung had been. Honda's thoughts were on the fourth of his 'imperative needs', colonisation, and he used his distorted population-theory merely as a bridge to this end.

(c) Colonisation

There was no subject to which Honda devoted greater attention than that of colonisation, which he termed the 'prime duty of the ruler'. His chief model in this was England:

Some of the prosperous nations of Europe are themselves small in area, but have extensive possessions; such countries are called 'great nations'. Among them is England, a nation about the size of Japan.[119]

Lists are given of English colonies in different parts of the world, and the benefits England receives from them are enumerated. The wonders of England itself are described, the implication being that there is no reason why Japan cannot follow in her footsteps and attain equal prosperity.

Honda outlined the order to be followed in colonisation:

First, ships are despatched to ascertain the location of the islands to be taken, and to measure their size. The natural products of the islands are investigated and the native population estimated. Then, when it is known about how many provinces the islands would make if they are settled, the actual work of colonisation is begun. If the natives of the islands are still living in caves, they are taught about houses. Dwellings should be built for the tribal chiefs. In the case of natives without implements and utensils, they should be supplied with them. By helping the natives and giving them everything they desire, one will inspire a feeling of affection and obedience in them, like the love of children for their parents. This is true because they are moved by the same feelings that pervade the rest of the world, even though they are considered barbarians.[120]

The suggestions are followed immediately by a discussion of the recompense gained by the coloniser in return for his trouble.

The way to compensate for the expenses involved in colonisation lies in taking the natural products of these islands and shipping them to Japan. Trading marks a

Life among the hairy Ainu

夷人ヤスヲ以テ
オットセイヲナ
ゲ突ニスル躰

ヤス

as pictured by Hayashi Shihei

(from *Sangoku Tsūran Zusetsu*, 1786)

beginning of compensation for the expenses. Even barbarians do not expect to ask favours and give nothing in return. The products they give represent a first form of taxation. Since every island has wooded areas, there will always be some value in the lumber which can be taken from it even after a good many years. The value of other products would be too great to calculate. It is the task of the ruler-father to direct and educate the natives in such a manner that there will not be a single one of them who spends even one unproductive day. This is a matter which should not be put off another moment.[121]

Honda's bald statement of the methods of exploitation of the natives would have put to shame any European contemporary! It is true that he did not advocate bringing the Word of Shinto to the benighted natives, but he was quite confident that the blessings of Japanese culture were sufficiently great to make the natives forget their enforced servitude.

The first places to be colonised were naturally enough those closest to Japan. Honda explained:

Japan is as yet unfamiliar with navigation, transport and foreign trade, and it will not be easy to begin without experience. Therefore Japanese should first sail to the Ezo islands, since they are possessions of ours . . . Trade at these places in Japanese goods will yield steadily-increasing profits. Everyone will desire to travel abroad, and this will permit the natural growth of 19.75 times in thirty-three years of which I wrote above.[122]

The Ezo islands, that is Hokkaidō, Karafuto and the Kuriles, were also well suited as the initial colonisation venture because the people were of the same race as the Japanese in spite of their hairiness.[123] The natives of the Aleutians, including Amchitka, the island where Kōdayū was wrecked, were of the same race, and Honda heard that the natives of

North America also resembled Japanese. The fact that the Ainu still referred to the Japanese as *kamoedono*—exalted beings—and that there existed a tradition of allegiance to Japan meant that Japan had an advantage over any other country wishing to colonise Ezo. However, if she did not act at once, it would be too late, for the Russians were steadily encroaching on the Ezo domains of Japan. If only Benyowsky's warning had been heeded, this unhappy situation need never have arisen! Every day that passed made the retaking of Ezo more difficult, for the natives were gradually being won over to Russian ways.

Honda's worries about the Russification of the natives may have come from his learning of conditions on Etorofu, one of the Kurile islands where Russian influence was strongest. One traveller had written:

When I went there in 1788 I had one of the natives called over to me, and I asked him what he had learned from the Russians. He said that the Russians had given him holy images and taught him prayers. He had been told that if he believed in them he would prosper in his fishing, would never be shipwrecked, and that he would not fail to get whatever else he desired. When I enquired about the prayers, the man stood up and, like a Russian, put three fingers together. Pointing at his forehead, chest and arm-pits, he three times recited 'Ohoppomipomira' and bowed down.[124]

Kudō Heisuke had earlier warned of just such a tendency. He had written that because of Japanese neglect of the Ezo islands, the natives, of the same race as the Kamchadales, already conquered by the Russians, were now obeying Russian orders, and Japanese wishes were no longer consulted.

Honda did not disapprove of the Russian attempts to civilise the Ainu. Had he known of the brutal Russian treatment of the natives, which had sometimes resulted in the annihilation of their villages, he would have been furnished with another argument for Japanese sovereignty over the islands, but as it was, he spoke only in the highest terms of their energy, which he contrasted with Japanese sloth. It was compassion for the natives which had induced the Russians to bring them the benefits of civilisation, and the Ainu accordingly regarded their conquerors as their parents. Views similar to Honda's were expressed by Habuto Seiyō, the first Magistrate of Hakodate, who wrote in 1803:

According to what I have heard of Russian state policies, countries which are already civilised and where a government exists are never invaded. All the Russians are doing is to educate those natives who at present do not even know the art of cooking their food.[125]

Habuto thus felt it needless to establish military defences in Ezo as long as Japan made it clear that she was bringing civilisation to the Ainu.

The desirability of colonising (or civilising) Ezo was by no means an undisputed issue. Although advanced writers like Kudō Heisuke, Hayashi Shihei and Honda Toshiaki favoured the immediate assertion of Japanese sovereignty in the north, persons closer to the government continued to voice opposition to any such undertaking. Nakai Chikuzan (1730–1804), one of the leading political writers of the time, wrote in 1789 that Japan should confine her activities in Ezo to the establishment of trading posts. Then, if the Russians attacked in strength, the posts could be abandoned with no military disgrace to Japan. He felt that there was no reason to put Japan to the expense and trouble of defending so worthless a place. If the Russians succeeded in capturing Ezo, there would be time enough to decide whether or not to do business with them there. Japan should consider it fortunate that this valueless, scantily-populated buffer existed between herself and

Russia. Any attempt to colonise Ezo would only bring about the deaths of officials and soldiers, and would destroy the favourable state of affairs.[126]

Honda branded such opinions as traitorous, and lumped together persons who considered Ezo a foreign country with those who thought that the inhabitants 'unlike other human beings, have only one eye, in the middle of their foreheads, which flashes like lightning.'[127] But his attempts to discredit Nakai and others of his school counted for little alongside the official patronage of such conservative doctrines by Matsudaira Sadanobu. Other shogunate advisers informed Matsudaira of the military power of the Matsumae clan, and he appears to have been persuaded that no real danger of invasion existed in face of such strength.

In an attempt to change Matsudaira's views, Honda submitted in 1792 a memorial on the advisability of settling Ezo. He gave five reasons why this should be done: (1) to establish a natural frontier between Japan and Russia and thus prevent Russians from roaming freely about Japanese territory; (2) to provide a place where criminals might lead useful lives; (3) the mines would yield valuable metals; (4) the land when cultivated would produce abundant crops which could help Japan in time of famine; and (5) the timber of Ezo could be used to build ships.[128]

The last three of these points need no comment; the first was obviously in answer to Nakai's opinion that Ezo served a useful function as a desolate 'no-man's-land' between Japan and Russia. Honda favoured a clear-cut frontier, and to make this seem desirable to the conservative officials in power, he pointed out that it would make it possible to keep out Christians who might otherwise drift into Japan. Honda's second proposal, to use Ezo as a place of exile for criminals, had an interesting background. In 1786 it was suggested to Tanuma Okitsugu that 70,000 *eta* be forced to migrate to Ezo. When the population of Ezo had increased sufficiently, it would then be feasible to send some of the *eta* colonists on to Tartary and Manchuria as well as to the remoter Kurile islands. This ambitious plan fell through because of Tanuma's dismissal from office, but Honda may have learned of it.[129]

Honda was aware of the difficulty of finding people willing to serve as colonists in lands whose reputation, in spite of his own efforts, was so unfavourable. At one time he suggested that those farmers from the northern provinces of Japan who visited Ezo every summer be compelled to remain there with their families (which, he believed, they secretly wished to do anyway). Idlers, robbers and other lawbreakers from parts of Japan where snow falls should be sent to Ezo, there to expiate their sins by leading honest lives as farmers or fishermen, and thus benefiting the country. Persons of similar description from parts of Japan where the snow did not fall should be sent to colonise southern territories like the Bonin Islands.[130]

Honda gave very detailed attention to the problems of colonists in the northern regions, even to prescribing the construction of the houses they were to use, the methods of heating and the best types of windows and doors. He also listed the steps to be taken in communicating Japanese culture to the natives. He realised that it would be impossible to convert them overnight to the Japanese way of life, and advocated retaining their good customs and only replacing bad ones with superior Japanese practices. 'Japanese customs should be spread very gradually among the natives, and the Japanese government also established gradually.'[131]

The Ezo controversy raged among Japanese scholars for many years with little fruitful result. Men before Honda (as early perhaps as the end of the seventeenth century) and men for many years after him continued to stress the advantages of Ezo, often in exaggerated terms, but the conservatism of the government was too great to be overcome by even the most persuasive of writers. Parties of exploration continued to visit the north, but it was unlikely that any real colonisation could take place as long as it was forbidden for Japanese to leave the country, circulate information about Japan abroad, or teach the Japanese language to foreigners.

In the writings of all the advocates of the development of Ezo there was a strong note of urgency: 'It will soon be too late; the Russians will beat us to Ezo!' was the cry of many patriots. When Honda learned of the death of Catherine the Great, he felt that the moment had arrived for Japanese action. The Russian empire would collapse on the death of so incomparably gifted a ruler, and the Japanese could easily extend their possessions up the Kuriles to Kamchatka, to Cape Thadeus beyond, and across to the continent of North America.[132] No show of force would be necessary if only advantage were at once taken of this unique opportunity. 'It will soon be too late!'

Nothing happened. The opportunity passed, and the voices most heeded by the government were those which called for maintenance of the status quo. When the Russians sent an embassy in 1804 to ask for trade, the most trusted shogunate councillor advised, 'It is the law of our ancestors not to permit trade with nations other than China and Holland.'[133] But if the Japanese missed their chance to gain an empire, as Honda believed, they did not suffer the invasion of their territories predicted by many writers since the time of Benyowsky. The benevolent Russian colonial administration, which Honda thought would soon be extended to Hokkaidō, found no favour with the Ainu, who knew it brought only death in the form of gunfire and disease. Those natives who survived the harshness of Russian rule rapidly degenerated, as may be seen even in this account by a Russian apologist:

Although their manner of living be most nasty, and their actions most stupid, yet they think themselves the happiest people in the world, and look upon the Russians who are settled among them with contempt: however this notion begins to change at present; for the old people who are confirmed in their customs, drop off, and the young ones being converted to the Christian religion, adopt the customs of the Russians, and despise the barbarity and superstition of their ancestors.[134]

It may be wondered whether the Japanese would have done better. When Captain Krusenstern contemplated the seizure of Saghalien from Japan, the nominal possessor of the island, he wrote:

The most essential objection would be, that such a capture was made without the approbation of the true possessors of Sachalin, the Ainos; and I honestly confess my doubts whether they would gain by such a change; for they appeared to me to be treated with great humanity by the Japanese.[135]

Such tribute would have surprised Honda Toshiaki, who could see only stupidity and inefficiency in Japanese practices as contrasted with the invariably enlightened usages of the West. His attitude has been much condemned by modern Japanese critics as showing an unseemly adulation of foreign things, but it was precisely this receptivity on the part of Honda, Shiba and other advanced men of their time which made it possible for Japan alone among Asian nations to rise to the challenge of the West. Perhaps Honda did go too far in his admiration for the West, but only by professing such extreme views could he hope to shake Japan from her long somnolence and reveal to her the possibilities of greatness.

NOTES

1. *Honda Toshiaki Sensei Gyōjō-ki* in *Honda Toshiaki-shū* (henceforth abbreviated *HTS*), pp. 399–404.

2. *Ezo Kaihatsu ni kansuru Jōsho* in *HTS*, p. 321.

3. *Cf.* Uno, p. 400. (In *HTS*.)

4. *Cf.* Smith and Mikami, *A History of Japanese Mathematics*, p. 208, and Hayashi, *Wasan Kenkyū Shūroku*, vol. 2, pp. 102–3.

5. In *HTS*, pp. 359–95. The letters here given date, with two later exceptions only, from the years 1799–1801.

6. Honjō: Introduction to *HTS*, p. 10.

7. Uno, p. 402. There is nothing in Honda's writings to indicate that he himself had visited Kanchatka in 1784, and there is much to make one think he had not. However, since Uno's statement was made while Honda was still alive, it cannot summarily be rejected.

8. Honjō: Introduction to *HTS*, p. 9. Zeniya was imprisoned for his unsuccessful attempt to develop marshland, and for having engaged secretly in foreign trade.

9. Uno, p. 404.

10. *Cf.* Honjō, *Kinsei no Keizai Shisō (Zokuhen)*, pp. 219–23. The 1888 edition of *Seiiki Monogatari* has become extremely rare. The excerpts given by Honjō indicate that it was a simplified version which attempted to recast Honda's crabbed style, sometimes to the detriment of the sense.

11. Ebina, *Honda Toshiaki no Tsūshō Kōeki-setsu*, in *Rekishi Chiri*, vol. 17. Honjō (Introduction to *HTS*, pp. 110–12) gives a list of articles about Honda and editions of his writings up to 1936.

12. *SM*, p. 129. It is curious that Honda gave 1,500 years since the Emperor Jimmu. This figure is surprisingly close to the one modern scholarship has fixed. By traditional dating, it would have been almost 2,500 years since the foundation of the country.

13. *Cf.* Morishima, *Kōmō Zatsuwa*, p. 454. Boxer (in *Jan Compagnie*, p. 171) quotes an account by Hayashi Shihei fixing the foundation of Holland at A.D. 6 The only Japanese who fully understood the Christian dating was apparently Miura Baien who visited Nagasaki in 1778. (*Kisan-roku*, p. 1064.)

14. Shiba, *Shumparo Hikki*, (henceforth abbreviated *SH*), p. 461.

15. *SH*, p. 403. For an account of Hiraga's career, see Irita, *Gennai Sensei no kotodomo* in *Hiraga Gennai Zenshū*, vol. 2.

16. Ishii, *Nihon ni okeru Yōfūga no Enkaku*, pp. 8–9.

17. *Ibid.*, p. 9. *Cf.* Shiba, *Seiyō Gadan*, p. 366. Shiba declared that *all* painting was artisan's work; the brush was a tool for making pictures.

18. *SM*, p. 155.

19. Ishii, p. 6.

20. *SH*, pp. 401–2.

21. *SH*, p. 421.

22. *SH*, p. 405.

23. *SH*, pp. 406–7.

24. Letter to Tachihara in *HTS*, p. 381.

25. *Nieuw en Volkomen Woordenboek van Konsten en Weetenschappen.*

26. Shiba, *Seiyō Gadan*, p. 369.

27. Ishii, p. 12.

28. *Groot Schilderboek.* Shiba, *Seiyō Gadan*, p. 367.

29. Morishima, p. 479.

30. Ishii, p. 16. The founder of the group was Araki Genyū, who attempted to blend Chinese and Western techniques. His son, Araki (or Ishizaki) Yūshi, possessed greater talent and was known for his oil-paintings on glass.

31. Arai, *Sairan Igen*, p. 814.

32. Gotō, *Oranda-banashi*, pp. 436–7.

33. Morishima, p. 474.

34. *SM*, p. 140.

35. Shiba, *Oranda Tensetsu*, p. 2a.

36. *SM*, p. 155.

37. Golownin, *Narrative of My Captivity in Japan*, vol. 1, p. 111.

38. *SM*, p. 156.

39. Shiba, *Tenchi Ridan*, p. 30. Among the fables Shiba translated were those of the Fox and the Crow, and of the Wolf and the Crane.

40. Hirazawa, *Keiho Gūhitsu*, pp. 58–60.

41. Itazawa, *Rangaku to Jugaku*, pp. 658–9. Itazawa considered this unfinished translation to have represented the highest level of *rangaku.*

42. Feenstra Kuiper, *Japan en de Buitenwereld*, p. 253.

43. Matsudaira, *Uge no Hitogoto*, p. 177.

44. Kaempfer, *History*, vol. 3, pp. 301–36. Kaempfer's conclusion was that it was more advantageous for Japan to remain 'shut up'.

45. *SM*, p. 152.

46. Itazawa, *Rangaku to Jugaku*, pp. 657–8.

47. Maeno, *Seiyō Gasan Yakubun-kō*, p. 1. The engravings were the work of Stradanus (1523–1605), possibly part of the series *Venationes ferarum, avium, piscium pugnae.* They were Flemish rather than French pictures: Maeno mistook the name of the publisher, Galle, for 'Gallic'. The date of the engravings makes it likely that they had been in the possession of the shogunate for many years.

48. Golownin, vol. 2, pp. 116–17.

49. Broughton, *A Voyage of Discovery*, p. 101. Could this Japanese have been Isokichi, Kōdayū's companion?

50. Itazawa, *Rangaku no Hattatsu*, p. 82.

51. Kondō, *Kōsho Koji*, pp. 242–59.

52. Kumazawa, *Daigaku Wakumon* (tr. Fisher), p. 325.

53. *SH*, pp. 422–3.

54. *SH*, p. 474.

55. *SH*, p. 453.

56. *SH*, p. 397.

57. Shiba, *Tenchi Ridan*, p. 87.

58. *Ibid.*, p. 120.

59. Ōnishi, *Shiba Kōkan no Sekai-kan*.

60. Shiba, *Dokushō Bōgen* (quoted in Muraoka, *Zoku Nihon Shisō-shi Kenkyū*, p. 253.)

61. *Ibid.*, p. 253.

62. Quoted in Muraoka, *Shisei no Tetsujin*, p. 18.

63. *SM*, p. 129.

64. *SM*, p. 132.

65. *SM*, p. 182.

66. *SM*, p. 136.

67. *SM*, p. 158. The facts ascribed to this priest belong to the careers of two actual priests, the Italians Sidotti and Chiara.

68. *SM*, p. 159.

69. *SM*, pp. 187–8. Honda believed that in the West it was always felt desirable for relatives (the closer the better) to marry, thereby keeping the good qualities of a family intact. 'If no suitable spouse may be found within a family, and a person from another family is taken, people declare that this calamity bespeaks the wrath of God. It is usual in such cases among the lower classes to point the finger of scorn at such marriages. Thus, even if a family has a great many children, it is attempted not to contract marriages more remote than with cousins, or with aunts and uncles if their age is suitable. This is considered to be destiny, and such marriages are praised all the more highly.' (P. 188.)

70. Muraoka, *Nihon Shisō-shi Kenkyū*, p. 327.

71. *Ibid.*, p. 322.

72. Hirata, *Shutsujō Shōgo*, p. 501.

73. Muraoka, *Nihon Shisō-shi Kenkyū*, p. 332.

74. Miura, *Kisan-roku*, p. 1073. Miura's informant was Matsumura Kiminori. *Cf.* Muraoka, *Shisei no Tetsujin*, p. 44.

75. *Kopperu Temmon Zukai*. In the earlier (1796) *Oranda Tensetsu* Shiba gave heliocentric theories, and only in conclusion did he express

preference for Copernican astronomy. (Vol. 2, pp. 5–12.) But by 1808 he was fully convinced of the newer theory.

76. Quoted in Muraoka, *Shisei no Tetsujin*, p. 46.

77. *SM*, pp. 130–1.

78. Sansom, *The Western World and Japan*, p. 234.

79. Golownin, vol. 2, p. 118.

80. The scholars of native learning, equating the sun with the deity Ame-no-minaka-nushi no kami, 'the god who rules the centre of the heavens', claimed that the Copernican theory was one of their most ancient beliefs. Other scholars, such as Asada Gōryū, claimed to have discovered the theory independently. *Cf.* Tōkyō Kagaku Hakubutsukan, *Edo Jidai no Kagaku*, pp. 7, 57, and Szczesniak, *The Penetration of the Copernican Theory into Feudal Japan*, p. 58.

81. Hirazawa, p. 88.

82. *SM*, p. 157.

83. *SM*, p. 134.

84. *SM*, p. 140.

85. Letter to Tachihara in *HTS*, p. 380.

86. *SM*, p. 139.

87. The daimyo were, of course, a special class of samurai, who ruled over fiefs of varying dimensions. Writers on economics seldom distinguish between the ordinary samurai and the daimyo in their discussions of the military class, and it is sometimes difficult to know whether their statements apply to both groups indiscriminately.

88. *Cf.* Borton, *Peasant Uprisings in Japan*, p. 9. 'Pawnshops, baths, and barber shops had all been established and were credited with bringing about the downfall of the country.' See also Claudel, *L'Impôt sur le Thé en Angleterre* for a discussion of similar criticisms levelled against the English farmers.

89. Quoted in Nomura, *Tokugawa Jidai no Shakai Keizai Shisō Gairon*, p. 97.

90. *Ibid.*, p. 130. The writer was an obscure ronin named Yamashita Kōnai.

91. The *shingaku* school was founded by Ishida Baigan (1685–1744).

92. Nomura, p. 214.

93. The 'outside lords' (*tozama*) were those who opposed the Togugawa family at the Battle of Sekigahara in 1600. Those who supported the family were known as *fudai*.

94. Nomura, p. 194.

95. *Ibid.*, p. 202.

96. Boxer, *Jan Compagnie*, p. 143.

97. *SH*, p. 471.

98. The 'ever-normal granary', though discussed in China centuries before, was first put into practice in 54 B.C. For a history of the theory to modern times, *vide* Bodde, *Henry A. Wallace and the Ever-Normal Granary*.

99. Nomura, p. 128.

100. *Ibid.*, p. 149.

101. Quoted in *ibid.*, p. 110.

102. *Keizai Hōgen* in *HTS*, p. 103. Honda attributed many curious feats to the Empress Catherine, including the conquest of Tartary by an army of elegantly attired Amazons led by herself.

103. *Hōka Jiryaku; cf.* Murdoch, *A History of Japan*, vol. 3, p. 266.

104. Quoted in Honjō: Introduction to *HTS*, p. 38.

105. Kōno, *Aka-Ezo, etc.*, p. 600.

106. *Keisei Hisaku* in *HTS*, p. 58.

107. Shiba, *Tenchi Ridan*, p. 104.

108. Quoted in Johnson, *Predecessors of Adam Smith*, p. 3.

109. Malthus, *An Essay on the Principle of Population*, vol. 1, p. 12.

110. *Ibid.*, vol. 1, p. 8.

111. Malthus, *First Essay on Population* (ed. Bonar), p. 134.

112. Malthus, *An Essay*, vol. 1, p. 215.

113. Hung, *I-yen*, in *Hung Pei-chiang Shih-wen Chi*, p. 48.

114. *Ibid.*, p. 49.

115. Such remedies as Hung did suggest—the prohibition of extravagance, suppression of Buddhist and Taoist monks, development of new lands, etc.—do not appear to have been real solutions for him. *Cf.* Lung, *A Note on Hung Liang-chi, the Chinese Malthus.*

116. These include most of the east and north of Japan.

117. *SM*, pp. 183–4.

118. *SM*, p. 186.

119. *SM*, p. 170.

120. *Keisei Hisaku*, p. 40.

121. *Ibid.*, pp. 40–1.

122. *SM*, p. 187.

123. *Chōki-ron* (in *HTS*), p. 209. 'Since they are all the descendants of the Emperor Jimmu, they are of the same race as ourselves.' This refers to the legend of Jimmu's visit to the Kuriles. Honda believed that in time Ezo could be developed to the 'city' level of society.

124. Kondō, *Henyō Bunkai Zukō*, p. 67. The words pronounced by the native are apparently 'O Gospodi Pomilui', the Russian for 'Oh Lord! Have mercy!'

125. Inobe, *Bakumatsu-shi no Kenkyū*, p. 462.

126. Honjō, *Kinsei no Keizai Shisō (Zokuhen)*, p. 56.

127. *SM*, p. 170. Andō Shōeki, an earlier thinker, had declared that the Ezo natives ranged from six to eight feet in height! *Cf.* Norman, *Andō Shōeki*, p. 237.

128. *HTS*, p. 317.

129. Tsuji, *Tanuma Jidai*, pp. 310–12.

130. Quoted in Honjō, Introduction to *HTS*, p. 48.

131. *HTS*, p. 323.

132. *Keizai Hōgen* (in *HTS*), p. 117.

133. Hayashi Junsai, quoted in Inobe, *Bakumatsu-shi no Kenkyū*, p. 391.

134. Krasheninnikov, *The History of Kamtschatka and the Kurilski Islands* (tr. Grieve), p. 180. Sauer (in *An Account of a Geographical and Astronomical Expedition*, p. 309) related, 'Of their former customs there only exist their lascivious dances, and their impure language, with part of the dress.'

135. Krusenstern, vol. 2, p. 69.

Chapter Five

HONDA'S WRITINGS

NOTE

THE translations here given include most of
the first half of *A Secret Plan for Managing the Country*
(*Keisei Hisaku*) and of the second volume of the *Tales of the
West* (*Seiiki Monogatari*). It may be wondered what principles were followed in selecting this part of Honda's
writings for translation. The *Secret Plan*, undoubtedly his
most important work, had naturally to be included, but its
second half, concerned chiefly with relatively minor matter,
'lesser needs' as Honda himself termed them, is no longer
of much interest today, and has therefore been omitted. The
first half has been translated almost in entirety; I have left
out only digressions and repetitions harmful to the sense
of the whole. The text I have used for this and other works
of Honda is that edited by Honjō Eijirō, entitled *Honda
Toshiaki-shū*. It was published in the series *Kinsei Shakai
Keizai Gakusetsu Taikei*.

The *Tales of the West*, a work of much looser construction,
could not have been given in full, or even in the type of
abridgment followed with the *Secret Plan*. Parts of it are so
confused that few readers would care to wade through
them. The second volume, however, possesses considerable interest, containing as it does Honda's best piece of

descriptive writing, his account of a journey through the famine-stricken northern provinces of Japan. The main ideas in the rest of the work, as well as in other of Honda's writings, have already been presented in the introduction.

If Honda's writings, even in this version doctored as above noted, appear somewhat illogical and unconvincing by Western standards, it must be remembered that he had no heritage of Greek logic to fall back on, and in his attempts to break away from the well-worn paths of Confucian doctrines he was very much a pioneer.

I. A SECRET PLAN FOR MANAGING THE COUNTRY

PART ONE

I am a subject, and other men are likewise subjects. Being thus of the same condition, our opinions might also be the same. This, however, is not the case, and I therefore cannot do otherwise than to discuss mine.[1]

Can it be that anyone born in Japan would fail to think of what is beneficial to his country, or rejoice in Japan's misfortunes and begrudge her good fortune? Rather it should be in the nature of every person born in Japan to share in the joy at his country's good fortune and the desire to promote it, as well as in the sorrow over her ill fortune and the desire to prevent it. Not only is this not true of present-day customs, however, but if ever there is anything which looks as if it will prove advantageous for the country and the people, there are always envious and wicked people who come forward to destroy it. It is the way of the world that good things are always weak, and bad ones strong, so that in the end the good cannot be accomplished. It is just like the fact that it is difficult to become wealthy and easy to remain poor. If one honestly seeks to discover whose fault it is that this situation has arisen, a few moments of silent thought will assuredly yield the answer.

We should be grateful that for the first time in the history of Japan the country is as peaceful as it now is. The people rejoice in the benefits of this fortunate condition, and the expression 'the joys of good government'[2] might well be used of these times. It is thus entirely to be expected that the population should show a tendency to increase in numbers steadily. There will then be insufficient food to supply the nation's wants unless food production increases in direct proportion to this growth of the population. For this reason, the entire land of Japan must be developed, even the waste areas and remote mountain-regions, and converted into farmland which can produce grain and fruit. If these measures prove inadequate and there is still not enough food to meet the needs of the people, some of them will starve in years of poor harvest or famine. Since most of those who starve will be farmers, the amount of farm produce will be still further reduced, and there will be disturbances in the country.

When the entire population is fed by the farmers and society is maintained along the class lines of samurai, farmers, artisans, merchants and idlers, there is stability, and the nation is peaceful. But if many of the farmers, who are the foundation of the nation, die of starvation, the stability is upset and calamities of every sort arise. If such trouble is suppressed in one place, it boils up in another; if put down in that place, it is felt in still another. These disorders arise because of poverty. Far-reaching consideration must therefore be given to the matter.

The chief object of such study should be how to keep from hindering the natural increase in numbers of the four classes of society. Towards this end, the four imperative needs should be made the prime consideration of the government. When the country is thus ruled, there will be no obstacles to increase, and the population will multiply and flourish. There will then no longer be widespread abandonment of good farmland such as now takes place. On the contrary, the amount of land under cultivation would increase, and with it the prosperity of the nation. If, mistakenly, the country is not governed in accordance with the four imperative needs, the unsuitability of these other policies to the well-being of the nation results in the steady increase of wasteland and its attendant disasters. Of such events there are numerous examples in both ancient and modern history.3

The four imperative needs are so called because they represent the four things which are most urgently required at present: that is, (1) gunpowder, (2) metals, (3) shipping and (4) colonisation. I have divided the four and will discuss each of them below.

(1) *Gunpowder*4

Gunpowder is of great use to a nation in times of peace as well as in war. For example, when conditions do not permit the use of river craft to ship goods, and the produce of a locality lies rotting on the ground as a result, the situation may best be alleviated by making the river usable by boats and thus enabling the produce to be transported to areas where it is needed. There may be rocks and boulders which form rapids in the rivers. These cannot be removed by human labour, but if gunpowder is used, the obstructions can be blasted and easily removed. A channel will then be open, permitting river craft to pass through taking products from one region to another.

Another peacetime use of gunpowder may be found in the following. If it is desired to improve a steep road through a mountain pass by cutting through great quantities of rock, gunpowder will easily bring this about where human efforts unaided would fail. Thus a thoroughfare can be opened which will mitigate the discomforts of the traveller.

Gunpowder is also effective in dealing with rocks hidden beneath the surface of the sea along the shipping-lanes, shoals which have been dreaded from ancient times. There are also submerged rocks in many harbours and anchorages. Sometimes, just when a ship is about to drop anchor at the end of a voyage, its cargo of food will be lost when it hits one of those rocks, and the lives of valuable citizens may also be lost. With gunpowder these rocks could be removed and such disasters averted.

It is impossible to complete any major construction undertaking without the use of gunpowder. That is why the European nations consider it to be a product of the greatest value and importance to their countries and make many uses of it. In Japan the mining of gunpowder is not being prosecuted seriously by the officials, nor do the ordinary people make any effort to mine it as it is not considered of value. When there are heavy rains, the gunpowder is washed into the sea to become salt, but if mined it can bring profit to the nation.

Certain expenses are involved in extracting gunpowder from the ground, but the incidental costs of extraction should not be considered, because of the product's importance. The money in any case will pass into the hands of Japanese and not foreigners, and will be like a gift to one's own children, a gift which will be many times repaid. If it is worth the people's while to mine gunpowder, they will make it their regular practice. Because of its importance, I have termed gunpowder the first imperative need.

(2) *Metals*

There are gold, silver, copper, iron and lead mines scattered throughout the country, but in spite of their great numbers, they are all abandoned and yield no profit. There are secret reasons which have brought about this abandonment as one may discover through investigation.

Let us examine the case of the copper mines. Several years ago, when I was travelling through a certain domain in Ōu,[5] I saw a man's head hanging on the prison gate of the castle town. I approached and looked at it. There was a sign saying that this man had been executed and his head exposed for having violated a national prohibition. I secretly made enquiry of a native as to the nature of the offence, and was told that the man had guided some strangers to mines within the domain and had therefore been punished. I asked then why it was so strictly forbidden to reveal the location of the mines, and was told that by law all copper extracted from the mines had to be turned over to the government. In return the government was supposed to pay the correct value of the copper, but when the costs of operating the mines were deducted, the payment was found far from sufficient, and there was some loss on every piece of copper mined. In recent years the daimyo of the domain had become impoverished on account of crop-failures, and the salaries of the miners had been reduced. The miners could not make a living on their reduced wages, and the production of copper had steadily decreased. At the time that I enquired it had ceased altogether. It was said not to be profitable, but this was actually only because the government payments were inadequate.[6]

This system of fixed prices for metals may appear to be unjust and unprincipled, but it is actually a good way of preserving the national strength. The fact that the locations of the gold, silver and copper mines in the country are enshrouded in mystery may be attributed to the fear of the system. If it did not exist, and these metals could be sold without restriction on the free market, there would be a scramble to exploit the mines, and their yield would then be sent abroad. This would amount to removing the bones of the country.[7] The fixed-price system thus has the fortuitous result of protecting the country's strength. If articles imported from abroad were all of permanent value, there would be no profit for the foreign countries in trade with Japan, but the gold, silver and copper used by Japan in payment are actually of great and permanent value, and thus the bones of the country. If they were exported without any annual limit being placed on them, it would result in a most unfortunate situation.

As a general rule it is of course desirable that those precious metals which have been mined in Japan be passed on within the families of the shogun and the daimyo, and stored by them in perpetuity for use in national emergencies. In the interest of the nation, the export of gold, silver and copper should be strictly prohibited.

When houses are constructed of wood they must later be repaired and rebuilt constantly, representing a tremendous waste of labour. If all classes of people including the lowest were permitted to use stone instead of wood for the pillars of their houses, and copper sheeting for the roofs, their dwellings would be permanent. Then even the lowliest person would be able to understand why it is that gold, silver and copper are the backbone of the nation. Then, if the export of precious metals to foreign countries were stopped, it would not prove unpopular; people would positively wish to aid in the enforcement. Laws should be enacted to keep the precious metals, which are vital in all things, from being removed from Japan.

It is a basic part of a ruler's duties as parent to the people to ensure that these articles of permanent worth are transmitted in perpetuity by the noble families. Another duty of the ruler is to insist that the miners be treated with consideration at all times, for the mining of precious metals involves long hours of work in caves. If a ruler is lax in this matter, he will be no better than a speculator out for profit, which is contrary to the calling of a ruler. The ruler's duty to the nation requires him to secure profit for the nation regardless of the expenses involved. Just as Aoto[8] looked for the coin he lost in the Nameri River, necessary expenses are like presents to one's own children as they only go into the hands of Japanese. Metals are thus so important that I have termed them the second imperative need.

(3) *Shipping*

By shipping I mean the transport of and trade in the products of the whole country by means of government-owned ships, and the relief of the hunger and cold of all people afforded by these instruments of supplying each region with what it needs. Shipping and foreign trade are the responsibility of the ruler and should not be left to the merchants. If shipping is left entirely in the hands of merchants, they will act as their greed and evil purposes dictate, thereby disturbing commodity-prices throughout the country. Prices then fluctuate enormously, and the farmers find it difficult to survive. If this situation is remedied by using government-owned ships for transport and trade, the prices of commodities will be stabilised naturally and the farmers relieved.

As long as there are no government-owned ships and the merchants have complete control over transport and trade, the economic conditions of the samurai and farmers grow steadily worse. In years when the harvest is bad and people die of starvation, the farmers perish in greater numbers than any other class. Fields are abandoned and food production is still further reduced. There is then insufficient food for the nation and much suffering. Then the people will grow restive and numerous criminals will have to be punished. In this way citizens will be lost to the state. Since its citizens are a country's most important possession, it cannot afford to lose even one, and it is therefore most unfortunate that any should be sentenced to death. It is entirely the fault of the ruler if the life of even a single subject is thereby lost.

All the many varieties of troubles, disasters and crimes found among the common people are a product of their unhappiness and anger over fluctuations in commodity-prices. Such fluctuations are caused by the inadequacy of sea transport, which in turn is caused by the fact that the ruler controls no ships, and there is no government service. It cannot be estimated how greatly the prerogatives of the ruler are thereby impaired. Shipping and trade are now the business of merchants. Under this system no distinction is made between the interests of the merchants and the duties of the ruler. By developing the techniques of shipping it would become possible to equalise prices throughout the country, thus helping both the samurai and the farmers. Food-production would increase steadily which, in turn, would make the nation prosperous.

It is obviously impossible to feed the thousands of people living in a great city with only the food that can be brought in by coolie-labour or on the backs of beasts; unless food is transported in ships the population will go hungry. But when shipping is controlled, as is at present the case, by merchants, it will lead in the end to disaster; this must be changed. Let me give an idea of the disasters which this condition has engendered. At present, when a most thorough search for bandits and robbers is supposed to be in progress, the inquiries are not getting anywhere; about a quarter of the rice being transported to Edo for the samurai is robbed on the way by the captain and crew of the rice-ships. Afterwards false affidavits are lodged and the matter is brought to a close. In the affidavits it is stated that the ship encountered a storm at sea and was damaged, that the cargo had been jettisoned in order to lighten the ship, and that they had barely been able to scrape through the storm with their lives. These affidavits are presented to officials who to themselves conjecture that the statements are false, but they have no way of establishing the truth because there are no officials aboard private vessels, and there are not even government supervisors or loading-inspectors. Since the officials have made it their practice not to press matters beyond the affidavits, the above condition prevails to the present.

An extreme case of this malpractice is to be found at Tonoura in Sado.9 The people there have a saying, 'This is no year to make any commitments—shipwrecks have been few and far between.' They will then postpone until the following year giving away a bride already promised, or taking into their household a son-in-law as previously arranged. They say, 'Next year if things are better we will go through with the marriage as we had planned as soon as possible.'

This is what they actually do. Whenever there has been a severe storm and ships at sea are tossed about, they climb to the top of the hill on the shore of Tonoura Bay and light bonfires there in the middle of the night. A ship seeing the bonfire may take it for the all-night beacon of a harbour or anchorage. The people on shore wait for the ship to be guided inshore by the light of the fire. Then, as soon as it runs aground they rush forward in great numbers with whatever implements they happen to have and, far from attempting to save the lives of the shipwrecked crew, they throw everyone aboard the ship into the sea. If any of the crew attempt to get ashore, they are beaten back into the water until they are all drowned. After this the people of Sado gather together and divide up the ship's cargo. Finally they set fire to the ship to remove the evidence.

This type of occurrence is not restricted to Tonoura, but happens at all out-of-the-way bays throughout the country. It represents the greatest peril to ships at sea, a first beginning of piracy which has arisen from a grave defect in the government of the nation. Some daimyo have now ceased to pay their retainers their basic stipends. These men have had half their property confiscated by the daimyo as well, and hate them so much that they find it impossible to contain their ever-accumulating resentment. They finally leave their clan and become bandits. They wander lawlessly over the entire country, plotting with the natives who live on the shore and thus entering a career of piracy. As they become ever more entrenched in their banditry one sees growing a tendency to revert to olden times.[10]

It is because of the danger of such occurrences that in Europe a king governs his subjects with solicitude. It is considered to be the appointed duty of a king to save his people from hunger and cold by shipping and trading. This is the reason why there are no bandits in Europe. Such measures are especially applicable to Japan, which is a maritime nation, and it is obvious that transport and trade are essential functions of the government.

Ships which are at present engaged in transport do not leave coastal waters and put out to sea. They always have to skirt along the shore, and can navigate only by using as landmarks mountains or islands within visible range. Sometimes, as it inevitably happens, they are blown out to sea by a storm and lose their way. Then, when they are so far away from their familiar landmarks that they can no longer discern them, they drift about with no knowledge of their location. This is because they are ignorant of astronomy and mathematics, and because they do not possess the rules of navigation. Countless ships are thereby lost every year. Not only does this represent an enormous annual waste of produce, but valuable subjects also perish. If the methods of navigation were developed, the loss at sea of rice and other food products would be reduced, thus effecting a great saving. This would not only increase the wealth of the nation, but would help stabilise the prices of rice and other produce throughout Japan. The people, finding that they are treated equally irrespective of occupation and that the methods of government are fair, would no longer harbour any resentment, but would raise their voices in unison to pray for the prosperity of the rulers.

By saving the lives of those subjects who would otherwise be lost at sea every year, we shall also be able to make up for our past shame, and will keep foreign nations from learning about weak spots in the institutions of Japan from Japanese sailors shipwrecked on their shores. Because of these and numerous other benefits to be derived from shipping, I have termed it the third imperative need.

(4) *Colonisation*[11]

If the islands near Japan were colonised they would make highly desirable places. By such colonisation numerous possessions—some sixty or more—would be created, which would serve not only as military outposts for Japan, but would also produce in abundance metals, grain and fruit, as well as various other products, thus greatly adding to Japan's strength. I presume that run-of-the-mill officials must be thinking that colonisation could be effected only at the expense of the ruler, and the authorities are not in the least inclined to spend any government money on developing farmland. This is the way mediocre minds always react.

The order to be followed in colonising territories is as follows: First, ships are despatched to ascertain the location of the islands to be taken, and to measure their extent. The natural products of the islands are investigated, and the native population estimated. Then, when it is known about how many provinces the islands would make if colonised, the actual work is begun. If the natives are still living in caves, they are taught about houses. A house should be built for the tribal chief. Those natives without implements or utensils should be supplied with them. By helping the natives and giving them everything they desire, one will inspire a feeling of affection and obedience in them, like the love of children for their parents. This is true because they are moved by the same feelings that pervade the rest of the world, barbarians though they may be considered.

The way to compensate for the expenses involved in colonisation lies in taking the natural products of the islands and shipping them to Japan. Trading marks a beginning of compensation for those expenses. Even barbarians do not expect to ask favours and give nothing in return. The products they offer represent a commencement of taxation. Since every island has wooded areas, there will always be some value in the lumber which can be taken from the islands, even after a great many years. The value of other products besides lumber would be too great to calculate. It is the task of the ruler-father to direct and educate the natives in such a manner that there will not be a single one of them who will spend even one unprofitable day. This matter should not be put off for another moment; it is a vital state duty.

At this point we must discuss the foundation of colonisation—the sciences of astronomy and mathematics. In Japan these sciences are not as yet fully known, and there are few men who understand their significance. Even in China the principles of astronomy and mathematics have roughly been understood since the arrival of a number of Europeans late in the seventeenth century.[12] If, in connection with colonisation projects, ships cross the seas without reference to the principles of astronomy and mathematics, there is no way to tell how much easier sea travel is than land travel. The name of the book in which the natural laws behind these principles are contained is *Schatkamer*,[13] a European work. One may learn from the latitude of a particular island what its climate is like throughout the year. Or, without actually visiting an island, one can predict in this way whether it will prove fertile. This may be done with certainty; false tales need not be believed.

The key to colonisation is to establish a system[14] with long-range objectives as to future profit and loss. By encouraging the good customs of the natives and eliminating their bad ones, it is possible to have them maintain human dignity. They should never be permitted to forget the generosity of the Japanese ruler. This is how colonisation should be set about, but Japan persists in her bad habit of imitating old Chinese usages. Very few of the government authorities possess any real knowledge of astronomy or mathematics, and it is because of their ignorance that whenever there is talk of colonising the northern territories, as occasionally happens, the project is never carried through. It is Japan's misfortune that her officials are misled by foolish tales about these great countries, which are actually far superior to Japan, and consequently do not take advantage of great opportunities for profitable ventures. This is a matter of especial regret because there have been Russian officials in the islands inhabited by the Ainu since about 1765.[15] They have displayed such diligence in their colonisation efforts that eighteen or nineteen Kurile islands and the great land of Kamchatka have already been occupied. Forts are said to have been built at various places and a central administration established, the staff of which is regularly changed, and which rules the natives with benevolence. I have heard that the natives trust them as they would their own parents.

In Japan, on the other hand, this system is as yet not followed. It is forbidden to carry from the country seeds for the five cereals or edged tools for use in building houses. It is forbidden to teach Japanese to any natives. These are supplemented by a host of other prohibitions. It is a most lamentable system which has as its object keeping barbarians forever in their present condition. Since the Russians operate under a system which provides that their own subjects are sent out to live among the natives, it is only to be expected that the Ainu look up to the Russian officials as gods and worship them.

There is a story which I would like to relate at this point. There was a European named Baron Moritz Aladar von Benyowsky[16] who was defeated and taken prisoner with his force of fifty men after an engagement with the Russians. His life was spared, but he was sent into exile at Kamchatka. In return for having his life spared, he was made to help in the colonisation of the Eastern Ezo islands, but he waited only the opportunity to escape. He managed to gain control of a government vessel and attempted then to sail back to his native country in Europe. After navigating in the waters east of Japan, he anchored at Awa where he requested fuel and water. In response to his appeal to the kindness of the daimyo of that province, he was presented with several hundred sacks of rice, and then set sail from Awa. Later he again called at a Japanese port, anchoring this time at Ōshima in Satsuma.

When he visited Japanese waters for a second time, he desired to express his gratitude for the kind treatment he had been accorded at Awa. He addressed a letter in European script to the Dutch factory director in Nagasaki in which, intending to demonstrate his good wishes towards Japan, he described the plans of the Russian emperor. This incident took place in 1771. The Nagasaki magistrate of the time, a certain Natsume,[17] discussed the document with his subordinates and various other people in order to determine its truth. It was a very difficult communication to handle, and it finally was left to disappear.

If one examines present conditions in the Ezo islands, one will observe that they are exactly as Benyowsky described them in his letter. All the islands are now Russian possessions. Until about 1765 dried salmon and fish-oil used to be obtained every year from Kamchatka. Seal skins, *kajika*,[18] and fish oil were sent from the Eastern Ezo islands and placed on sale at Matsumae.[19] The island of Ezo used to yield over 20,000 deer-skins alone, but at present, it should be noted, not a single deer skin is coming to Japan because they are all collected by the Russians. Weeping over this situation will not bring back our territories to us; we must save at least the island of Ezo. As this is a place which will prove very valuable to us, we must act at once and not be careless. If we abandon it, it will be just like attempting to keep out bandits without a fence. Nothing could be more dangerous.

The island of Ezo has a circumference of somewhat less than a thousand *ri*.[20] It lies between 40° and 43° North Latitude and enjoys a climate comparable to that of Shunt'ien-fu in China.[21] Since the southern tip of Kamchatka is located at 51° N. Lat., it follows that all the Kuriles lie between 40° and 50°. It is clear from their latitudes that they must be fertile lands where all varieties of grain and fruit will grow. Proof of this may be found in the fact that the capital city of Holland, one of the chief European countries, is located at 53° 23' N. Lat. Because it is possible to determine from the latitude of a place its climate and fertility, the first step in colonisation is thus achieved.

The harbour of Okhotsk is now being developed into one of the key-points of the East. I have been informed that a central administrative staff is sent there for regular terms of office from Russia to look after the area. Ships are sent out for purposes of trade from Okhotsk to the Kurile islands and to North and South America, supplying whatever is needed in each place. The king[22] rules the natives benevolently and is most generous to them in his capacity of father and mother to the people. Okhotsk is located around 55° N. Lat., and is thus an extremely cold place. Every year from April to September government-owned ships ply to and from Okhotsk in great numbers, but during the winter months the snows lie deep, and no ships can arrive or depart. During this time there is no work to be done. Okhotsk lies northwest of Kunashiri and Etorofu, and due north of Karafuto at a distance of about four hundred *ri* across the water.

Since no Japanese ever go abroad, and since most Japanese are ignorant of astronomy and mathematics, we shall be unable to win profits as great as those Russia obtains unless we undergo a complete awakening, so be-sotted is the nation by the foolish tales constantly spread by suspicious and ignorant people. This is a grave misfortune for Japan. I imagine it is because Japan has not been civilised for half so long a time as the nations of Europe that there are as yet very few men who are versed in the processes of government. It is to be expected that hence-forth there will be people who do possess this ability as more and more people gain familiarity with the sciences.

There is a large island called Karafuto in Western Ezo, located 67 *ri* northwest of Sōya on the western coast of Matsumae. Japanese merchants have been crossing over to this island for about 150 years to trade with the natives, and have built little houses, called *unjōya*, for this purpose.[23] They decide on the number of years they intend to trade at the place and it is calculated how much has to be paid to the house of Matsumae for the privilege. Whoever pays the tax becomes the local administrator and appoints the three groups of people who work there: the managers, the inter-preters and the guards. These people build houses on the island and engage in beneficial trade with the natives. This situation holds true of both Eastern and Western Ezo.

To the northwest of Karafuto is the country of Santan.[24] Beyond Santan to the northwest is Manchuria, which in ancient times was known as Tartary. The territory to the west of this country extends as far as Europe. Thus, how-ever far removed Europe may be, it is connected to Santan by a continuous land-mass; this in turn makes of Karafuto an important frontier. It is important because of the seem-ingly irresistible conquest of half the world by Russia in recent years which has resulted from the Russian policy of making colonisation the prime function of the state. A start should therefore be made from the trading stations which are on Karafuto now. They should gradually be improved and other stations added. Japanese will then come in steadily increasing numbers.

It is surprising that the trading stations were built so long ago. It would seem to show that even the merchants of the period after the civil wars were bolder than the samurai of today. Did they first cross over to Matsumae in the footsteps of Yoshitsune (who later went on to Tartary)?[25] There are even historical remains of the Emperor Jimmu in the Ezo islands.[26] No place in the world is of greater historical significance to Japan than this region, yet for the past ten years Russian officials have been stationed there.

Some years ago a complaint was directed to the Matsumae clan about the activities of the Russians in the area of the trading stations, and officials were accordingly despatched to investigate. They were told by the Russians: 'We were cast ashore on this island two or three years ago. Our ship was wrecked and we have been unable to return to our country. If you would be so kind as to take us back to Japan and send us on to Nagasaki it will be the best place from which to return since there are Europeans there. Grant us this favour and save our lives.' Thus they pleaded to the accompaniment of tears.[27]

On first hearing their story, one might think that these were unfortunate men deserving of help, but they were Europeans, whose nature it is to be very cunning. One should never take what a European says for the simple truth. To give an idea how skilled they are in deception, let me relate the story of a Russian named Simeon Drohevitch Izuyosov[28] who spent eight years in the islands from Etorofu to Kunashiri. Officials were sent from Matsumae who ordered him on several occasions to return to his country, but Izuyosov replied each time, 'I fled here because I was convicted of a crime in Russia, and I cannot return. Even now, if I were caught by a Russian official I would be executed. It is only natural in such circumstances that I have no desire of going back to my country. Rather than be driven from here, I would prefer that you cut off my head.' In so saying, he stuck out his head and did not withdraw it an inch.

The officials were at a loss what to do. They delayed deciding his case from day to day, but in May of the same year that Kōdayū, the sailor from Shirako-machi in Ise[29] was returned to Japan, a Russian envoy came for Izuyosov and they went back to Russia together. The story that he was a criminal and therefore could not return was thus so much deception and cunning.

This Izuyosov showed in his daily behaviour that he was no ordinary individual. He is reported to have been a courageous person, both learned and accomplished. I imagine that he was a Russian spy who had been selected for his heroism, conspicuous even in Russia, to keep watch on the government and people of Japan. In view of the fact that such persons as Izuyosov exist, it seems highly improbable that the Russians at present on Karafuto just happen to have been shipwrecked there. I believe that Benyowsky's warning meant that the Russians would resort to every variety of stratagem rather than withdraw. Grounds for suspicion exist already in the religious teachings being given to the natives of Etorofu and Kunashiri by Russian officials. Crosses over ten feet high have been erected in front of the thrones of the tribal chiefs and are worshipped morning and night. (The cross is called *kurusu*.) There are also three types of images—paintings, wooden statues and metal statues—in twelve aspects. They are called *teusu*.[30] I imagine that they are connected with that heretical sect which was proscribed at the end of the sixteenth century.[31] It is especially worthy of note that the tribal chiefs of Etorofu and Kunashiri have been taken by ship to Okhotsk where they have met high Russian officials and been given lavish presents. Many similar instances could be cited. For Japan such incidents at present constitute a minor disgrace, but I need not go into what may happen if things continue in this manner.

It is clear from the above paragraphs that when the Ezo islands are colonised they will make worthwhile places which will yield several times as much produce as Japan does today. Although there are other islands both to the east and west which should also be Japanese possessions, I shall not discuss them for the moment. At this crucial time when the Ezo islands are being seized by Russia, we are faced with an emergency within an emergency. When, as now, Japan does not have any system for colonising her island possessions, there is no way of telling whether they will be seized by foreign countries or remain safe. This is not the moment for neglect; such actions by foreign powers may lead to the destruction of our national defence. With the establishment of a system of colonisation, a knowledge of navigation will naturally develop among Japanese, but if navigation, shipping and trade continue to be considered the occupation of merchants, the natives of our island possessions are doomed to an eternal want of civilisation. The fact that the Ainu are living in a state of barbarity has been regarded by Russia as affording a fine opportunity for her to devote her energies to the colonisation of the islands, a timely undertaking. The lack of a colonisation system has kept Japanese rule from the island, and has meant that the natives are unaware of the goodness of the ruler of Japan. Because of this ignorance they have been quick to become subject to Russia.

So important is colonisation that I have termed it the fourth imperative need.

PART TWO

In Part One, the general outlines of the four imperative needs were discussed. When a county or province, or the whole country itself is governed in accordance with these needs, every part of Japan, even the wastelands and mountainous regions, can be turned into cultivated fields.

Villages will spring up about them and, as this trend increases in strength, there will finally be an overflowing to island possessions. Mines will be developed and all varieties of crops will be produced in quantities increasing each year. There will be no such thing as insufficiency in the country.

It is a good policy to rule the country in such a way as to permit the natural increase of the population. The ruler encourages this increase and is greatly pleased by it. By helping that which is bad and commending that which is good, he will avoid crippling the natural population-growth. His enterprises will all meet with success, and the nation will be rich and strong. This new development will accord with Japan's reputation as a country of great military prowess and will so impress nearby countries that they will come under Japanese suzerainty.

The cultivation of a national spirit which will complement the martial strength of the country is called 'paternalism.'[32] The method employed is valid in all situations. Whether one governs a province, a county or the whole country, it amounts to the same thing as governing the household of one of the common people. This spirit is found in the sentiment of being 'master in one's house' possessed by rich and poor alike.

The four imperative needs which have thus been elaborated are such important duties of the state that they should not be neglected for an instant; it is the height of the inexpedient that they have not as yet been adopted. If one were to attempt seriously to trace back their origins, one would have to go back over eight hundred years to the times when the country was divided by internal strife. At that time men were so intent on devoting all of their energies to military activity that they naturally did not have time to learn the art of government.[33]

Not until Tokugawa Ieyasu used his power to control the strong and give succour to the weak did the warfare that had lasted for three hundred years without a halt suddenly abate. Arrows were left in their quivers and spears in their racks. If now, in such a time of peace, the country were ruled in accordance with the four imperative needs, the prices of all commodities would be stabilised, and the discontent of the people thus cut off at the root. This is the true method of establishing a permanent foundation for the nation so that the people will become honest in their hearts and cultivate orderly ways even if they are not governed. It must have been because he realised how difficult it would be to preserve the empire for all ages to come if the people were not honest in their hearts that Ieyasu, in his testament,[34] exhorted shoguns who would succeed him to abstain from any irregularities in government, and to rule on a basis of benevolence and honesty. It was his counsel that the shoguns should serve as models to the people, and by their honesty train the people in the ways of humanity and justice. He taught that the shogun should not compel obedience merely by the use of force, but by his acts of benevolence should keep the nation at peace.

Ieyasu had the great lords of the empire leave their families behind in Edo, where they themselves had to be in attendance every other year.[35] In that way he could learn of the government of the domains. This is an example of the profound insight of Ieyasu. He taught the daimyo that the duties of a governor consisted in the careful attempt to guide the people of their domains in such a way as both to bring about the prosperity of the land and to encourage the literary and military arts.

However, in recent days there has been the spectacle of lords confiscating the allocated property of their retainers under pretext of paying back debts to the merchants. The debts do not then decrease, but usually seem rather to grow the larger. One daimyo with an income of 60,000 *koku*[36] so increased his borrowings that he could not make good his debts and there was a public suit. The court judgement in the case was said to have been over 1,180,000 *ryō*.[37] Even if repayment had been attempted on the basis of his income of 60,000 *koku*, the debt would not have been completely settled for fifty or sixty years, so long a time that it is difficult to imagine that the day would actually come.

All the daimyo are not in this position, but there is not one who has not borrowed from the merchants. Is this not a sad state of affairs? The merchants, watching this spectacle, must feel like a fisherman who sees a fish swim into his net. The daimyo then choose officials to harass and afflict the farmers, claiming this is in order to repay their debts, but the debts do not diminish. Instead, they go on making new ones every year. The officials are blamed for this and are dismissed as being incompetent. New officials then harass and afflict the farmers in much the same way as the old ones, and so it goes on. However talented the officials may be, they become disgusted and abandon the effort. Some pretend sickness and remain in their homes; others who are indiscreet die young.

No matter how hard the daimyo and his officials rack their brains, they do not seem to be able to reduce the debts. The lords have 'sunk in a pool of debts', as it is popularly said, a pool from which their children and grandchildren will be unable to swim. Everything will be as the merchants wish it. The daimyo turn over their domains to the merchants, for which they received an allowance with which to pay their public and private expenses. Such daimyo give no thought at all to Heaven,[38] to fulfilling their duties as samurai, or to the proper way of looking after the farmers.

Many fields have turned into wasteland since the famine of 1783 when thousands of farmers starved to death. Wherever one goes from the Kantō to Ōu, one hears people say, 'There used to be a village here . . . the land over there was once part of such-and-such a county, but now there is no village and no revenue comes from the land.' This condition prevails especially in Ōu where alone five counties have been left wastelands. During the three years of bad crops and famine which followed 1783, over two million people in the province of Ōu alone starved to death. When so many farmers starved, reducing still further their already insufficient numbers, the amount of uncultivated land greatly increased. If the wicked practice of infanticide, now so prevalent, is not stopped, the farming population will dwindle until it tends to die out altogether. Generous protective and relief measures must be put into effect immediately if this evil practice is to be stamped out.

A wise ruler could end this practice in short order and create an atmosphere favourable to the prosperity of the nation by establishing a system based on generosity and compassion. When a woman of one of the lower classes becomes pregnant, a government agent should be sent to investigate the situation. The mother of the child should then be given two sacks of rice each year from the month the child is born until he is ten years old. The practice of infanticide would then soon stop. Thus by spending a mere twenty sacks of rice over a period of ten years, the country would at the same time gain a good farmer and atone for the misery caused in the past.

When I say misery I mean that there are no words capable of expressing the feeling that everyone must have when he considers that there are people who kill with their own hands the children they have brought into the world. Dumb animals and birds all experience love and compassion for their young. How can it be that man kills his children? The Confucian scholars of ancient and modern times have talked a great deal about benevolence and compassion, but they possess neither in their hearts. Officials and authorities talk about benevolent government, but they have no understanding of what that means. Whose fault is it that the farmers are dying of starvation and that good fields are turning into wasteland? The fault lies entirely with the ruler. I am at a loss to describe the disloyalty and faithlessness of such actions. The rage that overpowers me when I consider how slow in coming is the punishment sent by Heaven is a sincere expression of my thoughts on the matter.

I have travelled three times through the provinces of the country examining conditions. Since I am a poor person I have at times been forced to sleep in fields or in the mountains. I have experienced all kinds of physical hardships and want. I have noted the conditions of farm roads in the provinces, roads which were so poor that produce was left to rot on the ground for want of a way to transport it. I have described such things as the location of mines, the activities of robbers in different places, and the secret disposal at some remote port of goods which were being shipped from one harbour to another and which had been robbed from the owner under the pretence of a shipwreck. These records I leave to future men of good will. The reason I have sought to give to the nation what I have come of myself to understand about the significance of the four imperative needs is that it is my humble hope that my plan will relieve the suffering of the farmers and help to bring about the gradual disappearance of the practice of infanticide. I am hesitant about leaving behind these crude writings when there are so many learned and brilliant persons in the world today, but if it is true as it says in the proverb that a three-year-old child can show the way over a dangerous crossing, persons who condescend to read these lines carefully may derive profit from them.

Of all the countries of Europe, Africa, Asia and America, the one with the longest history is Egypt, which lies on the eastern shores of Africa. Over six thousand years ago Egypt was civilised and knew the art of writing. The Egyptians had a calendar at that remote date and a system of time-notation was in use throughout the country.

There later appeared a man named Christ in a country called Judaea at the northwest end of Asia who established the Catholic religion, which spread northwards to Europe. In India, to the east, Sakyamuni appeared, and in China there were the sage-rulers Yao, Shun, Yu, T'ang, Wen and Wu. All of these men transmitted their own teachings. Although what they taught differed, their doctrines amounted in each instance to an explanation of the way countries should be ruled and kept at peace. The teachings differed from country to country, but in all cases their meaning could be reduced to the principle of encouraging virtue and punishing vice.

Every country has a system of writing with which it transmits the teachings of its sages. Our country adopted Chinese writing and philosophy. Thus there are persons who enjoy a reputation for wide scholarship when all they know is the origin and history of one country, China. China became civilised three thousand years ago, and was thus over three thousand years slower than Egypt. Because of this difference in antiquity there are many faults in Chinese state policies which time has not as yet corrected.

The great number and inconvenience of Chinese characters make them useless in dealings with foreign countries. There are now barely three countries besides China where they may be understood: Corea, the Loochoos and Japan, but even in these countries it is considered a difficult task to gain a thorough knowledge of them. The European alphabet has twenty-five letters each of which may be written in eight different forms.[39] With these letters one can describe anything in the world. Nothing could be simpler. If one tried to memorise all the hundreds of thousands of Chinese characters and devoted one's life's energies to the task, how many could one actually learn? One would be sure to forget a great many. Even supposing that some man could learn them all, the best that he could do would be to copy in Japan all the old Chinese stories. Rather than attempt to help the nation in this way, it would be simpler to turn to profit those resources with which Japan is naturally endowed.

There is a country called Italy at the southern end of

Europe, lying between 35° and 36° N. Lat. The good laws of Judaea, which is separated from the southern tip of Italy by the Mediterranean Sea, appear to have been transmitted there. Thus it was that an enlightened ruler established a benevolent rule in Italy which was cheerfully obeyed by the people. He was considered so wise a man that he was given the title of Emperor of Europe, and for many generations afterwards all Europe was under one sovereign. However, there came a foolish emperor whose regime was disordered. The subject countries then rebelled, and now all of the countries formerly under one emperor are independent.

The capitals of France, Spain, England and Holland have become thriving places. There are reasons for their prosperity which I shall attempt to explain by using the example of one of them. France long ago became the first country to manufacture cannon, and she also invented the method of making gunpowder for military use.[40] This gave her supremacy over her neighbouring countries. She afterwards used her inventions against those countries which were at war, thus compelling them to cease fighting. This was the great achievement of France. No matter how well-equipped a nation might be, even if it possessed mighty fortresses of steel, when French cannons were brought to bear against them or French privateers[41] attacked, not only would its fortresses fall, but very few of its people would be left to tell the tale. Thus, for fear of loss of human life France has not yet transmitted her inventions to other countries.

Europe was first with all other important inventions as well. Because astronomy, calendar-making and mathematics are considered the ruler's business, the European kings are well-versed in matters of celestial and terrestrial principles, and instruct the common people in them. Thus even among the lower classes one finds great men who show great ability in their particular fields. The Europeans have as a result been able to establish industries with which the rest of the world is unfamiliar. It is for this reason that all of the treasures of the world are said to be attracted to Europe. There is nowhere their ships do not go in order to obtain the different products and treasures of the world. They trade the rare products, superior implements and unusual inventions of their own countries for the precious metals and other valuable goods of other nations, which they bring back to enrich their own countries. Their prosperity makes them strong, and it is because of their strength that they are never invaded or pillaged by other countries, while there are countless examples of non-European nations which have been invaded by them. Spain has conquered many of the best parts of North and South America, and has moved her capital there.[42] Portugal, England and France also have possessions in the Americas. The islands of the Eastern Oceans such as Java, Sumatra, Borneo and Luzon are all European possessions. The Europeans have set up trading stations in those countries which have not as yet submitted to them where they trade with the local rulers, seeking only to obtain as great profits as possible. Thus, even those countries which have not yielded to European might, devote all their energies to producing things for Europe. The real objectives of the European nations are thus achieved anyway.

There is no place in the world to compare with Europe. It may be wondered in what way this supremacy was achieved. In the first place, the European nations have behind them a history of five to six thousand years. In this period they have delved deep into the beauties of the arts, have divined the foundations of government, and have established a system based on a thorough examination of those factors which naturally make a nation prosperous. Because of their proficiency in mathematics they have excelled also in astronomy, calendar-making and surveying. They have elaborated laws of navigation so that there is nothing simpler for them than to sail the oceans of the world.

There is no positive evidence as to when European ships first reached the nations of the Far East, but it would appear from the descriptions in the 'Foreign Events' section of the Ming History that they first came to China during the Wan Li era [1573-1620]. It cannot have been so very long ago, in any case, since they first came to the Orient. As far as our country's history is concerned, it was not until the opening years of the seventeenth century that Dutch ships came regularly every year for trade. It has been by such trade that the European nations have become so wealthy.

There is nothing to compare in size with the great bell of Moscow or the copper lantern of France.[43] Nor is there elsewhere in the world anything to compare with their practice of building houses of stone. These are a product of their achievements in sailing over the world. If it is attempted to complete any great undertaking such as some important state project or a powerful fortress on the resources of one country alone, it will be very difficult and will result in the exhaustion of the people, but by adding the resources of foreign countries there is no undertaking, however great, which cannot be accomplished. This is true in particular of those nations of Europe celebrated for their strength and prosperity. Because they are cold northern countries, they could not afford any large-scale expenditures if they had only the resources of their own country to depend upon. In spite of this example, however, the Japanese do not look elsewhere than to China for good or beautiful things, so tainted are the customs and temperament of Japan by Chinese teachings. Japanese are therefore unaware of such things as the four imperative needs because they do not figure in the teachings of the Chinese sages.

China is a mountainous country which extends as far as Europe and Africa. It is bounded by the ocean to the south, but water communication within the country is not feasible. Since it is impossible to feed the huge population of cities when transport can be effected only by human or animal strength, there are no big cities in China away from the coast.44 China is therefore a much less favoured country than Japan, which is surrounded by water, and this factor shows in the deficiencies and faults of Chinese state policies. China is not worthy of being used as a model. Since Japan is a maritime nation, shipping and trade should be the chief concern of the ruler. Ships should be sent to all countries to obtain products needed for national consumption and to bring precious metals to Japan. A maritime nation is equipped with the means to increase her national strength.

When it is attempted, on the other hand, to manage a country with only its own resources, it will grow steadily weaker. Such weakness will affect the farmers, and there will be a tendency for the number of farmers to decrease over the years. It becomes a grave national problem when this crisis is reached. To put the matter more bluntly, the policies followed by the various ruling families up to date have determined that the lower classes must lead a hand-to-mouth existence. The best part of the harvests of the farmers who live on the domains of the empire is wrenched away from them. The lords spend all they take within the same year, and if they then do not have enough, the farmers are oppressed all the more cruelly to obtain additional funds. This goes on year after year. It is thus no wonder that when, on top of the grave afflictions which have exhausted the farmers in recent times, there have come bad harvests and famines in the years since 1783, farmers from the Kantō to Ōu have starved to death, and good fields which could produce millions of *koku* of rice have been turned into wastelands. Is it not true that the people living on a daimyo's domains are imperial subjects left in his care? Is there any reason why even a single one of their precious lives should be left to the caprices of a lord? Is not caring for them the function of a governor and the concern of the ruler?

During the first twenty years of a man's life he is supported by the efforts of his parents, and consumes huge
quantities of food without producing any himself. If then,
he has reached manhood and is at long last at a point
where he can be of service to his country, it is the worst
possible loss for him to be left to die by his lord. Man, unlike other creatures, becomes of service to his country only
after twenty years have accumulated, and thus every single
subject is precious.

Is it not true that if the ruler fails to cherish his people,
he is remiss in his duties, and that the fate of the nation is
determined by his actions? The ruler who is lax in looking
after the people's needs will fall naturally into profligacy
and idleness, and his extravagances will mount without
limit. In extreme cases he may go so far as to destroy his
house and ruin his province, but even if this does not
occur, the gods will surely punish him for his wickedness.
He will sink into a pool of debts from which his children
and grandchildren will not be able to swim, and in this
manner his domains will pass into the hands of the merchants. He will be trapped and forced thus to satisfy his
debts. There is no point in my dilating further on the fact
that samurai who enjoy hereditary stipends are falling into
the traps of the stipendless merchants. The samurai pretend that this is actually not so bad, but it represents a
terrible state of affairs. The tribute paid by the farmers
of the domains, the product of their tears of blood and
their hardships of a year, is seized before it reaches their
lords and delivered directly into the hands of the merchants. The ruling class does not even dream that these
offerings are made only after great exertions and tears of
blood.

It is a great shame that such conditions prevail, but it is
said that 'even the thoughts of an ant may reach up to
Heaven.' Though their conditions differ, the highest and
the lowest are alike human beings, and the rulers ought

to think about those who are less fortunate than themselves. Soon all the gold and silver currency will pass into the hands of the merchants, and only merchants will be deserving of the epithets 'rich' and 'mighty'. Their power will thus grow until they stand first among the four classes. When I investigated the incomes of present-day merchants, I discovered that fifteen-sixteenths of the total income of Japan goes to the merchants, with only one-sixteenth left for the samurai. As proof of this statement, I may cite the following case. When there are good rice harvests at Yonezawa in Dewa or in Semboku-gun in Akita,[45] the price is five or six *mon*[46] for one *shō*. The rice is sold to merchants who ship it to Edo, where the price is about 100 *mon* regardless of the original cost. At this rate it may be seen that if one bought 10,000 *ryō's* worth of rice in Dewa, sent it to Edo and sold it there, one's capital would be increased to 160,000 *ryō*. If the 160,000 *ryō* in turn were used as capital, the return in Edo would be 2,560,000 *ryō*. Thus with only two exchanges of trade it is possible to make enormous profits.

It may be claimed that of this sum part must go for shipping expenses and pack-horse charges, but the fact remains that one gets back sixteen times what one has paid for the rice. It is thus apparent that fifteen-sixteenths of the nation's income goes to the merchants.[47] In terms of the production of an individual farmer, out of thirty days a month he works twenty-eight for the merchants and two for the samurai; or, out of 360 days in a year, he works 337½ for the merchants and 22½ days for the samurai. In view of these figures it may be seen that unless the samurai put aside grain it is impossible for them to offer any relief to the farmers in years of famine. This may be why they can do no more than look on when the farmers are dying of starvation. This situation comes about from the fact that the right system has not been established. It is a most lamentable state of affairs that the farmers have to shoulder the weight of this error and die of starvation as inevitably as 'water collecting in a hollow.'

The price of rice determines that of other cereals and also affects foodstuff prices as a whole, and as it fluctuates so will the others. One can thus judge its importance. It should not be left for the merchants to determine. Since the market price of rice concerns the ruler it must be controlled by the government authorities. The present attitude is that since trade involves buying and selling, and since buying and selling is the merchants' profession, involving a contest with the people for profits, the samurai are absolutely re-solved not to engage in trade. This is an unintelligent and ill-informed attitude.

Japan is a long narrow country which stretches over ten degrees of latitude from its northeast to southwest corner, a distance of about 550 *ri*. Thus, even in bad years, when the crops failed to ripen in one place, there has never been a case when the drought extended to every part of the nation. It is therefore the parental duty of the ruler towards the people to relieve their hunger by shipping grain from provinces with rich harvests to those with poor ones, thus ministering to their wants. This is imperative. There is a difference between this duty of the ruler and what the mer-chants do to make a living. The merchants buy up at low price the produce at the place where it is harvested and then store it. They wait for a drought or for other natural dis-asters to harm the crops and cause the price of rice to go up. They then sell the grain at the place where it was originally purchased at a price several times what they paid. In this way they struggle with the people in their greed for high profits. Gentlemen would never do this.

In the summer of 1787 the price of 100 sacks holding 35 *shō* of rice each climbed from 250 *ryō* to 300 *ryō* in the capital. There was a plot to make the prices go even higher. It was announced that the stocks of rice in the city had been exhausted. This was really not true; there was a perfectly adequate supply, but the merchants planned this so as to get even bigger profits. In view of the disgraceful motives which inspire merchants, it is impossible to live in security unless some plan is devised to deal with them once and for all. Trading stations should therefore be established at important inland- and sea-ports throughout Japan. Rice and other grain offered for sale should be bought during the year at the natural market price, as determined by the quality of the harvest, and stored at the station. A survey should be made of crop conditions in all parts of the nation, and the information obtained quickly circulated by couriers in boats. Every year each county should estimate the amount of food that it will need, and leave that amount in the appropriate station. The remainder will be transported on station ships to provinces which have had bad crops, and thus relieve hunger. In all provinces, including the capital, the normal price paid to the farmers during the previous year should be used as the price standard. If the price does not go up or down more than ten to twenty per cent from this level, the station will not buy or sell rice. If it rises above the limit, the station will sell, while if it falls below the limit, the station will buy rice. Buying and selling will thus maintain prices within ten to twenty per cent of the average price paid to farmers during the previous year. The stations can thereby keep the highest price of rice fixed at that of the price in the capital. It is inevitable that there will be some discrepancies arising from the difference in shipping costs to places nearer or farther away, but the prices will average roughly the same, and the people will be greatly helped. It will give the farmers a sense of having received a new lease of life.

Then, even if no formal regulations are made on the subject, the evil practice of infanticide will stop of itself. Within twenty years not only will there be a better race increasing in numbers, but the abandoned fields will gradually be cultivated again and return to their original fertile state. This is a plan which will permit millions of *koku* of additional income to be raised without persecuting the farmers. When a policy truly designed to bring peace and prosperity to the country is adopted, the people will show honest obedience, and they will share in the fifteen-sixteenths of the national income the merchants now take. Then in two or three years those provinces which are now so impoverished that infanticide is the general rule will be put on their feet, and the farmers rehabilitated.

Even during the short period that Hideyoshi[48] was in power, he managed to distribute 465,000 *ryō* (767,250 *ryō* in current exchange) among the lords of the empire in the fourth moon of 1588. If he had lived to attain old age, he would probably have succeeded in making even China a tributary nation of Japan, but unhappily he died in his sixty-third year on 15 September 1598. Because the country was at war at the time, he gave the money to the lords; if peace had prevailed he would have given it to the farmers for their relief.

Unless the ruler is possessed of great genius, the country will be poorly governed. Examples of this adage may be found thoughout the ancient and modern histories of both Japan and China. The present times are the first since Minamoto Yoritomo[49] founded the military order that the samurai have been in such a sorry state. This situation must be changed at once, and the old order of samurai, farmers, artisans, merchants and idlers restored. Trading-stations should be established steadily throughout the country, as I have above suggested, and extensive trading carried out. The wants of one section should be supplied with what another possesses by transporting the produce in government-owned ships. This will both help the people and cause the currency to revert to government treasuries. If the ruler becomes very wealthy without courting wealth and without seeking profit, proving himself thus worthy of the name 'richest in the land', he will preserve his authority and his fortune. This will be a most felicitous and extraordinary thing, and lay the cornerstone for ten thousand years of prosperity.

*

There are three sources of worry in Edo which make it impossible to feel secure there, and which make the city unsuited to be the location of the capital. These three sources of worry must by degrees be removed so that one may live there in tranquillity. The three sources of worry are (1) fire, (2) rice shortages, and (3) night robbery. Below will be found details concerning each.

(1) *Fire*

Although Edo is the largest city in Japan, it will not be fitted to be the site of the ruler's castle until houses are of permanent stone construction and everyone can dwell there in safety, without fear and suffering from fire and floods. In Edo, however, for several *ri* around there are rows on rows of highly-inflammable wooden structures which present a very flimsy appearance. Every year, whenever there has been a dry spell, it is so hot that the earth is parched and the wells dry up. If at that time a wind strong enough to stir up sand and pebbles should spring up, and then by mischance a fire broke out somewhere in its path, the fire would soon become a great conflagration, and would burn everything to the ground. When there is just a slight wind and a small fire it is possible to extinguish the fire quite easily, but it is humanly impossible to cope with the combination of a strong wind and a roaring conflagration. The heavy damage resulting from such fires is attributable to the wooden construction of the houses. In the large cities of Europe the houses of rich and poor alike are built of stone. Thus, even when, as it rarely happens, there is a fire, only the wooden articles inside the house are burned, and the neighbouring houses are not even aware that there has been a fire.

Even in Europe they have probably not always had houses built of stone. They presumably learned the lesson of building with stone only after they had suffered from many fires. Since there have been no major fires in Edo, apart from those of 1657 and 1772, people have become careless and do not fear what they should fear. They are also unaware of the uses of stone. During the present period of peace, now of over two hundred years' duration, there has been a large-scale construction of Buddhist temples, palaces, monasteries and luxurious private dwellings, but these have either been destroyed by fire or have had to be kept under ceaseless repair. For this reason the nearby mountains have all been deforested, and the woodsmen are heading towards the remoter mountains. In olden times there were places where no human being had been, but none such are left. Sooner or later all the trees which can be used for posts will have been cut down. Then there will be no alternative to building the frames of houses with stone. Circumstances thus favour the use of stone. No longer will human energy be wasted on account of fires. The government will also be spared the expense of giving relief to those who have been victims of fires. Unless, however, the people want such houses to be built, they will not survive, so the chief thing is to win popularity for them.

All the bridges in Bizen are already built of stone. This must be one of Kumazawa's[50] achievements, and is a fore-taste of the time when houses will be of stone instead of wood. If such examples of stone construction are praised, the practice will gradually spread, and eventually building in stone will be general.

Small-minded officials will probably say that although it may be a good thing to build with stone, the costs are so high as to be prohibitive. This may be true of houses for the common people, but the rulers and high dignitaries should not hoard their gold and silver as if they were priceless treasures. It is only by using them that they acquire value. If it were the case of foreigners coming in and getting paid for work done, the money would indeed be lost, but since only Japanese subjects would be involved, giving them wages and goods amounts to giving money to one's own children. Since this is putting money into circulation which is destined to return in the form of yearly levies and duties, it should be released to the people. They will cheerfully accomplish any enterprise, however great, in an honest and conscientious manner.

The ruler, however, must be wise and capable. Even when he is virtuous and talented he must also have men to carry out the functions of government. Since the regulations insist that administrators be chosen from among persons of high rank, it is natural that there are few men of ability among them. If they were selected instead from among the many government officials of lesser rank, there would certainly be some of ability. When the ruler is provided with administrators and officials who are fitted for their tasks and for the times, there is no project which will not succeed.

However, even if the ruler and the subjects are not on such a high plane of wisdom, there is one thing which must be dealt with at once: the building of houses of stone to remove the danger of fire. Fires are therefore called the first source of worry.

(2) *Rice Shortages*

Over 90,000 *koku* of rice are consumed daily in Edo. In ten days this amounts to over 900,000 *koku* and in a month it totals 2,700,000 *koku*. If rice is transported on vessels carrying 1,000 *koku* of rice each, ninety ships must enter port every day in order to supply the needs of the people of Edo. In addition, ships must bring in such articles as saké, soy-sauce, salt, oil, candles, cereals and cloth, as well as firewood and lumber. These commodities thus require an additional number of ships. Because the samurai do not own any ships, everything must be brought in by merchant vessels. There is no greater danger than for the people to be dependent on the merchants for their food.

Pirates lying off the Izu Shichitō,[51] the Bonins, the islands off Nambu or the islands northwest of Saga could easily watch for shipping and attack it unexpectedly. They would board the vessels, kill the unarmed captain and crew, and then plunder the cargo. Or they would intimidate and scatter the sailors with guns and then make off with the cargo. Up to the end of the sixteenth century there were pirates renowned for such practices all over Japan and even in foreign countries. The nation was at the time involved in wars, and as there was no one to control the pirates, they roamed the seas as they wished. Once the country was unified, however, piracy naturally died out.

What we now call the *bahan* was another name for the pirates of that time. The word is written with the characters of Hachiman.[52] The pirates were called 'the *bahan* of Japan' because they always used to hoist a flag with the name Hachiman on it whenever they sailed for piracy. The neighbouring countries were terrified of them.

The daimyo are now all impoverished and unable to pay their retainers their stipends. The farmers are exhausted by severe taxation, and practise infanticide in order not to add mouths to feed. It is certain then that both the lords and the farmers hate the ruler. There are at present large numbers of bandits roving over the countryside. The daimyo and the representatives of the shogunate sometimes confer on this problem, but they never get beyond mere formalities, and no one is actually apprehended. The authorities keep this matter a dark secret for an interesting reason which I shall not disclose here for fear of digressing too much.

This is probably the first time in the history of Japan that the samurai and farmers have been in such sore straits. If changes are not made at once, it will be tantamount to inviting disaster. Only by giving due consideration to the problem may this disaster be averted. The reason that the samurai and farmers are in so unfortunate a position is to be found in the error stated above of permitting the merchants to carry on all shipping and trade. The merchants are now getting fifteen-sixteenths of the Japanese national income and are the only wealthy people in the country. They are thus the most powerful of the four classes. Who would not be enraged that such a situation is tolerated? Unless the merchants are brought under the ruler's control, the wrath and pent-up indignation of the samurai and farmers will burst forth, and anything may happpen. Conditions will revert to those of former times, and piracy will become as prevalent now as it was then in the hope of robbing some of the merchants' wealth.

There are rich merchants in every province, but a large percentage of them is concentrated along fourteen or fifteen *ri* of the coast between Settsu and Harima.53 The most prominent of them have incomes of several hundred thousand *koku*, while the others have lesser fortunes. Most of the merchants of great wealth live in Osaka; the chief of them was named Kōnoike Zenemon.54 His fortune was beyond compare; he was said to possess incalculable stores of gold and silver, and his income was as great as that of ten provinces.

The port of Osaka, now the most prosperous in Japan, has been increasing in importance ever since Hideyoshi built his castle there.55 Rice from all parts of Japan must be shipped to Osaka for trade before it can be disposed of. It is a sign of the power of money that the produce of the entire nation is sent to Osaka for pricing instead of Edo; the influence of Hideyoshi may be detected here. But though the produce is first shipped to Osaka, it must be sold in Edo in order to obtain a good profit. That is why most of the ships that enter Edo harbour every day with rice and other commodities (as I have above described) come from the coast around Osaka.

There has been no change in the past two hundred years in the methods of supplying Edo with food. Now when the samurai are impoverished and the farmers reduced to penury, it may well happen, as I have already mentioned, that they will attempt to seize the cargoes of ships at sea. If it should happen that even one ship were attacked by pirates, rumours about this happening would be fed by lie on lie until they reached enormous proportions. Sailors would be terrified by such rumours, and soon there would not be a single ship sailing for Edo. But if the ninety rice-ships alone did not enter port each day, life in Edo could not go on. In two or three months food supplies would be exhausted not only in Edo itself, but in the whole region. A famine would soon occur, and the lower classes would create serious disturbances. They might attempt looting, and there would then be no rice left for sale in the city. The daimyo in residence would make some excuse and return to their domains, and other city-dwellers who originally came from the country would return in increasing numbers to their former homes. The people of all classes would soon be on the point of revolt. This grave situation would have arisen because of the mistake made in permitting the merchants control of shipping and trade. Even supposing, however, that nothing of the sort occurs, it is too paradoxical a thing that the samurai should have to depend on the merchants to protect their lives by supplying them with food.

(3) *Night Robbery*

At present the houses of the great lords are left unlocked, even the bedroom-doors. Seven or eight years ago there was a robber named Inaba Kozō[56] who used exclusively to break into the houses of the high and mighty of Edo. For several years he escaped detection, but his luck finally ran out, and he was captured. He was turned over to the authorities for examination, and his guilt was established. Later he was subjected to public exposure and executed. According to what I have heard of his confession, he admitted having entered the mansions of over 260 lords and wealthy men in Edo. He stole gold and silver objects in the bedrooms and swords as well. He never took clothing because it was too easy to be detected. Under torture he confessed that he had once entered a governor's bedroom and stolen his sword of state. This he attempted to sell after dismantling, but the sword was too magnificent, and as no one would purchase it, he was forced to bury it in the ground. Some officials dug it up, and I have seen it myself. After Inaba was sentenced he no longer had anything to fear, and he freely disclosed the particulars of the luxurious life he had led up to then.

There are no locks on the houses of the lords living in Edo. They have guards who are supposed to watch over them, but the guards take no heed of what happens in any room other than the particular one with which they have been entrusted. This is the universal practice of samurai; apart from their special duties, they are like the three monkeys who see not, hear not and speak not. It is thus very easy for robbers to sneak in late at night, and there is no house well enough guarded to give them a moment's anxiety. Once they have begun to rob the great houses, they are said never to break into the homes of ordinary people again.

However peaceful an age this may be, there is far too much carelessness. I believe that the houses of the great administrators of the country should be so built that they are free from worry about fire or robbery. Even if all the houses in the neighbourhood burn down, an important official's house must not be destroyed by flames, because it is a place where government business is conducted. His house, unlike those of the common people, should be imposing. Otherwise the people will not fear and obey him. This is a good way of exhibiting authority to the nation and should be adopted by rulers and nobles. Because of its importance, I have termed night robbery the third source of worry.

*

By means of the plans outlined in the account of the four imperative needs and the three great sources of worry, the present corrupt and jejune society can be restored to its former prosperity and strength. The ancient glories of the warrior-nation of Japan will be revived. Colonisation projects will gradually be commenced and will meet with great success. A capital city will be built in Eastern Ezo for northern Japan. The central capital will be at Edo, and the southern one at Osaka. The capital of the entire nation will alternate among these three locations. Then, under enlightened government, Japan can certainly be made the richest and strongest country in the world. This is because Japan, unlike other nations, has ample deposits of gold, silver, lead and iron.

Everything depends entirely on the course of action adopted. If it is a good one, the outstanding men of the country will come forward to serve the ruler and demonstrate their loyalty. The precious metals of the country will gravitate towards the ruler and circulate as he chooses. The people will all seek to be perfectly loyal to the ruler, and will direct their faithful attentions towards him. Everyone will sincerely desire to help the programme. Since there will be no opposition to the government, there will be few criminals. When the country is ruled by force against the will of the people, many in their hearts will oppose this compulsion and become criminals. All these blessings depend on finding men who are talented and able, and who are versed in the laws of Heaven, earth and man. If the rulers are lacking in these talents, the people will not have faith in their decrees.

The above secret programme may seem like outspoken criticism of the government because it goes down to the origins of contemporary practices and openly discusses their merits and demerits. This is a matter of which I am deeply afraid. However, if in consideration of that fear I wrote with deference and reverence, the important principles might appear shallow, and so I have recorded my thoughts plainly even at the risk of having spoken in a manner unbefitting my status.

PREFACE TO TALES OF THE WEST

This book is one that describes Japan, China and the West as they actually are. It will probably thus arouse much controversy, but I have not hedged on that account. If one hedges too much, the rights and wrongs become confounded and cannot easily be told apart. I have therefore not taken into consideration what dangers may be involved and, in the interests of my country and the people, I have come out directly to call right what is right and wrong what is wrong, leaving out all roundabout expressions and falsifications. What I have said may sound like slander or abuse, and I realise that it will be impossible for me to escape censure for having, as an inferior, criticised my superiors. It has been customary since olden times to call wise men those people who are wary of this and keep to the approved way; such people have won the world's acclamation. Those who have not so acted have all met with misfortunes and perished. The severity of government regulations is responsible for this.

Since this book, in which vital matters are discussed, has not been written in the approved spirit, I too may thus be unable to escape misfortune. But even if the book falls into the hands of people who may be my enemies, if its contents are carefully read and examined to determine whether it was written for personal profit or for the benefit of the nation, they will find that it was conceived in good-will, and whatever merits it may have will also become apparent. To write with such an intention is what is to be expected of every person born in Japan. I have come to grips with the natural principles insofar as my limited intelligence has permitted, and I have described without ornamentation the general features of Japan, China and the West, mixing the three together. I have entitled the work *Tales of the West*. Although the book actually treats the three regions, the facts about China and Japan are known to everyone, and I have therefore mentioned only the West in the title.

This is to serve as preface.

September 1798.

*   *   *

VOLUME TWO*

The Dutch have been coming to Japan for over a hundred and fifty years. They must have included many amusing things in the descriptions that they have written for the people in their own country of the Japanese religious and popular observances which they have witnessed during this time. I shall relate a few of the things which I have heard. When they go into temples and see peculiarly shaped images like those of the Blue Sage King, the Wild God or Shōten, with three eyes, six or seven arms sticking out of their backs, and their whole bodies coloured vermilion and green; or like Fudō, with fire flaming from his back, they think that these must all be false gods, and that the Japanese people is a race which believes only in empty idols. Japan harbours an exceptionally great number of foolish customs, but among them the one of having the common people pray to such things must count as the most absurd. However, since this practice is of many years' standing, I suppose that nothing can be done about it now.

* See page 159

Among the factory directors who have come to Japan was one named Kaempfer. He remained in Nagasaki for three years and studied Japanese history with the interpreters. After he had sailed home, he wrote a book about events in Japan, from the Age of the Gods to the present. Later, when Natsume, Lord of Izumi, was governor of Nagasaki, a factory director named Arend Willem Feith visited Edo twice. He was especially familiar with Japanese institutions and wrote a book called *Amoenitatum*.57 When I examined this book, the first thing I saw was an account of the imperial palace. It gave a detailed description of various ceremonies observed, of the appearance of the lords assembled in the palace on the occasion of a performance of Nō and kyōgen, and of various minor matters as well.

In certain of their books of miscellaneous essays of the variety of the *Tsurezure-gusa*,58 they include illustrations of everything from people and beautiful scenery down to implements. These pictures, which are copper-plate engravings of the type used in Holland, are actually even more beautiful than the real things. Since there have been a number of Japanese in times past who have left Japan for good and never returned, the Westerners have been able to learn everything about our country from them.

Someone asked me, 'Are there formal, running hand, and cursive forms to the European letters?' I answered, 'In Europe they do not use characters such as we have in China or Japan. They have only twenty-five letters, and these have eight forms which differ from one another in much the same way as the formal, running hand, and cursive scripts do. These twenty-five letters suffice for writing anything. In Japan there is a particular character used for every single thing, in imitation of Chinese usage, which means that there is an inconveniently large number of characters. For example, *ten* in Japanese is written with one character, while in Dutch it is *hemel*, four letters.59 *Chi*

in Japanese is another character, while *aard* has four letters.
It might seem simpler to use one character than four
letters, but if a man were to attempt to memorise the tens
of thousands of Chinese characters, he might not succeed
in doing so even if he devoted his life's energies to it. This
would certainly be a great waste of time. Even supposing
there were someone who could memorise them all, I doubt
whether it would be of any service to the nation. It must
have been because the Europeans realised this fact that
they adopted a simpler method. Since the chief function
of writing is considered to be the recording of facts and
opinions, it would be far more expedient to do so with our
Japanese *kana* instead of attempting to memorise all the
thousands of Chinese characters.

A person may acquire the reputation of being a great
Confucian scholar and yet not be really familiar with the
affairs of even one country. However, I understand that in
the West a man who has a reputation for wide learning
will know the languages of over thirty foreign countries,
and will be perfectly acquainted with their conditions and
products as well. This must be because, having few letters
to learn, they can devote all their energies to the study of
more important things.

In Europe a large goose-quill is used for writing. The
Europeans sharpen the end to a point and fill the opening
with ink. They start writing from the top left, and write
across to the top right. The sentences are written under-
neath one another in layers. Most of the world uses this
kind of writing. Chinese characters are used only in Corea,
Loochoo and Japan (to the east of China), in the various
provinces of Manchuria (to the north) and in Eastern
India. European letters are used in the countries of Europe,
of America, in the countries along the southern and western
coasts of Africa, from the islands south of Eastern India
to the islands south of China, in the islands south of Japan,
in the Eastern Ezo Islands, in the area of Kamchatka, and

as far as the continent of North America. All of these places use twenty-five letters in writing. Although each country has a different language, all of them may be recorded with the twenty-five letters. The alphabet resembles the Japanese *kana*, but the latter has twice as many symbols as there are letters. One might expect that any sound could be recorded exactly by means of the *kana*, but this is not the case. The *kana* is inadequate to represent the 43 tables of sound changes listed in the *Mirror of Sounds*,[60] and these are still not all the possible sounds.

If a careful study is made of their system of writing and ours, it will become apparent which one is correct and which false. Because of the deficiencies in our system, people spend most of their time in idle and elegant pursuits, the number of which constantly increases. They are forgetful of themselves, and when they reach old age it is too late for them to repent. It was fortunate for the Westerners that they foresaw this eventuality and took steps to avoid a system of writing so profitless to the nation.

'Why is is that European painting differs from Japanese and Chinese painting?' someone asked. I replied, 'European paintings are executed in great detail, and it is attempted to make them resemble exactly the objects portrayed, so that they may be of some use. There are rules of painting to achieve this effect. They observe the division of sunlight into light and shade, and also what are called the rules of perspective. For example, if one wishes to depict a person's nose from the front, there is no way in Japanese painting to represent the central line of the nose. In the European style of painting, shading is used on the sides of the nose, and one may thereby realise the height of the nose. Again, if one wishes to draw a sphere, there is no way to make the centre appear to stand out in Japanese painting, but the Europeans shade the edges to permit one to see the height of the centre. In Japan this is called *ukie*. Since it is the custom in Europe to consider above all whether something is of use to the nation, there is an academy which examines all books before they are printed so that no books of a frivolous or indecent nature will be published.'

In Europe and Africa are the huge edifices known as the Seven Wonders, considered the most remarkable sights of the world. The pyramids of Egypt and the tower of Babylon were both built for worshipping God. The latter was constructed of stone and ornamented with sculptures. It was round in shape, and of a splendour difficult to describe. One ascended gradually to the summit by means of a spiral staircase. When one reached the top it was very broad, with balconies giving in all directions; one was there truly above the clouds. Looking out from this vantage point, the mountains and oceans could be seen before one's eyes. These two wonders were both located in countries at the eastern end of Africa.

There was also the Colossus of Rhodes, which stood astride the mouth of the harbour of that island. It is said that large ships with full sail could pass between its legs. It was built because ships travelling to and from the island at night were apt to run aground on the concealed rocks in the Mediterranean some six or seven miles around the harbour mouth, and thereby damage their bottoms. The Lord of Rhodes, deploring this situation, decided to erect an all-night beacon. For this purpose he had a human figure built with two bodies, holding aloft beacons on both sides. It was so constructed that ships had no trouble in sailing through. Some years ago, when war broke out in that country, the Colossus was destroyed, and it is no longer standing. Its remains are nevertheless very considerable, and people from many countries come to view it. Even in Europe, the nations were thrown into disorder whenever they were unable to obtain natural good government, a condition similar to that which prevailed in Japan up to the end of the sixteenth century.

The wonders which still exist at present are the Great

Bell of Muscovy and the Stone Bridge of London. When Kōdayū returned to Japan a few years ago after having seen the Great Bell, he said that it looked like a small mountain. In the capital city of London there is a broad river called the Thames. A stone bridge spans its width of about three *ri*, and at both ends there are markets and temples. Large ships with sails raised can pass under the bridge. The magnificence of the stone embankment along the river and of the construction of the bridge itself is such that it is said that one doubts that it was accomplished by human labour. When it comes to grand edifices, no country in the world can compare with England.

There is also no country comparable to England in the manufacture of very fine things. Among the articles which have been imported into Japan by the Dutch, there have been none more precious than the watches. Some of them are so exquisite that hairs are split to make them. London is considered to produce the finest such workmanship in the world. Next comes Paris in France, and then Amsterdam in Holland. In these three capitals live people virtually without peer in the world, who are the handsomest of men. The houses in their towns and cities, even in the outskirts, are built of stone. They are from two to five storeys tall and surpassingly beautiful. Why is it that the people of these three cities, who are human beings like everyone else, have attained such excellence? It is because many centuries have elapsed since they were civilised and because their political institutions are founded on the principles of natural government. Their nations are thus very prosperous, so that even among the commoners one finds many wealthy persons. That is why they do not begrudge expenses but insist that even the smallest parts of their implements be made with the highest degree of skill.

Since the merit system is practised in Europe, talented and capable people all flock to these three capitals, and it is because of the efforts that they pour forth that the three capitals stand unique in the world. It would seem that the inhabitants of these cities must be possessed of some special cleverness, but the secret of their supremacy is not to be found apart from the above. Their prosperity is probably entirely due to the excellence of their political system and the great number of years of experience that they have had. This is not an isolated instance, and the excellence of their whole society cannot be conjectured from Japanese and Chinese equivalents.

(The following are some miscellaneous reports.)

There are books entitled *Buys, Chomel, Kunstkabinett*, etc.[61] in which are listed in detail the methods to make un-usual devices. These are most friendly books which seem to lead one by the hand. Although there are parts of the explanation which are difficult to understand, it has been attempted to make them as clear as possible by means of the illustrations. We are really fortunate to possess such books. In contrast to usage in the West, however, Japanese keep good things for themselves, and are reluctant to pass them on to others. It is a shameful state of affairs when people think only how they can profit themselves.

I have been told that in the Edo Observatory is kept a map of the world about seven feet wide and ten feet long which is a copper-plate engraving coloured in gold, silver, red and green. The precision and splendour of this map are said to surpass all description. It is extremely difficult to make an engraving of so great a size. Sometime during the 1650's several hundred copies of this map were made. Each of them was rolled up and placed in a box sealed with cloth and pitch. The boxes were then thrown into the Atlantic and Pacific Oceans as presents for the world. I have heard this story and imagine that the maps were thus distributed because it was desired to teach the world that the various nations were located as shown on the map. From this one thing we can appreciate how lofty their national spirit is. One of these maps floated ashore in

Satsuma and has been kept there by the daimyo as his secret possession. The map in the Observatory was obtained as a present from Holland when Yoshimune was shogun.

Some years ago a Roman was taken prisoner when he landed on Noushi Island in Chikushū.[62] He was brought to Edo where, in accordance with a shogunate order, the scholar Hakuseki interrogated him with the aid of this map. The Roman was greatly surprised that there was a copy of this map in Japan, and said that copies were rare even in his own country. The Roman was able to converse in Japanese. He had arrived here with his head shaved in the Japanese manner, bringing with him about 1,000 *ryō* in gold and silver coins, both old ones and of Kan'ei[63] mintage. He had been selected by the Emperor of Rome to sail to Japan and to give instruction in the Catholic religion as well as in the principles of natural government. He was not to prepare the people for a conquest of the country as the Portuguese had done, but came in order to transmit the benevolent and merciful institutions of the Roman emperor. He stated that he had come to Japan knowing all along that there was a severe prohibition in this country against Christianity, but repeatedly declared at great length how different his intent was from that of the Portuguese. His explanations were never accepted by the shogunate, probably because the troubles with the Portuguese were still recent. He lived in Japan for more than forty years, and finally died of illness when over eighty without having succeeded in his plans. He was buried in the Muryō-in in Koishigawa.

When he was on the point of death he said, 'Now that I have attained to so great an age, my death may come today or tomorrow. I should like now to transmit to the Tairō-sama[64] the greatest thing in the world, in return for the kindnesses I have received for so many years. The thing of which I speak is a system of laws which will keep the country free from disturbances for all time to come, even if no precautionary measures are taken. It is because Japan has not yet learned the true method of government that the spirit of bloodshed still prevails, and that one must always take precautions here. It was my desire to inform the Tairō-sama of this system, but to the end he has not wished to hear me. This is the source of the greatest regret to me.'

The spirit of bloodshed has still not vanished, and that is why it is so difficult for the people to feel a sense of security. In the midst of peace the farmers are gradually being impoverished, and this situation will in the end lead to unrest within the country. A way exists to remedy this condition. When this way is taught and understood, all classes of society in Japan will greatly rejoice. Furthermore, whoever puts it into effect will leave a name for all generations to come as a great leader. The benevolent and merciful system of the Emperor of Rome will naturally be founded. If this happens, the two nations will be friendly, ships will go back and forth between them, and considerable profits will accrue to both countries. Since the two nations lie at corresponding degrees of latitude, it is likely that their products and people are also similar. It is indeed a pity that there should be this war because of a difference in religion.

The bloodthirsty spirit of war vanishes when the world's religious teachings are good, and this spirit flares up when they are bad. There is thus nothing more valuable or loftier in the world than religious teachings. This great leader changed his name while in Japan and called himself Okamoto Sanemon.[65] This was in accordance with a shogunate order. It was unfortunate and unkind that this person, who could have helped the nation, was cruelly neglected during the forty years he lived in Japan.

'I have heard that in all the prosperous countries of Europe the houses are built of stone. How are they constructed?' I replied to the person who asked me, 'As I have said before, there are many countries in Europe, including

England, France, Holland, Germany, Poland, Italy, Spain, Portugal, Turkey and Russia. Houses are built of stone in all of them. Their method of construction is the following. [One paragraph omitted.]

'The roofs are covered with tiles cast of copper or iron. The interiors are made of wood as in Japan. The grounds of the houses are spacious and, as they have a way to prevent plants and flowers from dying in the cold seasons, there are flowers blooming all the year round. Because they have ample facilities for heating their houses, they do not wear heavy clothes when it is cold, nor do they wear night-clothes in bed even in the depths of winter. They use three or four quilts stuffed with kapok, which is most luxurious.'

A Dutchman said, 'Children who are born in Japanese-style houses are like grass. They have feeble intelligences and are undistinguished. Children born in houses of stone are like metal; they have keen intelligences and are gifted. Having travelled all over the world and been a student of human nature, I have found this always to be so.'

These words are exaggerated, but there is nevertheless more than enough reason to believe them.

*

I have a story to relate at this point. In the summer of 1783 Mount Asama in Shinano[66] erupted and ashes fell in such quantities on the surrounding provinces as to render farming impossible. This had already created famine conditions when in 1786 a volcano erupted on Ōshima in Izu,[67] and all summer long the sky was overcast. In the middle of the seventh moon, there were great falls of hail and floods in twelve provinces from the Kantō to Ōu, the Etsu's[68] and Shinano, and a grave famine resulted. In Edo the price of 100 sacks containing each thirty-five *shō* rose from about 250 gold *ryō* to 300 *ryō*. The retail price of polished rice rose in the towns to 100 *mon* for 3/10 *shō*. When the stocks of rice on sale were finally exhausted, grave disorders broke out among the common people, who were hard pressed to survive, but these quieted when the government gave the people relief.

When I passed through the domain of Aizu in Ōu during the tenth moon of that year on business, foodstuffs were scarce and expensive. One seldom saw any of the local people going about, and there were empty houses everywhere. I arrived at a place called Hara-yado as it was growing dark, and I looked around from place to place, thinking that there would surely be an inn in the town where I could spend the night. At last, when it must have been about eight hours in the night, I saw a light, and smoke rising from a large house. I thought then that I would ask to spend the night there, but when I knocked at the door there was no reply. I wondered what kind of house this might be, and went inside. I called out what I had come for, and then an old woman appeared and said, 'Your request is a very moderate one, but we have no food, no bedding, nor anything at all. If you are willing to accept these conditions, you may do as you please here.' She went within and made no sign of looking after me.

There was now no alternative to spending the night in this house, and so, without food, bedding or light, my servant and I lay down in the utter darkness of what I imagined was a drawing room. I could not sleep on account of the pangs of my empty stomach. As I turned over the situation in my mind, I felt that there was something mysterious about the place, and I got up and went farther back into the house towards the kitchen, thinking that I would have a look into what was going on in the house.

When I reached the kitchen and looked about, I could see six or seven emaciated figures, who might have been either men or women, huddled about the edges of an oblong brazier. I went up to them, thinking I might ask for some hot water to relieve my thirst, and then I saw that they were all women. They might have been young, but in appearance they were aged, and their features were like those of monkeys. I cannot describe the grief and pity I felt on seeing their emaciated state.

Barely able to hold back my tears, I asked them how they had come to this unfortunate condition, but no one answered me. When I had asked a second and a third time, one of them, a girl of fourteen or fifteen, answered, 'Don't you know? This is not our house. We are people from the mountain villages fifteen miles around here. We have had a famine ever since the ashes began to fall. At first we got along eating things we were never meant to eat, but gradually we became thin, and gradually began to die. Now there is no one left in the villages. I could not bring myself even to tell you what we have gone through in these three years of suffering—it has been too sad, too cruel for my words. The men, perhaps because they have always worked so hard, are weak in the face of death. I have no words to tell you the sorrow of seeing them die. We women, unfortunate creatures that we are, have been left behind, but we too are gradually dying away, and now all that is left is the whitened bones of our parents, children and kin.' She wept as she said these words. I too was so filled with tears that I could not speak.

Then I said, 'This is indeed most pitiful. Has it been thus with all you ladies?'

'We seven women come from seven different places, all who were left living in those villages, gathered together, living from one day to the next, uncertain of the morrow, spending our days in hunger: thus are we seven. This year we had planted a little rice, but, as in other years, it did not ripen. We cut it when it withered still green. There were no ripe ears, but only blasted ones like straw, which we parch on the fire and pound in mortars. We make it into a kind of flour paste, round it into dumplings and boil them in salt water. A bowl or two of this we eat a day, and with this food, more fit for horses than for human beings, we are barely able to prolong our lives from one day to the next. But it is not likely we will be able to last through this winter until the spring when the flowers bloom.'

When I heard these words said in tears, I could not control my grief. 'I think I may have a plan,' I said to the seven women. 'We shall be returning presently to Edo. If I escorted all of you there, you could somehow make a living in Edo. If you are willing, I shall do whatever I can to help you on the way.'

They answered me, 'Thank you for your kindness, but we are all sinners who have escaped death when we should have died with our parents, husbands and brothers. Our duty was to die with them, and, however much we regret it now, it will always be true that they died before us. Why, then, should we now go to Edo or wherever it may be? To die here is the proper thing for us, even if it must be of starvation.' They refused my offer with these words. However much I tried to coax them, they refused, which moved me greatly.

I felt that there was nothing I could do, and so I took out what little money I had and gave it to them, saying, 'This is only a little money, but please buy something with it for yourselves.'

They answered me, 'It must seem very strange for us to refuse when your wish comes from such deep compassion, but here, even if one has money, it is of no use. There is nothing at all being sold. Up until last year there was a little to be had, although at high prices, and the money would have been of use. This year the money is useless, since everyone for fifteen miles around is dead, and there would be no one to buy, even if there were something to sell. A traveller has nothing to depend on save his money. Please keep it for your own needs.' These words they said and would not talk further on it. So stubborn were these good people that I could do nothing for them, and I withdrew, wringing my hands.

The next morning my servant and I got up, muttering to ourselves because we had had no means of filling our empty stomachs. We set off in the direction of Sendai.[69] On the way I noticed that almost all the houses in the villages were empty, and if rarely we met a villager, it would be a woman who, to judge by her face, emaciated and with feeble eyes, looked as if she might collapse at any moment. We did not come across a single man. They say that when faced with starvation, it is the men who die first, and I thought that the statement must be true.

Next we passed through villages in the domain of Sendai. If all those mountain villages had been put together, they would have made over five counties in which everyone was dead, and where only empty houses stood. We headed from there towards the interior, which was still an area of great famine. It was the same in the domains of Sōma, Iwaki, Nambu and Tsugaru, and in the area of Semboku County.[70] Alongside the roads were many whitened human bones. I thought that I have never heard of such a thing happening in former ages.

I stopped at a certain inn. While I was there the woman of the house told me, 'There is a strange woman living in this village. She had a boy who was two this year, who already could say a few words, and was just at his loveliest. She had always been poor, and what with the famine of the past few years, she had nothing at all left to eat this year. There was no food left on sale, and she was in a desperate plight. Her little boy wanted to suck her breast, but she no longer had any milk to give. She said, "If I abandon him, he is weak and will die. I have no way to keep him alive. If I die and he is left behind, he will be eaten by wolves. It is better that he die before me. Since he originally came from my belly, he should go back again into my belly." She took the boy by the head and twisted it off. Then she ate him, bones and all. I have heard in stories of olden times that when there was a great famine people would eat one another, but now such stories must be told of the present.'

In another village where I stopped, there was a family cat in the inn. Some of the village people came and said, 'Please let us have your cat.' They seized it, and then produced 700 *mon* as 'compensation' for it. They said, 'It will save you the bother of feeding the cat,' but the owner would not agree to the arrangement. While they were arguing over it, I excused myself and went out. It is impossible for me to describe how these wretched people looked. I recall that at the time I thought how lucky I was to live in the capital. This reflection served as a warning for my life. I realised after having seen these things that if I valued my life I should return to Edo at once. A woman of the town said to me, 'Things are still worse farther on. Instead of continuing on this dangerous journey, you should return at once to Edo and look to leading your full span of life.' I then turned back and hurried on to Edo. Thus I managed to save my life.

In the two provinces of Ōu alone, the number of persons who died of hunger is said to have reached two millions during the years 1783–6. This figure must be true. I was astonished when I saw the amount of wasteland in both provinces. If these facts were made known to the Europeans, would they not despise us? They would say that it is because people who live in wooden houses are stupid and of feeble intelligence that so many citizens have been lost.

There was an old man who once said to me, 'For years you have been saying that a maritime nation must be familiar with the sciences of astronomy, geography and navigation or else it will suffer from grave famines and the loss of its citizens. Do you have any plan for relieving the hunger of the people in these times of suffering? If you do have one, please explain it to me in detail so that I can write it down for future reference.'

I answered, 'I certainly do have a plan which, if used to help the people, will mean that not even one man in 10,000 will die of hunger. Japan is a maritime nation and, as it is located between 31° and 41° North Latitude, there is an equable amount of cold and heat, and the climate is excellent. That is why all varieties of cereals and fruit grow here. In countries like China, which is bounded on three sides by other nations, the transport facilities are poor, and widespread relief activities would be difficult to carry out because of the many obstacles. Japan, fortunately, is an island nation. The fact that the country is surrounded by water means that even if famine extends to every part of Japan, there need not be a single death because of starvation, nor need there be any obstacle to the normal industries of the people. They would be able to go about their business in good cheer. However, imperial authorisation must come for this to happen.

'If the sanction comes, and it is made the governing principle of the nation, the sorrow of famine will never be known again. The people will then steadily multiply, and this will lead, as I have before mentioned, to the settlement of the islands around Japan. There are also secret matters concerning the various plans to be followed towards this end which I am afraid to discuss in detail here at this time, for one should not speak loosely. If we exchange oaths and go into a private room, I will give you a detailed explanation which you can write down.

'There is, however, a difficulty. In order to comprehend the plan in its details, you must be capable, virtuous and skilled. Since you are greatly read in Chinese studies, I presume you are both capable and virtuous, but the factor of skill is the difficult one. I mean by it a knowledge of the sciences of astronomy, geography and navigation. If you are not versed in these, you probably won't be able to understand anything, however much I explain. If you were to apply yourself to the task of saving the country, you wouldn't understand how to set about it, and you would be blocked at every turn. What do you say to this?'

When I asked him this question, the old man, probably because he could not go so far, gave a great sigh and said no more.

If present practices continue to be observed, there is certain to be another famine which will afflict the people as widely as this one has, and it is not likely that the harm done can be made up for. One should not think that because there has only been one great famine since the country was founded we shall probably never again see people dying before our eyes. If we make this mistake again, how indeed shall we be able to excuse ourselves to the gods? We must take precautions now. These precautions will be in the nature of reforms. I should like to say what such reforms would involve, but they are most difficult matters to discuss. They must be based on just principles or else the people will not be satisfied with them, and they must take into account the two million people who died of starvation. Some plan must be worked out to save the people from experiencing famine again. Then the time will come for considering projects of colonisation.[71]

*

The greater part of the precious metals mined in the various Japanese deposits during the past three hundred years has been exported to foreign countries, and the little that now remains here has passed into the hands of the merchants.[72] As an example of this tendency, we may cite the money obtained from the sale of unrefined sugar produced in the domains of the Lord of Satsuma. The value of the amount sold in Edo every year is from 280,000 to 300,000 *ryō* of gold. So great a sum pouring into Satsuma each year, it is natural that some of it also overflows into the Loochoo Islands. There the market price is one gold *ryō* coin for about 4,700 *mon* of Kan'ei copper cash.[73] The unscrupulous Nagasaki merchants therefore secretly load copper cash aboard ships, and send them off to the Loochoo Islands, where they can make great profits by trading them for gold coins. Of course there have been prohibitions placed on such activities for many years as being piratical, so that if by some chance these merchants are caught, they are punished with death. But, with full cognisance of the hazards, they perform their risky business in the hope of profit. It is bad enough that they break the laws, violate the borders, and disobey the government, but they are also deficient in their loyalty to Japan. The ships of the Lord of Satsuma are said to load merchandise for China in the Loochoos and then sail for trade to ports in the area of Cha-p'u and Chekiang.74 A great deal of gold coin among other things, must be carried off in this way.

It is a most unfortunate situation when no measures are taken to prevent this sapping of our nation's strength. The situation shows no signs of improving; eventually all the gold and silver will have been exported, leaving none in Japan. It will then be recounted as a tale of days gone by that once there was something called gold coin which was used as money. If that happens, far from building our houses of stone, we may eventually find that even wood has become so scarce in Japan that it is not possible to build houses of it. Then people may begin to show a fondness for the old cave-dwellings.

Here is a suggestion. In former days, the nation was torn by wars that lasted for many years, and the administration of the government was not unified. Finally, in the late sixteenth century, peace was established, but the usages of the period of warfare were still retained. That is why many provisional laws, which were designed as temporary expedients, continue to be used in governing the country. They have been left just as they were, without any attempt having been made to determine their value or good in later years. They must now be changed, or the farmers will be exhausted and incapable of survival. I believe that a solution exists for the problems of our times, one that is simpler than any other to inaugurate, and which will bear fruit. Wise rulers, however, are rare. When, for want of a wise ruler, everything is left entirely to the wisdom of aged counsellors, there may be inferior persons in office before projects can be seen through. Over and over in the course of history one reads of persons of considerable talent who devoted themselves to their country's welfare, only to have things turn against them before they could accomplish anything, and who have thus spent their lives pointlessly; this is the highest good fortune that they may hope for! One does not read of more fortunate officials. Since such is the case, the sovereign and his ministers must work together. They must acquire a good knowledge of conditions and exert themselves in taking suitable steps to improve them. The people should be informed that whatever is done for them by anyone is a result of the sovereign's great generosity. The ministers should not assert their own preferences in even the smallest respect, but, showing perfect obedience in all matters, take care not to deviate from the way of good subjects. Thus, by having whatever good things happen each day attributed to the ruler, the people's confidence will be directed towards the government, and all plans may then succeed. This is a general outline of the way to begin the task.

Some of the prosperous nations of Europe are themselves small in area but have extensive possessions. Such countries are called 'great nations'. Among them is England, a country about the size of Japan, which extends only from 50° to 60° North Latitude, and is no more than ten degrees broad from east to west. It is a far colder country than Japan. The great country called Kamchatka, in Japan's Eastern Ezo territories, is also situated between 51° and 70° North Latitude, and thus has a climate similar to England's. Japanese, even some learned philosophers, say that the interior of Matsumae is so cold that cereals will not grow there, and that no one could live in such a place. Some go so far as to claim that Ezo is a foreign country, declaring that the inhabitants, unlike other human beings, have only one eye, in the middle of their foreheads, and that it flashes like lightning! They say moreover that if ships make port there, they never return to Japan, and that it is so cold that the extreme severity of the winters would freeze anyone to death. There are quite a few of these people who are very worthy men, who understand the principles of things and teach others about them, and who, even after an uncomprehending reading of a book, feel qualified to give instruction on it. This is the situation which prevails today; is it not scandalous? It arises because such men are ignorant of the sciences of astronomy, geography, and navigation. A person who is ignorant of these sciences has no possible way of knowing about the basic principles of colonisation.

Matsumae is located at 40° North Latitude. Since its climate is similar to that of Shun-t'ien-fu, the capital of China, the same great variety of cereals and fruit will grow in both places. When this territory, which is somewhat less than 1,000 ri in circumference, has been settled, it will yield as much produce as now grows in all of Japan put together, and when this produce is brought into Japan, there will be double the present amount of food. Ezo would be of great help in creating abundance within Japan; it must not be neglected. If we abandon Ezo, it will fall to foreign countries. The proper attention can keep it Japanese. If this care is given, the development of Ezo will eventually be accomplished, which will be in keeping with the basic policies of national defence. A natural frontier between Japan and foreign nations will be formed, which will meet the requirements of affording protection to the nation.[75]

It is hard to estimate the extent of the disasters which may some day occur if we continue our negligence. When it is a national obligation to attempt to increase the size of the country, even if this involves invading other countries, it makes me speechless with despair when I realise that we have permitted all of our possessions to be snatched away by another country.

How may Japan become the greatest nation in the world? She should profit by the arts of civilisation which she has learned during the 1,500 years that have elapsed since the time of the Emperor Jimmu. She should move her main capital to the country of Kamchatka. (It is located at 51° N. Lat., the same as London, so the climates must be similar.) She should build a great stronghold on Karafuto. She should trade with Santan and Manchuria, giving what they need in return for what they have to offer. The large ginseng roots are a product of the neighbouring regions of Chien-chou and Chiang-ning-fu,[76] and it will thus be possible to obtain as much of this product as desired at low prices to meet the nation's needs. Gold and silver will not be necessary in carrying on this trade. There will instead be a barter exchange of goods, the amount to be determined by how much is needed. The lower classes will feel that they have been helped, and great profits will accrue to the government. Such an arrangement will prove highly advantageous for all concerned. It will be 'getting good things with both hands', as the proverb goes.

The people of Santan have had the custom of sailing two or three boats a year to Soya, a place at the western end of the island of Ezo, by way of the southern coast of Karafuto. There they trade with the natives such articles as ceremonial coats (popularly called 'Ezo brocade', the court costume of Manchuria), green stones (known as 'insect nests') and various luxury items, all of which have come to be commonly used among the Ainu natives. Japan, on the other hand, sends the Ainu such things as pans and ironware, receiving in return the skins of sea and land animals. If routes were opened to facilitate this trade, Karafuto would soon be very prosperous. Since it is a larger country than

Japan, it will probably develop into an even better place. In Japan one can as yet obtain no detailed information about Karafuto. Some say that it is connected in the northwest to Santan; others say that a broad river divides them.77 Its area is probably twice that of Japan, but its exact size is not certain. However, there is positive evidence that it is a very large country. Karafuto must also possess many gold and silver deposits, for it is located a bare two days' sailing northwest of Sado.

To a person ignorant of navigation Karafuto must seem like a very distant place, but to one who is versed in the science, it is much closer than Nagasaki. The development of Karafuto is an urgent matter, especially because it concerns our frontiers. As the proverb says, 'Finders, keepers'. What sensible person would fail to give this matter his consideration? We must not let Karafuto slip through our fingers. The existing *unjōya* should be made the starting point for continued developments. Karafuto will eventually become a land of great cities, and there will naturally also be great strongholds there.

Once great cities spring up in Karafuto and Kamchatka, the momentum will carry on to the natural development of the islands to the south, and the growing prosperity of each of these places will raise the prestige of Edo to great heights. This, in turn, will naturally result in the acquisition of the American islands, which are Japan's possessions manifestly.

There are two of these islands lying in a northeasterly direction from Hitachi.78 Put together, they are probably about half the size of Japan, and they have a large native population. East-northeast of these two places are a great many other islands, one of which is Amchitka, where the vessel *Shinshō Maru* was wrecked. The captain of the ship, Daikokuya Kōdayū from Shirako-machi in Ise,79 was rescued along with his crew by a Russian official making a tour of the region. Kōdayū was returned to Japan by way of Russia, and has now been pensioned by the government. Since he actually saw what he reported, the facts may be taken as certain.

Kōdayū stated that between Karafuto and Santan there is a large river which flows into the northern sea, and that there is an island at the mouth of the river about as big as Shikoku and Kyūshū combined. This island is called Saghalien. From there it is about 5,000 *chō*[80] due north to the port of Okhotsk, from where Kōdayū sailed back to Japan. Okhotsk is Russian territory, and is a key point in the transport of all commodities to the islands to the east. The crews of the Japanese ships which have been wrecked in this area since the Enkyō era [1744-7] have all been given funds by the Russian government, and now live in Siberia, Russia and Okhotsk. It is a fact that they have all married women of these countries and have had children by them.[81] Although the *Shinshō Maru* was the fourteenth ship to be wrecked in the region, the only sailors to have been returned to Japan were Kōdayū and Isokichi. There has been a report of four other shipwrecks in Kamchatka since the *Shinshō Maru's*, and it is said that the crews of these vessels have been helped by the government of Kamchatka and are living there, but this report is not verified.[82]

There are many other islands not far from Japan, but it is impossible to gain any information about them because the science of navigation is as yet unknown in Japan.

Each of the chieftains of the twenty Eastern Ezo islands sends native boats laden with the special products of his island to Okhotsk by way of offering tribute. Since there are always Russian officials resident in Okhotsk, the chieftains offer their presents when they appear for an audience. Gifts from the Emperor of Russia are then bestowed on them. It will probably be a difficult matter to change the customs of the natives who have been thus befriended by Russia, but it is a tradition among them, transmitted from the days of their distant ancestors, that their islands belong to Japan, and the practice of respectfully addressing the Japanese as *kamoedono*[83] has not died out to this day. Before this practice disappears, Japanese vessels should begin sailing and trading there throughout the year. Then a benevolent rule can ensure that they are supplied with what they need, and that their surplus products are carried off in trade. When such beneficial trade is performed, it will be very easy to get the natives to submit to us. It has barely been twenty-five years that the Russians have been in the Ezo islands. If, then, this policy is put into effect now, before all the old natives are dead, and if talented officials are sent there who will get the old natives to tell the others about days gone by and keep the old gratitude to Japan alive, before many years have elapsed they will yield to and obey Japan.

There is a reason why this is true. Russia, first of all, is a distant country, accessible only over land; it is thus impossible to transport things back and forth with the requisite ease. If it were attempted to use ships for transport, the only way they have is to sail from their own country, pass through the North Sea and the Straits of Dover, double round the Cape of Good Hope, and then head for Eastern Ezo.

Russia may have some more immediate plan than the general vague one I have indicated, but she would probably not go so far as to attempt to take the Eastern Ezo islands if it necessarily involved her in a war. But even if Russia attempts only to relieve the suffering of the natives of the area around Okhotsk, the transport of products from the distant home country is blocked by many mountains. It would seem that good use might be made of the great rivers within the roughly 5,000 miles of land, but there are numerous obstacles in the form of narrows and ravines. That must be why the Russians decided that the best way to foster the development of the Eastern Ezo islands was by trading with Japan. The fact that Kōdayū was accorded high rank and sent back all the way from Russia at great expense shows more clearly than words how thoroughgoing their policy is, and how carefully they cultivate the role of parents towards all people. But however intelligently they act, they have found it impossible to carry out their plans satisfactorily because of Japanese laws. This has probably been fortunate for Japan.

It may be that to further her plans in this connection Russia has selected officials and sent them to Japan as crew-members of Dutch ships.[84] They may even have come to Edo, visited the castle, and examined conditions. On returning to their country they may have reported that if, when transport facilities are improved in Ezo, it is established as the frontier, there will be no disputes in the future about the border between Japan and Russia, and that it would be most practical to foster the development of Eastern Ezo by using Japan's abundant resources. This was apparently the plan underlying the desire to return Kōdayū, but things have not gone in accordance with their plan. The Russians were informed that they might visit Nagasaki and trade there and obtained documents of authorisation before they returned home, but they have yet to visit Nagasaki. This is presumably because their plans have been upset.

Since, as I have written, the nature of their country is such that transport is most difficult, the Russians have not been able to do as much for the natives of Ezo as they wished. Now, while this remains true, is the time to take the islands back. If we plan secretly, we can make them Japanese Ezo islands, as they used to be. If these plans are put into effect, there is no doubt but that there will be two most prosperous and powerful countries in the world: Japan in the East and England in the West.

England is located between 50° and 60° N. Lat., lying to the northwest of France, from which country it is separated by a channel barely six *ri* wide. To the west of England is the

Atlantic Ocean; to the south are Portugal, France, Germany, etc.; and to the east are the territories of Russia. To the north, lands of night succeed frozen seas, and civilisation there comes to an end. England is an island, a land of great cold. It produces little food. Perhaps by diligent study one may be able to discover in general how it was possible for this wretched island without a single redeeming feature to become so splendid a nation. With this information we would have the means to make Kamchatka as well into a great country.

Kamchatka lies between 51° and 70° N. Lat. and is thus in a location similar to England's. Since its climate, produce and people must also thus be comparable, it should become as fine a country as England. It has been by the system of education that the clever and the stupid have been divided; by virtue of the natural law that the wise makes use of the foolish, England is a master nation with island and continental possessions. The proper behaviour for rulers and subjects is followed, which is the way of virtue on earth.

Kamchatka is superior to England in that it extends to America to the east, where there are numerous as yet uncivilised islands. Consider, for example, the natives of Amchitka who live in caves instead of houses.[85] For clothes they wear in summer cloth made from the bark of trees; in the winter they wear the skins of land and sea animals. Their food consists of fish in spring, summer and autumn, while in the winter they eat lilies with black blossoms gathered, dried and stored in the previous seasons. They boil the flowers in salt water. The men have hair all over their bodies. The women look like Japanese. They have two horns on their foreheads which look as if they have grown naturally, but which are actually artificial and made of fur. At night they take them off. The people are of the Japanese race—that is to say, like the Ezo. They have no writing or calendars, and there is thus no conception of dates or time. They mark the years only by the fall of the snow; the natives tell their age by the number of first snows they have seen. Since they have no money, trade is entirely by barter.

To the south are twenty-two islands called the Eastern Ezo, as well as Matsumae Island, Japan and the Loochoos. The twenty-two islands and Matsumae are all populated by uncivilised Ezo, as above described. To the west are Okhotsk, Saghalien and Karafuto. These places are also inhabited by Ezo, but in recent years there have been important Russian officials residing at Okhotsk, and a beginning of civilisation has gradually been made. The usages, however, are all Russian. The writing, calendar and currency of Russia have all been adopted, but are by no means widespread. If we push on there, the natives will follow our ways, while if we neglect them, they will eventually obey Russia. Russia is far off, but is connected by land and has stationed high officials there. In general, we may say that Japan is at a standstill while Russia is moving ahead. Because of our tendency towards ineptitude in all things, Russia has become master of standstill Japan's Kamchatka. The reason why the barbarians of islands east, south and west of Kamchatka all seem to be attracted like ants to the sweetness of the Russian system is that the Russians have made capital out of their experiences of struggle and toil during the past 1,500 years.

NOTES

1. This first paragraph is very obscurely worded in the original, and the translation is thus only approximate.

2. An expression derived from the Chinese philosopher Chuang Tzu.

3. I have omitted here a digression on a scheme of inflation-deflation.

4. Gunpowder for Honda apparently meant both the material used in making it (saltpetre?) and the powder itself.

5. Ōu is a region in the northeast of the island of Honshu.

6. An identical example from the province of Dewa is here omitted.

7. An image derived from Arai's *Hōka Jiryaku.* See above, p. 133.

8. Aoto Fujitsuna (13th century) was known for his thrift. The simile does not seem entirely appropriate here.

9. Sado is an island in the Japan Sea off the northwest coast of Honshu.

10. A reference to the *bahan*, Japanese pirates who were at their strongest in the fifteenth and sixteenth centuries.

11. Although this section in the original is placed at the conclusion of the entire volume, it most properly belongs at this point.

12. Honda is a century out—late 16th century would be more accurate.

13. Possibly the *Schatkamer of te Konst der Stuur-Lieden* by Klaas de Vries, a navigator's handbook frequently reissued in Holland. The book was known in Japan before the country was opened. *Cf.* Hayashi, *A List of some Dutch Astronomical Works*, p. 44.

14. *Seido*, here translated 'system' is a difficult word; it means more or less that which can be established by means of laws.

15. See above, p. 46.

16. See above, Chapter III.

17. Natsume Izumi-no-kami Nobumasa, in office 1770-4.

18. A large fish (*cottus pollux*) used for food and medicinal purposes.

19. Matsumae was the name of the clan which ruled over the island now called Hokkaidō. In Honda's time the island itself was sometimes called Matsumae, but more frequently Ezo. By Matsumae Honda here meant the town at the southern end of the island (modern Fukuyama), which was the seat of the clan.

20. One *ri* is about 2.5 miles, but Honda's figures are not to be trusted.

21. Shun-t'ien-fu was an administrative area including Peking.

22. Presumably the Russian official in charge at Okhotsk.

23. *Unjōya* was the name given to the trading stations in Ezo.

24. By Santan, Honda meant the region of the Siberian maritime provinces.

25. There was a legend that Minamoto no Yoshitsune (1159-89) escaped to the island of Ezo, from where he made his way to Mongolia and established himself as Genghis Khan.

26. Another legend.

27. This apparently refers to the mission of 1786 described in the *Ezo Shūi*. See above, p. 47.

28. Conjectural reading of a Russian name. This man is mentioned in the *Ezo Shūi* and elsewhere, but I am unable to establish his identity. Honda heard of him from Mogami Tokunai, who was with the 1786 mission.

29. Ise is southwest of modern Tokyo. For Kōdayū see Chapter III. The year mentioned by Honda was presumably 1792.

30. I.e. *deus*. Pictures of the Russian icons discovered are included in the *Ezo Shūi*.

31. Christianity—not prohibited, however, until 1636.

32. *Buiku*, literally, to 'instruct soothingly' or 'govern clemently'.

33. I have omitted at this point a long and essentially irrelevant retelling of the main events of Japanese history.

34. Translated in Murdoch, *History*, vol. 3, pp. 796–814.

35. This was the *sankin kōtai* system. See above, p. 125.

36. A *koku* is about 5 bushels; the incomes of daimyo were calculated in terms of the number of *koku* of rice they received a year.

37. A *ryō* was a gold coin. It is extremely difficult to ascertain modern equivalents for the value of the *ryō* and other 18th century coins, but fortunately it is not usually necessary.

38. That is, to the punishment they will receive from Heaven for their improper conduct.

39. By this Honda meant capitals, miniscules, italics, etc.

40. There is a confusion here between *furanki*, an old name for fire-arms and *Furansu*, the name for France. See Pelliot, *Le Hôja et le Sayyid Husain*, pp. 204–5.

41. *Dokujinsen*, literally, 'solitary fast ships'.

42. Possibly Honda, hearing of the Viceroy of Peru and his court, imagined that the Spanish capital had been moved from Madrid to Lima.

43. A confusion for Pharos? The lantern of Pharos was one of the wonders of the world.

44. A curious error on Honda's part; perhaps here again his desire to propagandise overcame his better knowledge.

45. Dewa and Akita were provinces in northern Honshu.

46. A *mon* was a copper coin. A *shō* was about 3.2 pints.

47. Honda's figures here go quite astray; again, his desire to make a point leads him to make unreasonable statements.

48. Toyotomi Hideyoshi (1536–98), one of the great men of modern Japan.

49. Minamoto Yoritomo (1147–99), founder of the Kamakura Shogunate.

50. Kumazawa Banzan (1619–91). See above, p. 122. Kumazawa was one of two predecessors praised by Honda, the other being Ogyū Sorai (1666–1728).

51. Izu Shichitō are islands lying south of Tokyo Bay.

52. The name *bahan* is a Japanese approximation of *pa-fan*, the Chinese pronunciation of the characters for Hachiman, the Japanese God of War.

53. The Inland Sea coastline in the general area of Osaka.

54. Kōnoike Zenemon (1667–1736) served as financial agent to over thirty clans and amassed incredible wealth in so doing.

55. Osaka Castle was built in 1583.

56. A famous burglar (1756–89) whose Robin Hood-like exploits made him a popular hero.

57. This work was actually by Kaempfer, not Feith, and does not contain any illustrations of the imperial palace. Probably a triple confusion, involving Kaempfer's *History*.

58. A book of short essays by Kenkō Hōshi (1283–1350).

59. Honda either could not count the number of letters in *hemel* (heaven) or else there has been a misprint in the text.

60. *Inkyō* (in Chinese, *Yün-ching*), a late T'ang work on phonetics.

61. Buys' *Dictionary* and Chomel's *Encyclopaedia* have been mentioned. (See above, pp. 88, 97.) I am not sure of *Kunstkabinett*.

62. The career of this 'Roman' combines facts from those of Giovanni Batista Sidotti (1668–1715) and Giuseppe Chiara (1606-85).

63. The Kan'ei era was 1624–43.

64. An honorific title for a high shogunate adviser. The office was vacant at the time that Chiara supposedly made his request (1685).

65. The name that Chiara was given after he had apostasised. See Anesaki, *Kirishitan Kyōshi no Nihon Sennyū*, pp. 739–41.

66. A province in central Honshu.

67. Ōshima is one of the islands of the Izu Shichitō.

68. Echigo, Echizen and Etchū were three provinces on the Japan Sea coast of Honshu.

69. Sendai is a port northeast of Tokyo.

70. All places in northern Honshu.

71. At this point follows an inaccurate summary of Japanese trade relations with foreign countries, here omitted.

72. A short digression on the sorrows of the farmer is omitted.

73. Copper coins (*sen*) issued 1624–43.

74. Cha-p'u, more commonly called Ningpo, and Chekiang are places in central China.

75. At this point is given again the story of the Russians in Ezo and of Benyowsky's warning—deleted.

76. Places in Manchuria. Ginseng is a root widely used in the Far East for medicinal purposes.

77. It was Mamiya Rinzō who first explored the river. See above, p. 115.

78. Hitachi is northeast of Tokyo. The identification of these islands is not clear.

79. See above, Chapter III.

80. One *chō* equals about 119 yards.

81. The 1786 expedition came across Feodor, the half-caste son of Tokubei, a castaway. Feodor told them that all the earlier castaways had married Russian women and were supported by the Government. (*Ezo Shūi.*)

82. There follows a description of several unidentifiable islands.

83. *kamoe* is an Ainu word derived from the Japanese *kami*—'exalted being'.

84. One of Honda's alarmist rumours.

85. Amchitka was the Aleutian island on which Kōdayū was shipwrecked. (See above, p. 62.) The description of the natives given by Honda probably thus originated with Kōdayū.

BIBLIOGRAPHY

Note—In the bibliography I have made use of the following abbreviations:

AEL : *Annales de l'Ecole Libre des Sciences Politiques*, Paris.
IB : *Iwanami Bunko*, Tokyo.
JAOS : *Journal of the American Oriental Society*, New Haven.
KKS : *Kokusho Kankōkai Sōsho*, Tokyo.
NAW : *Nieuw Archief voor Wiskunde*, Amsterdam.
RC : *Rekishi Chiri*, Tokyo.
SZ : *Shigaku Zasshi*, Tokyo.
TASJ : *Transactions of the Asiatic Society of Japan*, Yokohama and Tokyo.
YB : *Yūhōdō Bunko*, Tokyo.

(A) *Japanese*

1. Amenomori Hōshū, *Tawaregusa* (in *Meika Zuihitsu-shū*, vol. 2), YB, 1926.
2. Anesaki Masaharu, *Kirishitan Kyōshi no Nihon Sennyū*, SZ vol. 40, 1929.
3. Arai Hakuseki, *Sairan Igen* (in *Arai Hakuseki Zenshū*, vol. 4), KKS, 1906.
4. Ebina Kazuo, *Honda Toshiaki no Tsūshō Kōeki-setsu*, RC vol. 17, 1911.
5. Gotō Rishun, *Oranda-banashi* (in *Bummei Genryū Sōsho*, vol. 1), KKS, 1913.
6. Harima Narayoshi, *Rokoku ni okeru Nihongo Gakkō no Enkaku*, SZ vol. 33, 1922.

BIBLIOGRAPHY

7. Harima Narayoshi, *Rokoku Saisho no Kennichi Shisetsu Rakusuman*, SZ vol. 34, 1923.
8. Harima Narayoshi, *Rokoku Saisho no Kennichi Shisetsu Adamu Rakusuman Nisshi*, SZ vol. 34, 1923.
9. Hayashi Fukusai, *Tsūkō Ichiran*, KKS, 1913.
10. Hayashi Shihei, *Jōsho* (in *Sendai Sōsho*, vol. 2), Sendai, 1923.
11. Hayashi Shihei, *Kaikoku Heidan* (ed. Muraoka), IB, 1939.
12. Hayashi Tsuruichi, *Wasan Kenkyū Shūroku*, Tokyo, 1937.
13. Hirata Atsutane, *Shutsujō Shōgo*, YB, 1921.
14. Hirazawa Kyokuzan, *Keiho Gūhitsu* (in *Kaibyō Sōsho*, vol. 6), Kyoto, 1928.
15. *Hokkaidō-shi* (New Edition), Tokyo, 1937.
16. Honda Toshiaki, *Honda Toshiaki-shū* (ed. Honjō), Tokyo, 1935.
17. Honjō Eijirō (ed.), *Honda Toshiaki-shū* (in *Kinsei Shakai Keizai Gakusetsu Taikei*), Tokyo, 1935.
18. Honjō Eijirō, *Kinsei no Keizai Shisō* (*Zokuhen*), Tokyo, 1937.
19. Inobe Shigeo, *Bakumatsu-shi Gaisetsu*, Tokyo, 1930.
20. Inobe Shigeo, *Bakumatsu-shi no Kenkyū*, Tokyo, 1927.
21. Inobe Shigeo, *Matsudaira Sadanobu to Ezo-chi Kaikō*, SZ vol. 45, 1934.
22. Irita Seizō (ed.), *Hiraga Gennai Zenshū*, Tokyo, 1935.
23. Ishii Hakutei, *Nihon ni okeru Yōfūga no Enkaku*, Tokyo, 1932.
24. Itazawa Takeo, *Rangaku no Hattatsu*, Tokyo, 1933.
25. Itazawa Takeo, *Rangaku no Igi to Rangaku Sōshi ni kansuru ni-san no Mondai*, RC vol. 59, 1932.
26. Itazawa Takeo, *Rangaku to Jugaku* (in Fukushima, *Kinsei Nihon no Jugaku*), Tokyo, 1939.
27. Itō Takeo, *Honda Toshiaki no Haka ni tsuite*, RC vol. 40, 1922.
28. Katsuragawa Hoshū, *Hokusa Bunryaku* (ed. Kamei), Tokyo, 1937.
29. Komiyama Fūken, *Fūken Gūki* (in *Hyakka Zuihitsu*), KKS, 1917.
30. Kondō Morishige, *Henyō Bunkai Zukō* (in *Kondō Seizai Zenshū*, vol. 1), KKS, 1905.
31. Kondō Morishige, *Kōsho Koji* (in *Kondō Seizai Zenshū*, vol. 3), KKS, 1906.
32. Kōno Tsuneyoshi, *Aka-Ezo Fūsetsu-kō no Chosha Kudō Heisuke*, SZ vol. 26, 1915.
33. Kōno Tsuneyoshi, *Anei Izen Matsumae-han to Rojin to no Kankei*, SZ vol. 27, 1916.
34. Maeno Ryōtaku, *Seiyō Gasan Yakubun-kō* (in *Kaibyō Sōsho*), Kyoto, 1928.
35. Matsudaira Sadanobu, *Uge no Hitogoto*, IB, 1942.
36. Miura Baien, *Kisan-roku* (in *Baien Zenshū*, vol. 1), Tokyo, 1912.

BIBLIOGRAPHY

37. Morishima Chūryō, *Kōmō Zatsuwa* (in *Bummei Genryū Sōsho*, vol. 1), KKS, 1913.
38. Muraoka Tsunetsugu, *Nihon Shishō-shi Kenkyū* (Revised Edition), Tokyo, 1940.
39. Muraoka Tsunetsugu, *Shisei no Tetsujin Shiba Kōkan* (in *Shiba, Tenchi Ridan*).
40. Muraoka Tsunetsugu, *Zoku Nihon Shisō-shi Kenkyū*, Tokyo, 1939.
41. Nakamura Kiyozō, *Edo Bakufu no Kinsho Seisaku, Shirin* vol. 11, Kyoto, 1926.
42. Nomura Kanetarō, *Tokugawa Jidai no Keizai Shisō*, Tokyo, 1939.
43. Nomura Kanetarō, *Tokugawa Jidai no Shakai Keizai Shisū Cairon*, Tokyo, 1934.
44. Ōnishi Iwao, *Shiba Kōkan no Sekai-kan, Kokumin no Tomo* no. 233, Tokyo, 1894.
45. *Oranda Mondō* (in *Kaibyō Sōsho*, vol. 2), Kyoto, 1928.
46. Ōtsuki Gentaku, *Ransetsu-ben* (in *Bummei Genryū Sōsho*, vol. 1), KKS, 1913.
47. Ōtsuki Gentaku, *Rangaku Kaitei* (in above volume).
48. Satō Genrokurō, *Ezo Shūi*, Cambridge University Library MS, Siebold 300.
49. Shiba Kōkan, *Kōkan Saiyū Nikki* (in *Nihon Koten Zenshū*), Tokyo, 1927.
50. Shiba Kōkan, *Oranda Tensetsu*, Edo, 1796.
51. Shiba Kōkan, *Oranda Tsūhaku* (in *Zuihitsu Bungaku Senshū*, vol. 6), Tokyo, 1927.
52. Shiba Kōkan, *Shumparo Hikki* (in *Meika Zuihitsu-shū*, vol. 2), YB, 1926.
53. Shiba Kōkan, *Seiyō Gadan* (in *Zuihitsu Bungaku Senshū*, vol. 2), Tokyo, 1927.
54. Shiba Kōkan, *Tenchi Ridan*, (ed. Muraoka), Tokyo, 1930.
55. Shimmura Izuru, *Shiden Sōkō*, Tokyo, 1934.
56. Shimmura Izuru, *Zoku Namban Kōki*, Tokyo, 1925.
57. Sugita Gempaku, *Rangaku Kotohajime* (ed. Nogami), IB, 1939.
58. Tōkyō Kagaku Hakubutsukan, *Edo Jidai no Kagaku*, Tokyo, 1938.
59. *Tokugawa Jikki* (ed. Kuroita), Tokyo, 1934.
60. *Tokugawa Kinrei-kō* (ed. Kikuchi), Tokyo, 1932.
61. Tokutomi Iichirō, *Bakumatsu Bunkai Sekkin Jidai*, Tokyo, 1936.
62. Tsuji Zennosuke, *Tanuma Jidai*, Tokyo, 1915.

(B) *Chinese*

1. Ch'en Ch'ang-heng, *Chung-kuo Jen-k'ou Lun*, Shanghai, 1932.
2. Hung Liang-chi, *Hung Pei-chiang Shih-wen Chi*, Shanghai, 1934.

BIBLIOGRAPHY

(C) Western

1. Barthold, V. V., *La Découverte de l'Asie*, Paris, 1947.
2. Benyowsky, M. A. von, *Memoirs and Travels*, London, 1790.
3. Bodde, Derk, *Henry A. Wallace and the Ever-Normal Granary, Far Eastern Quarterly*, vol. 5, no. 4, New York, 1946.
4. Borton, Hugh, *Peasant Uprisings in Japan of the Tokugawa Period*, TASJ, 2nd Series, vol. 16, 1938.
5. Boxer, C. R., *Jan Compagnie in Japan 1600–1817*, The Hague, 1936.
6. Boxer, C. R., *Rin Shihei and his Picture of a Dutch East-India Ship*, TASJ, 2nd Series, vol. 9, 1932.
7. Boxer, C. R., *'The Mandarin at Chinsura'*, Amsterdam, 1949.
8. Broughton, W. R., *A Voyage of Discovery to the North Pacific Ocean*, London, 1804.
9. Ch'en Fu-kuang, *Sino-Russian Diplomatic Relations since 1689* (in *Chinese Soc. and Pol. Sc. Rev.*, vol. 10), Peking, 1926.
10. Claudel, Paul, *L'Impôt sur le Thé en Angleterre*, AEL, vol. 4, 1889.
11. Du Perron, E., *De Muze van Jan Companjie*, Bandoeng, 1948.
12. Droppers, Garrett, *The Population of Japan in the Tokugawa Period*, TASJ, vol. 22, 1894.
13. Feenstra Kuiper, J., *Japan en de Buitenwereld in de Achttiende Eeuw*, Gravenhage, 1921.
14. Feenstra Kuiper, J., *Some Notes on the Foreign Relations of Japan*, TASJ, 2nd Series, vol. 1, 1924.
15. Golder, F. A., *Russian Expansion on the Pacific 1641–1850*, Cleveland, 1914.
16. Golownin, W. M., *Narrative of My Captivity in Japan*, London, 1821.
17. Haren, O. Z. van, *Van Japan*, Zwolle, 1775.
18. Hayashi, T., *A List of some Dutch Astronomical Works Imported into Japan from Holland*, NAW, 2nd Series, vol. 7, 1907.
19. *History of the Internal Affairs of the United Provinces*, London, 1787.
20. Honjo, E., *The Social and Economic History of Japan*, Kyoto, 1935.
21. Johnson, E. A. J., *Predecessors of Adam Smith*, London, 1937.
22. Kaempfer, Engelbert, *The History of Japan*, Glasgow, 1906.
23. Klaproth, J., *San Kokf Tsou Ran To Sets*, Paris, 1832.
24. Krasheninnikov, S. P., *The History of Kamtschatka and the Kurilski Islands*, Glocester, 1764.
25. Kropf, L. K., *Benyowsky*, (in *Notes and Queries* for 27 April 1895), London, 1895.
26. Krusenstern, A. J., *Voyage Round the World*, London, 1813.
27. Kumazawa Banzan, *Daigaku Wakumon* (tr. Fisher), TASJ, 2nd Series, vol. 16, 1938.

28. Lagus, Wilhelm, *Erik Laxman*, Helsingfors, 1880.
29. Lefèvre-Pontalis, G., *Un Projet de Conquête du Japon par l'Angleterre et la Russie en 1776*, AEL, vol, 4, 1889.
30. Lensen, G. A., *Early Russo-Japanese Relations*, Far Eastern Quarterly, vol. 10, no. 1, Ithaca, 1950.
31. Lesseps, J. J. B. de, *Travels in Kamtschatka*, London, 1790.
32. Lung, C. F., *A Note on Hung Liang-chi, the Chinese Malthus*, T'ien Hsia Monthly, vol. 1, no. 3, Shanghai, 1935.
33. Malthus, T. R., *First Essay on Population 1798* (ed. Bonar), London, 1926.
34. Malthus, T. R., *An Essay on the Principle of Population* (6th ed.), London, 1826.
35. Mikami, Yoshio, *On Shizuki's Translation*, NAW, 2nd Series, vol. 11, 1915.
36. Murdoch, James, *A History of Japan*, London, 1925–6.
37. Norman, E. H., *Andō Shōeki and the Anatomy of Japanese Feudalism*, TASJ, 3rd Series, vol. 2, 1949.
38. Norman, E. H., *Japan's Emergence as a Modern State*, New York, 1940.
39. Pelliot, Paul, *Le Hôja et le Sayyid Husain de l'Histoire des Ming*, T'oung Pao, vol. 38, Leiden, 1948.
40. Playfair, W., *Inquiry into the Permanent Causes of the Decline and Fall of Powerful and Wealthy Nations*, London, 1805.
41. Ramming, Martin, *Russland-Berichte schiffbrüchiger Japaner*, Berlin, 1930.
42. Sakanishi, Shio, *Prohibition of Import of Certain Chinese Books*, JAOS, vol. 57, 1937.
43. Sansom, G. B., *The Western World and Japan*, London, 1950.
44. Sauer, Martin, *An Account of a Geographical and Astronomical Expedition*, London, 1802.
45. Semyonov, Yuri, *The Conquest of Siberia*, London, 1944.
46. Smith, D. E., and Mikami, Y., *A History of Japanese Mathematics*, Chicago, 1914.
47. Szczesniak, Boleslaw, *The Penetration of the Copernican Theory into Feudal Japan*, Journal of the Royal Asiatic Society, 1944.
48. Strahlenberg, P. J. von, *An Historico-Geographical Description of the North and Eastern Parts of Europe and Asia*, London, 1738.
49. Thunberg, C. P., *Travels*, London, 1795.
50. Vixseboxse, J., *Een Hollandsch Gezantschap naar China in de Zeventiende Eeuw (1685–1687)*, Leiden, 1946.
51. Vondel, Joost van den, *Werken*, Amsterdam, 1929–37.

INDEX

INDEX

INDEX

INDEX

246

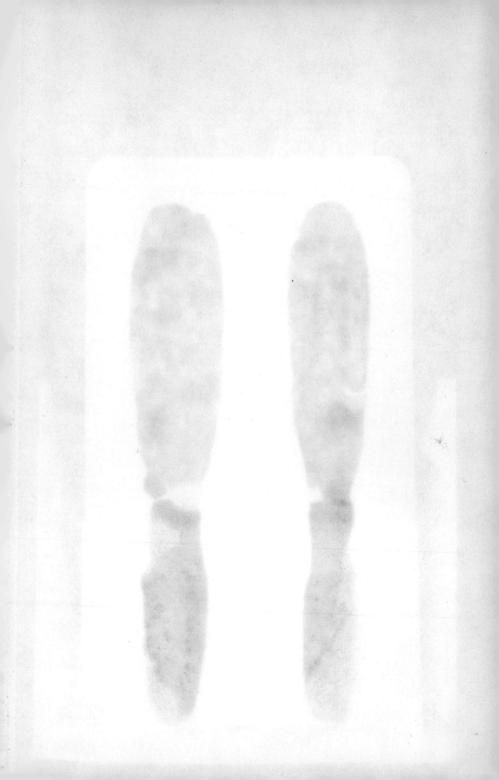